THE VEGETARIAN FEAST

THE VEGETARIAN FEAST

Martha Rose Shulman

Illustrations by Beverly Leathers

HARPER & ROW, PUBLISHERS

NEW YORK, HAGERSTOWN, SAN FRANCISCO, LONDON

THE VEGETARIAN FEAST. Copyright © 1979 by Martha Rose Shulman. All rights reserved. Printed in the United States of America. No part of this book may be used or reproduced in any manner whatsoever without written permission except in the case of brief quotations embodied in critical articles and reviews. For information address Harper & Row, Publishers, Inc., 10 East 53rd Street, New York, N.Y. 10022. Published simultaneously in Canada by Fitzhenry & Whiteside Limited, Toronto.

Designed by C. Linda Dingler

Library of Congress Cataloging in Publication Data

Shulman, Martha Rose.
  The vegetarian feast.
  1. Vegetarian cookery.   I. Title.
TX837.S468   641.5'636   78-2166
ISBN 0-06-013997-8

81 82 83 10 9 8 7 6 5 4 3 2

For Mary and for Max
with love and gratitude

CONTENTS

PREFACE

My neighbors are finally convinced that they needn't hide the pork chops when I drop in at dinnertime, because I am not "against" eating meat. So why am I a vegetarian? The answer has little to do with moral or philosophical considerations. When I was growing up, there was plenty of meat on the dinner table. I ate double portions of it (thanks to my mother's excellent cooking). But when I began to cook for myself, I gradually lost interest in meat. Around that time, I was becoming increasingly concerned with matters of health and ecology. The quality of meat was declining, and there were always plenty of foods available for vegetarian eating. So eventually I stopped eating meat altogether; I didn't really *decide* to give it up.

I did, however, make a decision to become a professional cook. Ever since childhood, when I was lucky enough to travel a great deal, I've had total recall of the new and extraordinary foods I've eaten. I remember having shrimp curry at a Jamaica hotel; tasting my first taco on a beach in Mexico; and, at the age of sixteen, eating three-star meals every day in France, when I spent a month living at the embassy with my friend whose father was the ambassador. There I was treated to my first cheese soufflé in a rich cream sauce (I had no idea what it was, but it almost knocked me off my chair). We had the most delicate salads, glorious wines, exquisite artichokes with hollandaise, and one of "Chef's" amazing specialties: fruit ices served in the skins of the fruits from which they were made.

The next year, when I was seventeen, I began cooking with a passion. I loved having friends to dinner and re-creating my favorite meals. When I stopped eating meat, in 1972, I read every vegetarian cookbook and nutrition book I could get my hands on. Every week I gave a dinner party; I baked bread for a local food co-op; I even took a job in a restaurant. Soon I was developing my own recipes—Black Bean Enchiladas (page 144), Italian Soybean–Grains Casserole (page 181), Mixed Grains Bread (page 38)—and then, during one of those joyful, exciting food parties, I realized that cooking was my calling. I began to teach classes in vegetarian cooking, and I opened a private "supper club" in my home. Every Thursday for two years I prepared a sit-down dinner for fifteen to thirty-five people, by reservation only. My cozy "home restaurant" allowed me all the fun and few of the headaches of running a public restaurant, and at the same time gave me a place to experiment and develop a repertoire of dishes to showcase my creations, and to learn about cooking for a crowd. From that point it wasn't long before I was taking meals into other people's homes in the form of a catering service—ranging from dinners for two to wedding receptions for a hundred and fifty to conferences for four hundred.

All along I've been working to integrate two undeniable pleasures: good eating and good health. Of course, one needn't give up meat to enjoy either of these, but since I'm a vegetarian, and I'm the cook, my cuisine is a meatless one.

Far from limiting one's choice of foods, vegetarianism gives the avid cook a wide range of dishes from every culture. That's why I wish there were some word other than "vegetarian" to identify a meatless bill of fare. Aside from the ascetic, faddist, and moralistic overtones of the word, "vegetarian" suggests a cuisine unto itself (originating in the mysterious land of Vegetaria?). But a quick survey of international foods will reveal that many of your favorite foods are *already* vegetarian.

From Mexico, for example, there are garlic soup—Sopa de Ajo (page 103) and Tortilla Soup (page 100), and the popular Guacamole (page 242). *Chalupas* and enchiladas are sometimes made with meat, but they're readily adaptable to the vegetarian table (I use black beans instead of meat, without any loss of authenticity). The raw ingredients of Middle Eastern cooking are ideally suited to my purposes: sesame seeds, olive oil, garlic, garbanzo beans, cucumbers, yogurt, and mint are used to create tantalizing dishes like Hommos (page 57), Tabouli (page 240), Baba Ganouch (page 61), Fallafels (page 197), and Turkish Cucumber Soup (page 139). Italy, of course, offers its exquisite, fragrant tomato sauces, its comforting pastas, full-bodied Minestrone (page 118), hearty pizzas, Eggplant Parmesan (page 179), and delicate Stracciatella (page 95). India—with its millions of vegetarians—has delightful curries, spicy *dahls*, and cooling *raitas*. Chinese delicacies—egg rolls, won tons, subtle vegetable combinations—are well known and loved here in the United States. Japanese cooking makes extensive use of tofu, or bean curd, a versatile food that's light and high in protein; it's a staple in my own diet, and I use it in all my stir-fries and tempuras. And the cuisine of France, my greatest source of inspiration, offers sublime sauces, a wide range of salads, and eminently useful culinary basics—the soufflé, the quiche, the omelet, and the crêpe—which give any cook a seemingly limitless framework.

I could go on and on, but instead I'll let the recipes inspire you. You'll find that there's something refreshing going on here, because in the last ten or fifteen years an awareness of nutrition has arisen in this country, and along with it a marvelous array of unadulterated foods has become available. As a result I've been able to develop a repertoire encompassing both the old and the new. Most of the tastes and aromas here will be familiar to you, and some of the classic dishes are identical to the ones you know and love. Others are more nutritious and less fattening (but no less delicious) than their classic counterparts—if a more healthful ingredient or technique can replace another, I employ it. Why use cream in a quiche when milk enriched with nonfat dry milk will produce virtually the same effect? Why use three tablespoons of butter when one will do? Honey can almost always replace sugar, and a whole-wheat pastry is not only more nutritious than a white-flour pastry, but also has much more character. Some of the original dishes in this collection will offer your senses combinations of textures, smells, and flavors that you never even dreamed of. A friend once said my food was "vegetarian but you'd never know it." It's for you, whether you're vegetarian or not, because it's for anyone who loves good food.

Every cook needs eaters. Marianne, Barbara, and Terry, faithful recipe testers and recipients of leftovers, have been my most constant aides. They always let me monopolize the kitchen and have been behind me all the way. I also thank those who came regularly to my "supper club" (where I began to develop this cuisine), my cooking students, and everyone who's ever come to dinner. I thank Drew for renting me his house above the lake the summer that I began writing. Much of the writing was done in a beautiful apartment in Tours, and I thank Richard for letting me stay there.

Every writer needs editors. I'm indebted to Frances McCullough and to Liz Johnson for finding her for me, and to Vance Muse for directing me to Liz Johnson. I was very fortunate to have my manuscript fall into Alice Rosengard's hands; she has worked long hours and chopped many an onion to help me bring this book to completion. And I am indebted to Margery Tippie.

My brother Peter and his wife, Leslie, were my hosts and main eaters in France, where I finished the first draft of this book. They thought they were just coming to dinner all those times, but they were actually testing recipes for me.

Out of pure love and devotion my sister Geri has subjected herself to a task I know she hates—washing lettuce—many times over the years. I thank her for that, but more profoundly for the love and devotion.

Ever since I told Mary how I'd learned to embellish canned ravioli, she's been enthusiastic about my cooking. A devoted mentor, she started me out in the kitchen years ago with Mary's Basic Salad Dressing, and upon my request guided me through her cookbooks. When I became a vegetarian, once she saw that I wasn't becoming feeble or scurvy-ridden and wasn't seeking converts, she was supportive: she threw out her processed foods; she bought kasha and whole-wheat bread. Whenever I visit there's tofu and yogurt for me in the refrigerator. I thank her for her mother's love and her wisdom.

M. R. S.

February 1979

THE VEGETARIAN FEAST

INTRODUCTION:
VEGETARIANISM UNMASKED

First I'd like to clear up a few myths and mysteries about vegetarianism. Besides the obvious question about all those "strange" ingredients and where they can be found (the answer to which lies in the following chapter), the questions I am most often asked are: How does one obtain enough protein? Isn't vegetarian cooking time consuming? Is the diet a very fattening one?

Getting Enough Protein

I follow the principles of "Protein Complementarity" set forth in Frances Moore Lappé's *Diet for a Small Planet*.[1] One obtains complete protein from eight "essential amino acids," which must come from the foods we eat in relatively equal proportions and must all be absorbed at the same time. Every protein food contains these amino acids, but in lesser or greater amounts. A "complete" protein is high in all of them. Meat, fish, fowl, dairy products, eggs, and soy products are such foods. Other foods—grains and flours, nuts and seeds, legumes (beans), fruits, and vegetables are low in some amino acids and high in others. To obtain balanced, complete protein, one simply combines foods from these groups. Vegetables and fruits are better as sources of vitamins, minerals, and sugars—which are essential for the *utilization* of proteins—than as protein sources. So the meatless diet relies on the combination of grains, legumes, and dairy products, foods with varying or *complementary* amino acid patterns, to provide complete protein.

It isn't necessary to go to a source book on nutrition or to study compli-

[1] Rev. ed. (New York: Ballantine Books, 1975).

1

cated charts to understand protein complementarity and to figure out how to compose your meals. There are two simple things to remember: legumes and grains complement each other, and dairy products and eggs, complete in themselves, complement everything. Nuts and seeds have amino acid patterns similar to grains, but they are so relatively high in fat that as a source of protein they should not stand alone—that is, be used in large quantity—to be complemented by legumes or dairy products. They are, however, an excellent source of supplementary protein in a dish. With most dishes and meals we do this instinctively: beans and grains (or breads) have been peasant staples for centuries; pasta is made with eggs and is often served with cheese. A soup can be enriched with egg, a cold soup garnished with yogurt. It's easy to "sneak" protein into dishes—roasted soybeans or hard-boiled eggs in a salad, hard-boiled egg yolks, tofu, yogurt, or buttermilk in the salad dressing, yogurt in the vegetable dip. Any dish made with dairy products or eggs will be packed with protein, and this includes desserts. If you're worried about the protein content of your meal, serve a soufflé or a cheesecake for dessert.

The "Time-Consuming" Myth

One of the biggest myths of vegetarianism is that the meals take hours to prepare. It's true that one can cook up a steak or a chop in a few minutes; but if you really want something simple for dinner, the trusty omelet will take less than a minute, and you can fill it with any number of ingredients you happen to have on hand. You can prepare a complete, varied meal of grains, Chinese vegetables with a sauce, a blender soup, and a salad in forty minutes if you remember to start the rice first.

The notion of the time-consuming aspect of the vegetarian diet comes from the fact that it takes beans so long to cook, bread so long to rise, and grains a certain amount of time to cook. But all of this cooking is *unsupervised*, and can be done in advance. Any kind of cooking demands organization, and in this case you do have to be organized enough to remember to soak your beans before you cook them and cook them before you need them and store them in the refrigerator; and you can always cook twice as much as you need and freeze some. When you bake bread, bake four loaves and freeze three; wrapped tightly in plastic they will keep well.

There are many things that can be done in advance. As a professional caterer, teacher of cooking, and owner of a "supper club," I have always had to get as much as possible done ahead of time. Those of you who work all day and are then beset with the challenge of feeding self, family, and friends will appreciate knowing what you can do beforehand, and how long beforehand, *without sacrificing the quality of your meal*. In the recipes that follow, if steps can be taken in advance, I will tell you.

Of course many of these recipes will demand a certain amount of time, but that has nothing to do with vegetarianism. The food will reflect the time spent in its preparation. But if you don't have the time, or don't particularly like to spend hours in the kitchen, you will still be able to find plenty to cook here, and some of it will make your family and friends *think* you spent hours in the kitchen.

The High-Calorie Myth

Because brown rice and beans have been the source of vegetarianism's starchy reputation, some people assume that it is a very fattening diet. It's true that the whole grains and legumes are high in starch calories, but one doesn't tend to overeat them, because they are filling. And because they are very low in fats, they are usually much lower in calories than an equivalent cut of beef. The total grams of protein may be lower, but the calories in starches and sugars are much easier for your body to burn than those in the saturated fats in meat.

Also, you don't need to eat heavy grains and beans or rich cheeses every day. I was an overweight child, and my cooking and eating habits reflect the fact that I never want to be "chubby" again. Now I'm a light eater and get most of my protein from soy products and from light dairy products such as yogurt, buttermilk, cottage cheese, and ricotta. The most difficult calories for the body to use up come from fats and refined sugars, so I use a minimum of cream, butter, and rich cheese in my cooking (there are some dishes where they are essential, but one can pick and choose), and virtually no refined sugar. For sweetening I use honey and try to cut it down to a minimum, often relying on the sweetness of the fruits and extracts. Oils and nuts are, of course, very high in fats. You will find nuts and seeds in several of the recipes here, but often they will be the only highly saturated food in the dish. If you are very concerned about calories, balance your meals accordingly. Don't serve a dish saturated with olive oil along with the Almond-Cheese Stuffed Crêpes on page 174. Serve a light soup and a fruity dessert with a heavy main dish. If you can't resist a rich dinner menu, eat as lightly as you can at breakfast and lunch. And get lots of exercise.

As you experiment with these recipes, you will begin to experience an overall sense of lightness. Meat takes hours to digest, and a rich, heavy meal is often still with you the day after you eat it. And who knows how long it takes processed foods to work their way through your system (if they ever do, completely)? Even the heartiest dishes in this collection will not sit with you for long.

INGREDIENTS

Much of the mystery of vegetarianism revolves around ingredients you may have never heard of. These are, for the most part, grains, legumes, soy products, nuts and seeds, and some seasonings (see the next chapter for more detail). The natural foods industry in this country has grown tremendously in the past ten years; you should have no trouble obtaining most of the foods called for in this book.

If you live in a small town, check to see if there is a natural foods store nearby; if you live in a city, you will have no problem finding them. But it will be worth your effort to try to find out if there are food co-ops. By now they exist in most cities. They operate on varying principles, some asking membership fees and labor hours from their members, others just membership fees, and some are open to the public. These stores are usually oriented toward natural foods and have wide selections, including dairy products, eggs, produce, and often unadulterated meat. The prices are usually lower than regular retail stores, and most of the products, including spices, are sold in bulk. What you can't find in a food co-op you can usually find in a natural foods store. If you don't want to join a co-op or there isn't one nearby, you can always form a group with friends and order grains, flours, legumes, and so on, in bulk from the nearest distributor.

Produce, eggs, and dairy products: It is sad to see the decline in quality of American produce, dairy products, and eggs. Produce is now grown for shipping more than for eating, eggs are mass produced, and milk and cream are "ultrapasteurized." Cream is often so highly processed that it will not whip.

Since the basis of a good dish is its ingredients, it's worth finding the best, which means fresh produce in season and fresh dairy products. Local

6

farmers do still exist, and co-ops and neighborhood stores and fruit stands are more likely to carry their produce than the supermarket chains. Co-ops and fruit stands often stock fresh eggs; even fresh "cage" eggs (from caged chickens, as opposed to chickens that run loose in a yard) are more suitable than mass-produced eggs that sit on supermarket shelves. I can't overemphasize the superior quality of fresh eggs. Crack a noncommercial egg into a bowl next to a commercial one. It will be shades yellower—the commercial egg will look almost white in comparison—and it will hold its shape. It's heartbreaking to have your omelet refuse to hold its shape simply because the eggs are old. You'll also notice that fresh eggs taste richer.

Shop around for dairy products, too. If you can find milk and cream that have not been "ultrapasteurized," buy them; they're sure to have more nutrients. Cottage cheese varies from brand to brand, as does yogurt; look at the carton and buy the brand with the least amount of additives (and the latest date). It may not last as long as the more processed brands, but what's the sense of eating week-old food that had little food value in it to begin with? You don't have to be a fanatic to want to avoid putting food additives into your system, and if you have a choice, take advantage of it. You will taste the difference.

Fresh herbs: Some of the recipes in this collection call for fresh herbs. They are sometimes difficult to obtain, so your only alternative is to grow them. Herbs will grow well in little pots in a sunny window if you have no space for them outside. Dried herbs can often be substituted, but there is nothing like the taste and aroma of herbs freshly picked. Try growing basil, coriander (*cilantro*), dill, mint, rosemary, tarragon, and thyme. It's nice to have parsley around, too, but that's the one herb you can always find in the grocery store. My favorite book on this subject is Irma Goodrich Mazza's *Herbs for the Kitchen.*[1] It's chatty and fun, with excellent instructions for growing, caring for, and using herbs.

Basic Ingredients

I have listed on the next few pages the grains, flours, legumes, nuts and seeds, oils, and miscellaneous items that you will find in my recipes. You'll see many more products in natural foods stores, but I've narrowed it down to what will be called for in the pages that follow.

[1] 3d ed. rev. (Boston: Little, Brown, 1976); paperback ed. (New York: Arco Publishing Co., 1973).

Grains: Store in tightly covered containers on shelves or in a pantry. They look nice in glass jars. Grains are susceptible to weevils if kept too long. Your store of grains should include:

Brown rice
Millet
Wheat berries
Cracked wheat
Bulgur (partially cooked cracked wheat)
Buckwheat groats
Rolled or flaked oats
Couscous (partially cooked hard-cracked semolina)
Rye

Flours: Store in tightly sealed containers on shelves or in the refrigerator. Wheat germ *must* be refrigerated, as it gets rancid very quickly. Other flours should be refrigerated if you live in a very warm climate, or if you don't use them up quickly, as they are vulnerable to weevils. Flours include:

Whole wheat
Whole-wheat pastry
Unbleached white
Wheat germ
Soy
Rye
Cornmeal

Legumes: Store in tightly sealed containers on shelves or in a pantry. Again, glass jars are fine. Beans will keep for a long time. Peanuts, however, should be refrigerated.

Adzuki, or azuki, beans (small red Japanese beans)
Black beans
Black-eyed peas
Garbanzo beans or chick-peas
Kidney beans
Lentils
Mung beans (for sprouts)
Navy beans and small white beans (can be used interchangeably)
Peanuts
Pinto beans

Soybeans

Soy flakes (split, partially cooked, and dehydrated soybeans; they cook faster than whole soybeans and can be substituted for soybeans)

Soy grits (cracked, partially cooked soybeans; a good supplement with grains, cooked along with the grains)

Nuts and seeds: Sesame seeds last a long time in covered containers on shelves. I refrigerate the rest of my nuts and sunflower seeds to ensure freshness; they can also be kept in the freezer. Basic nuts and seeds include:

Almonds
Brazil nuts
Cashews
Pecans
Pignolia (pine nuts)
Sesame seeds
Sunflower seeds
Walnuts

Oils: Cold-pressed oils, which can be found in natural foods stores, contain no preservatives and *must* be refrigerated upon opening. They get rancid quickly, which is something you can't always taste. Unless an oil says it is cold-pressed, there is no need to refrigerate; I keep my imported olive oil in the cupboard. Oils to have around are:

Olive oil (a rich, tasty oil used in salad dressings and in Italian, French, and Middle Eastern cooking)

Peanut oil (strong tasting; good for Oriental and Indian foods)

Safflower oil (the best all-purpose oil, very mild flavor)

Sesame oil (very tasty, but strong and rich; good for stir-fries)

Soy oil (strong tasting, cheap; good for stir-fries and tempuras)

Sunflower seed oil (strong and rich, like sesame oil)

Below is a list of other ingredients called for in the book, each followed by a short explanation:

Alfalfa seeds: Very small seeds that make excellent sprouts. Found in natural foods stores; will keep indefinitely in a covered jar.

Arrowroot powder: A white powder, like cornstarch, used to thicken sauces. Proportions of arrowroot to liquid for a glaze or thickened sauce are 1½ tablespoons arrowroot to 1 cup liquid. To prevent lumping, dissolve the arrowroot in some liquid before adding it. It is found in supermarkets and natural foods stores along with the spices, and can be used interchangeably with cornstarch. Keeps indefinitely in a covered container.

Buckwheat noodles: Nutty-flavored noodles made from buckwheat. Found in Oriental import stores and natural foods stores.

Carob powder: Also known as "St. John's bread," this product consists of finely ground pods from a leguminous evergreen. Very low in fat compared to chocolate, for which it is a substitute. Found in natural foods stores; will keep indefinitely in a covered container.

Chia seeds: Small seeds that are very high in protein. Add to breads to enrich. Found in natural foods stores; will keep indefinitely in covered containers.

Dried mushrooms: Dehydrated mushrooms, which, when simmered in water or stock, provide an aromatic broth. Found in Oriental import stores and some supermarkets. Store in tightly covered containers, refrigerated.

Filo dough: A thin strudel dough found in import stores and Greek markets. Comes in long packages of two sizes, both consisting of paper-thin sheets of dough that are dusted with flour, stacked, and folded up. The 2-ounce packages contain four to eight sheets per package; these are larger than the sheets in the 1-pound packages and are more heavily dusted with flour. Keep refrigerated; can also be frozen.

Gingerroot: A spicy root used mostly in Oriental and Indian dishes, either freshly grated or dried and powdered. Fresh ginger can be found in supermarket produce departments and Oriental and Spanish markets; the dried powder is readily available in supermarkets. Store fresh gingerroot, once cut, covered with sherry in a jar in the refrigerator; it will keep indefinitely this way.

Honey: Always use mild honey; see pages 275–76.

Marmite: A yeast extract imported in small jars from England and Canada. A very viscous spread, high in protein and B vitamins, used in this book as a flavoring for stocks and Soya Pâté (page 58). Can be found in import stores, natural foods stores, and on gourmet shelves. Keeps indefinitely in a sealed jar; no need to refrigerate.

Miso paste: A fermented paste made from soybeans and grains. High in protein; very salty. Used in soups, spreads, dressings, and sauces. Sealed in plastic or in a jar, it will keep indefinitely; I keep mine refrigerated. Found in natural foods stores.

Molasses: See page 276.

Postum: A powdered coffee substitute, somewhat sweet, made from grains and molasses. Found in supermarkets on the coffee shelves and in natural foods stores; will keep indefinitely in a covered jar.

Rose hips: The fruit of the rose plant, which, when dried, makes a good tea; rose hips also make a good soup and can be used to flavor fruit soups and compotes. High in vitamin C. Found in natural foods stores; will keep indefinitely in a covered jar.

Savorex: A yeast extract like Marmite, produced in this country by Loma Linda products. Available in many natural foods stores. Because it isn't imported it doesn't cost as much as Marmite.

Sea salt: Salt from evaporated sea water; higher in trace minerals than regular table salt. Found in natural foods stores.

Sesame tahini: Raw sesame butter, used in many Middle Eastern dishes, in sauces, dressings, and spreads. Delicious by itself on bread, like peanut butter. Can be found in natural foods stores and import stores. Keep refrigerated once opened if the container specifies. Tahini (especially the canned variety) sometimes separates. The ground sesame seeds will be on the bottom, very hard and dry, with about an inch of oil floating on top. If this happens, just blend the contents of your can in a blender or food processor and put the unused tahini back into the can. It shouldn't separate so drastically again.

Spray-dried milk: A highly concentrated powdered milk, about twice as concentrated as commercial brands. Comes whole or skim; can be found in natural foods stores. Good for enriching milk; I use it instead of cream in quiches and soups. Keeps indefinitely in a covered container.

Sprouts: Tender young shoots of seeds, beans, and some grains. Very high in simple proteins, sugars, vitamins, and minerals. Crisp and tasty; a wonderful, nutritious addition to salads, main dishes, and soups, also a beautiful garnish. My favorites are alfalfa, lentil, mung bean, and sunflower seed; each has a distinctive taste. For sprouting directions, see pages 26–27. Sprouts can be stored in sealed plastic bags or jars in the refrigerator.

Sugar: See page 275.

Tamari: A very strong soy sauce with a distinctively rich flavor. You will quickly note the difference between it and commercial brands. Found in natural foods stores; will keep indefinitely in a covered jar or bottle.

Tofu: Bean curd or "cottage cheese" made from soybeans and molded in solid cakes. Comes packaged in water and must always be kept in water in the refrigerator. Contains more protein and less fat per gram than any other food. By itself it is very bland, but it absorbs flavors beautifully because it is very porous, and it's fun to cook with. It is my own favorite source of protein. Found in natural foods stores, some supermarkets in the produce section, and Oriental import stores. If your city has an Oriental population, you can probably get it fresh, and fresh tofu is unbelievably light and delicate.

Vegetable bouillon cubes: These are bouillon cubes that dissolve in boiling water to make a simple vegetable broth. Can be found in some supermarkets and most natural foods stores and co-ops. There are several brands, and they vary in price and also in the number of preservatives they contain, so shop around. When pressed for time, use with tamari for Tamari-Bouillon Broth (page 91) instead of vegetable stock.

Vegetable salt: Seasoned salt made from salt and dehydrated herbs and vegetables. Found in natural foods stores and co-ops. The two brands I am familiar with are Herbamare and Vegesal, but there are more. Use along with or in place of salt or sea salt as a seasoning.

EQUIPMENT

If you're an experienced cook, you may want to skip this section, as you probably know what you need. The novice should remember that it takes—or should take—a while to acquire a *batterie de cuisine*. A friend of mine who is also a professional cook was recently fired from her job teaching cooking at a gourmet cookware store. The reason she was asked to leave was that she wasn't selling their expensive gadgets—Cuisinarts, crêpe pans, fancy utensils. Instead she urged her students to invest their money in a good set of knives and learn to use them, and to figure out what they should have in their kitchen as they went along.

You can begin to cook with a minimum of equipment: a couple of mixing bowls, one set of measuring cups and spoons, one or two good knives, one or two pots and pans, a skillet or wok, and a baking dish. I was cooking *professionally* for three years before I invested in an expensive set of pots and pans; it took me that long to know what kind of cookware would best suit my cooking.

When I began, I was cooking on a very low budget and bought many of my first items at secondhand stores, garage sales, and auctions. These are excellent sources for beautiful old utensils at very low prices. The blenders I've bought for five dollars at garage sales have outlived the fancy multispeed blender I bought new last year.

If you've never been to a restaurant supply house, I urge that you go. You'll be amazed at all the different kinds and sizes of equipment—not only cookware and cooking utensils, but also glasses, plates, flatware, serving utensils, pitchers, and salt shakers—all at unbeatable prices.

As my cooking became more refined, I began to know what I wanted and needed, and what to choose in restaurant supply houses and gourmet cookware stores. Good equipment *does* make a difference; but it's silly to buy it before you know what you need, and you can discover that only through cooking.

Here's what I have in my kitchen:

Cutting and Chopping Equipment

Knives: A paring knife, an all-purpose 6- or 8-inch, and a 10-inch. I rarely use the 10-inch except when I'm cutting several things at once; if I were to have only one knife, I'd choose the 8- or 6-inch. Mine are French Sabatier carbon steel. Other excellent brands are Zanger-Icel, J. A. Henckels–Solingen, Trident, and Forschner. I prefer the carbon steel because they keep a sharp blade for a long time and are easy to sharpen on a stone or steel. They rust, so choose stainless if you tend to forget to dry things.

Also, a cleaver (for chopping nuts and vegetables); a stainless-steel all-purpose knife (for fruits and acidic vegetables and potatoes); a serrated bread knife.

Utensils

Wooden spoons: Have three

Whisks: A medium size can serve as an all-purpose whisk. There's a nice flat whisk that is good for sauces—(see the illustration)—as the shape allows you to scrape sauces up from the sides and bottom of the pan while whisking.

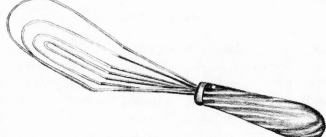

Balloon whisk or egg beater

Spatulas: A flat wooden or metal one, a rubber or plastic one.

Pastry brush

Graters: A four-sided hand grater and a Mouli grater; a nutmeg grater

Food mill

Garlic press

Mortar and pestle

Pepper mill

Citrus juicer

Pastry cutter

Pastry board

Pastry board scraper

Rolling pin: A large, heavy one, preferably with ball bearings. If you make many pie crusts, it's worth the investment.

Candy thermometer

Flame-tamer: Asbestos or metal

Kitchen timer

Kitchen shears

Bowls: A set of stainless-steel mixing bowls—3-quart, 2-quart, 1-quart, and 1-pint—and a large bowl for bread dough.

Colander and sieve

Measures

Individual measuring cups: One-cup, ½-cup, ⅓-cup, ¼-cup.

Measuring spoons: Have two sets, so you don't have to use the same spoon for wet and dry ingredients.

Pyrex measure: A 4-cup or a 2-cup, with a lip for pouring.

Pots and Pans

There are now a number of different kinds of pots and pans, many of which I haven't used, on the market. Aluminum should be avoided because it ionizes in boiling water and reacts with acids, and the aluminum particles get into the food. I prefer the enameled cast-iron pans—Le Creuset or Copco—because they're heavy and retain heat so well. I urge you to rely upon your taste, your pocketbook, and your experience.

Wok: If I had to reduce my entire *batterie de cuisine* to one pot or pan, I would hang onto the wok. It's a very versatile item; with its cover, it can be used for quick stir-fries or slow-cooking soups, stews, and pilafs. You can also use it for sauces. If it doesn't have a wooden handle (or if the handle comes off), you can place it in the oven. I prefer the cast-metal woks to the stainless steel, as they are heavier, and iron is a better heat conductor than stainless steel. Season your new wok by oiling it and heating it on a low flame for half an hour, then wiping it clean. You can wash your wok with soap after you use it, but wipe it dry with a towel and rub oil into it each time until it has a nice oil finish. Woks are not expensive and can be found in cookware stores or departments as well as Oriental import stores.

Frying pan: A 9- or 10-inch, with a lid.

Saucepans: Three, a 1-quart, 2-quart, and 4-quart.

Dutch oven or bean pot: Choose a 5-quart, one that can also go in the oven. I recommend heavy-bottomed equipment, enameled cast iron being my favorite. Heavy stainless steel is good. Soapstone and earthenware are beautiful, but breakable.

Large stock pot: For boiling water for pasta and corn on the cob, for steaming large amounts of vegetables, for cooking beans, and for incubating jars of yogurt. Thin enamel is fine; it's light and inexpensive.

Omelet pan: Use a 6 to 7-inch pan for a two-egg omelet, a 9- to 10-inch pan for three eggs, and a 12-inch pan for five. The 6- to 7-inch pan is most useful. Choose from traditional French cast iron (season and use only for omelets), heavy aluminum, the nonstick varieties (I use these), and stainless (Cuisinart makes a nice one).

Crêpe pan: Standard 6-inch French, or the inverted American type.

Steamer: Either a metal fold-up steamer that will fit in various-sized pots, or a tiered Chinese bamboo or metal steamer.

Chafing dish: For fondues and table-top cooking.

Baking Dishes

Baking pans: One square or rectangular 1½ quart baking pan, one or two 2- to 4-quart, rectangular or oval ones. Either Pyrex, stainless steel, enameled, or, as a last resort, aluminum.

Pie pans: Two, 9- or 10-inch, metal or pyrex.

Bread pans: Four, 8½ x 4½ x 2½ inches. Aluminum, tin, Pyrex, or dark metal.

Baking sheets with rims: Have two or three; these double as jelly-roll pans.

Soufflé dish: The straight-sided ceramic kind, 2-quart size.

Bundt cake pan: Ten-inch size.

Spring-form pans: For cheesecakes. Have two 8-inch or one 10- or 12-inch.

Serving Utensils and Dishes

Large wooden salad bowl and servers
Serving platters: Have several, in assorted sizes.
Bowls: In assorted sizes, for molding pâtés and presenting spreads and herb butters.
Molds: Have one or two or even more, 2-cup to 1-quart capacity. Your choice of shape.

Electrical Appliances

Blender: For pureeing, for chopping nuts, cracking grains, mixing drinks, and on and on. Remarkably low-priced, and worth the money. This is the one piece of machinery I couldn't do without. Don't buy an unfamiliar brand; Osterizer and Waring make the best. It's difficult to find one without multiple speeds, but the two-speed blenders actually last longer.

Electric mixer: A time-saver, but not necessary for most of the recipes here. Especially useful in baking and for herb butters. The most versatile and heavy duty is the KitchenAid.

Food processor: A magic gadget, with uncanny speed and efficiency. Hardly necessary unless you do a great deal of cooking, or hate to cook (as it saves so much time and enables you to make dishes you wouldn't think of attempting without one). Remember, though, that food processors are *not* cooks.

Arranging Your Cookware

The way you arrange your cookware and utensils depends largely on the size of your kitchen and on how much you cook. I like cookware to be easily accessible, hung on a pegboard or from a ceiling rack. Measures and utensils can be hung on nails or hooks on pegboards or in small spaces on kitchen walls. Molds look pretty hanging against a wall. My kitchen is very small, especially for a professional kitchen, and I get around my space problem by hanging tiered basket-trays for spices, with hooks on the bottoms for utensils. It depends, of course, on your personal taste; some people like things on display, others don't. The more you work in your kitchen, with your equipment, the more you will know what your requirements are.

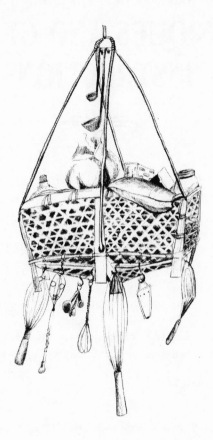

SOME SOUND ADVICE: TECHNIQUES AND GENERAL INSTRUCTIONS

I'm not one of those people who believe that long, tedious hours in the kitchen will result in a better meal; for me, the easiest method is usually the best. After all, working against the clock is an integral part of teaching and catering; you must simplify and develop special tricks as you go along. I've learned many techniques from other cooks, and have designed many of my own for the student—for the person who may not feel confident enough with a knife to do the quick chopping we associate with professional cooking. An efficient shortcut reduces kitchen time just as effectively as a quick hand.

This section is not a complete course for the novice cook. It's a list of techniques that will facilitate or clarify instructions that recur throughout the collection.

Cutting and Chopping, Slicing and Seeding

Always use stainless-steel knives for fruits, potatoes, and eggplant. Carbon steel reacts with the acidity and turns the fruit black on the edges, while the fruit or vegetable discolors the knife.

The cell structures of fruits and vegetables are arranged in a definite pattern; you'll notice lengthwise lines in onions and a lengthwise cellular grain in green peppers. All vegetables are constructed this way, but it's more discernible in some than in others. You can dice vegetables easily if you cut first along the grain, then across it.

Onions: To chop or dice onions, cut in half lengthwise (along a line). Cut off the ends and remove the skin from each half. Lay one half flat side down and cut into strips lengthwise along the lines, holding the onion together with your fingers. As the knife nears your fingertips, you will be beset with the problem of steadying the onion without cutting off your fingers. The way to get around this is to turn the onion around, holding onto the cut side, and work again from the other side toward the middle. Once the onion is sliced, turn it a quarter turn and cut across the slices at a right angle to dice. Repeat for the other half.

For onion rings, don't cut the onion in half. Cut the very ends off and remove the skin. If you have trouble peeling the onion, cut a lengthwise slit one layer deep down one side. You can then remove the layer of skin easily, taking with it a layer of onion (see illustration page 20). Slice rings across the grain, holding onto the onion carefully.

Green peppers: To chop or dice, cut in half lengthwise and gently remove the stem, seeds, and membranes. Proceed as for onions, cutting the pepper into lengthwise strips and then crosswise into dice. For rings, cut the top off crosswise and dig out the seeds with your fingers. Slice rings crosswise, against the grain.

Tomatoes, eggplant, turnips: Treat these and other roundish produce like onions and green peppers, even if you can't recognize the cell structure so easily. To dice, make an extra lengthwise slice or two after you cut the vegetable in half lengthwise (see illustration page 20). Lay the half vegetable flat side down, as if it were still intact, and proceed as for onions and green peppers.

Carrots, zucchini, celery, cucumbers: This method of slicing applies to long vegetables to be sliced crosswise or on the diagonal. Using a large knife, hold several vegetables side by side on your cutting surface and slice several at once as if they were one item (see illustration page 20).

Avocados: This eliminates the messy task of peeling. Cut the avocado in half lengthwise. Twist the two halves apart and remove the seed. Hold a half in one hand and, with a sharp knife, cut three or four strips lengthwise through *to* the skin but not through it; then cut several strips crosswise if you wish to dice the avocado. Take a soup spoon and carefully scoop out the flesh. With this method, you can scoop out precut slices or dice and keep their edges smooth.

Cucumbers: To seed a cucumber, cut it in half lengthwise. Cut in half lengthwise again so that you have spears. Run a sharp knife between the seeds and the cucumber pulp.

Pineapples: To peel, hold the pineapple so that the place where the leafy top joins the fruit is flush with the edge of your table and the leaves extend over the edge. Hold onto the pineapple with one hand and push down on the leafy top with the other; it should break right off (see illustra-

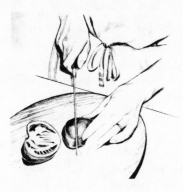

Dicing a tomato

Slicing an onion

Slicing celery

Peeling and dicing a pineapple

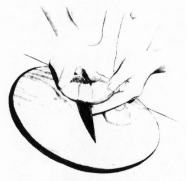

Peeling and dicing a melon

Coring an apple

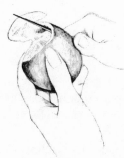

Peeling an orange for slicing

Peeling an orange for sectioning

Preparing an eggplant for quick-steaming

tion page 20). To peel quickly and neatly, use a stainless-steel knife to cut the ends off; cut the pineapple in half lengthwise, then into quarters (quarters are easy to handle). Run a smaller knife down between the skin and the outer edge of the flesh (see illustration page 20). Now run a knife down between the core and the flesh. For small chunks, cut the now neatly peeled quarters in half or in thirds lengthwise, then dice crosswise.

Melons: Cut in half lengthwise and remove the seeds. Slice in lengthwise strips; cut small crosswise sections down *to* the skin but not through it (see illustration page 21), the same way you do with an avocado (see page 19). Now run a knife along the inside edge of the rind and the pieces will fall right off.

Apples: Cutting the apple straight down each side of the core, make four cuts, and the core will be removed (see illustration page 21). Then slice or dice each piece. (Place, by the way, in water with lemon juice to hold and prevent discoloration.)

Corn on the cob: Remove the kernels from the cob by standing the cob upright on a plate and running a knife down between the kernels and the cob.

Herbs: Chop herbs on a board with quick, rapid strokes. Use a small, sharp knife; hold the handle in one hand and rest your other hand on top of the blade. Mince rapidly, pushing the herbs back to the center of your surface as they spread out.

Nuts: Don't try to do more than half a cup at a time. Use a cleaver or a large, sharp knife; hold the handle in one hand and the top of the tip down with the other hand. Keeping the tip end down, lift the handle of the knife up and down, pushing the nuts back to the center of the work surface as they spread out. If they begin to fly off the board, work more slowly and deliberately. To chop fine or grind, use a blender or food processor; they will grind up in seconds.

Peeling

Tomatoes: Bring a medium or large pot of lightly salted water to a boil. Drop in the tomatoes. Wait, with the heat still on, for 1 minute. Drain and run under cold water until cool enough to handle. The skin should peel off easily.

Garlic: Put the clove on a flat surface. Pound it once with the bottom of a jar or the flat side of a knife or cleaver. The skin should burst and practically pop off, or come away from the clove of garlic enough to allow you to remove it without getting your fingernails full of garlic.

If you have a lot of garlic to peel, as you would for a recipe like Sopa de Ajo, the garlic soup on page 103, you could peel the cloves by pouring boiling water over them, allowing them to sit for 5 minutes, and then rinsing with cold water. The skin should now peel off easily.

Almonds: To "blanch" almonds, bring a pot of lightly salted water to a boil. With the heat still on, drop the almonds in for 1 minute, then drain and rinse under cold water. Pop the skins off, one by one.

Oranges (and other citrus fruits): To remove all the white membranes with the skin, use a very sharp knife (serrated knives work well) to cut the skin off carefully in a spiral (see illustration page 21), taking with it all the white membranes. The outside edge of the orange will be quite juicy. This is a good method for oranges you would then slice, say, for Oranges Grand Marnier (page 279). The most efficient way to peel an orange for eating or sectioning is to quarter it just through the skin with a sharp knife. Peel the skin off in neat quarters (see illustration page 21); it will come off easily.

Blanching and Steaming

Eggplant: Most directions for handling eggplant before cooking involve salting and weighting, and careful rinsing to draw out the liquid. An excellent chef in Austin, James Taylor, taught me the following method; essentially it's quick-steaming at very high heat, which is effective not only for drawing out liquid, but also for bringing out the wonderful redolence of eggplant cooked in olive oil.

Preheat the oven to 500 degrees. Cut the eggplant in half lengthwise. With a very sharp knife, make two lengthwise slits in each half, cutting through *to* the skin but not through it (see illustration page 21). Oil a baking pan generously. Place the eggplant flat side down in the pan and bake for 15 minutes; remove from the oven. The skin will have shriveled and the eggplant will be soft and fragrant. When it is cool enough to handle, proceed with your recipe.

Spinach: To blanch spinach, wash and stem it. Bring a large pot of lightly salted water to a boil. Drop in the spinach and slowly count to 20. Drain immediately and rinse under cold water to stop the cooking.

Cauliflower, broccoli, carrots, and green beans: These and other non-leafy vegetables should be left in the boiling water as described above for 1 minute.

Vegetables for color: To steam a vegetable to bring out the color, place on a rack above 1 inch of water in a saucepan. Cover. Bring the water to a boil, and when you see the steam escaping from the pan count 60 seconds.

Drain the vegetable and rinse under cold water. Vegetables can be blanched or steamed before you need them, and held in cold water in the refrigerator for up to a day.

If you want the vegetables *very* crisp, drain and rinse as soon as you see the steam escaping.

Stir-Frying

This is quick-frying in a little oil or butter. Always heat the pan first, then add the oil or butter. Add just enough to give the food something to cook in—*not* to swim in. Don't add the food until the oil is hot, or it will just sit and soak the oil up. Use a paddle or wooden spoon to keep it moving, and don't overcook. You can also keep the food moving by shaking the pan vigorously. Use whichever method you prefer.

Deep-Frying

The most important thing here is to heat the oil (which will be at a depth of from 2 to 4 inches, depending on what you are cooking) sufficiently; it should be a constant 380 degrees. Drop your food in; it should float to the top quickly. Remove as soon as it is a golden brown and drain immediately on paper towels.

General Cooking Directions for Grains and Legumes

One part grains cooks up to two and one-half parts. One cup uncooked grains feeds four to six people (allowing ½ cup per person).

Brown rice, barley, soy grits: Use one part grains to two parts water or stock; add ½ teaspoon salt per cup of grains.

Combine the grains, water or stock, and salt and bring to a rolling boil. Cover, then reduce the heat and simmer for 35 minutes, until most of the liquid is absorbed. Remove the lid and cook, uncovered, for 10 minutes longer to separate the grains. Soy grits can also be cooked along with other grains.

Millet, buckwheat groats: Use one part grains to two and one-half parts water or stock. Add ½ teaspoon salt for each cup of grains.

Cook millet in the same way as brown rice (see above). Cook buckwheat groats as for kasha (see page 67).

Wheat berries, whole rye, and soy flakes: Use one part grains to three parts water; add ½ teaspoon salt for each cup of grains. Soy flakes can be cooked along with wheat berries or whole rye. Cook in the same way as brown rice (see above). When the grains are tender, pour off the remaining water.

Bulgur: Use one part bulgur to two parts water, ½ teaspoon salt. Combine the bulgur and salt in a bowl. Bring the water to a boil and pour over the bulgur. Let sit until the water is absorbed and the bulgur is soft and fluffy, not more than 30 minutes. Pour off excess water.

Couscous: One part couscous to two parts lukewarm, salted water. Pour the water over the couscous and let sit for 10 minutes. Fluff with a fork.

Legumes (beans of all kinds, including soybeans): You can soak beans for two or three days in the refrigerator before you cook them, or freeze them in the soaking water. Consider cooking double what you need and freezing the other half.

Use one part beans to three parts water, with 1 teaspoon salt per cup, or more to taste. Soak the beans in the water for several hours. Set over a high flame, bring to a boil, and add the salt. Cover, reduce the heat, and simmer for 1 to 2 hours, until tender.

To make a more flavorful pot of beans, sauté a chopped onion and some garlic in a little oil. When the onion is tender, add the beans with their water and the salt and proceed as above.

Quantity Cooking Instructions for Grains
(Brown Rice and Millet)

For large quantities of rice, you can avoid making pots of mushy, gummy rice if you use the steaming method instead; this will result in a drier, fluffier rice. The same method can be used for millet. Use one part rice or millet to four parts water, with ½ teaspoon salt per cup of grains. Combine the grains, water, and salt in a large stock pot and bring to a boil. When the water starts to boil, test the rice for tenderness. If you can bite through the kernel—that is, if the hard center part is somewhat tender—the rice is ready to be steamed. If the kernels are still hard, continue to boil for another 5 to 10 minutes, until you can bite through.

Now place a colander over another large pot. Drain the grains into the colander and place the pot, now full of hot water, on the stove. Place the colander of grains in the sink. Fill the pot you just drained with cold water and pour over the grains (this will separate any grains that have begun to stick together). Rinse two more times.

Place the colander of partially cooked, rinsed grains over the pot of hot water on the stove. Bring the water to a boil and cover. (If the handles of the colander prevent the lid from fitting tightly, seal the spaces with a towel.) Making sure the colander doesn't touch the boiling water, steam for 30 minutes, or until the grains are tender.

General Cooking Directions for Dried Pasta

You should have a large pot of salted water simmering. About 10 minutes before serving, bring to a boil, add a tablespoon of oil and the pasta. Cook for 7 to 10 minutes for whole-grain noodles; less time will be required for semolina. When the pasta is just about tender, drain.

If you are cooking a large quantity of pasta and need to cook it in "shifts" (to avoid large clumps of noodles sticking together), have a second pot ready with a colander or strainer resting on it. Pour the spaghetti into the colander, then place the second pot of already steaming water on the stove. Bring back to a boil and continue to cook the pasta and drain in this fashion.

See page 187 for the cooking directions for fresh pasta.

General Directions for Sprouting

Place 2 tablespoons your choice of alfalfa seeds, mung beans, lentils, adzuki beans, or sunflower seeds in a wide-mouthed pint or quart jar and cover with water; let soak overnight. Cover the jar with cheesecloth, fixing it to the jar with a rubber band (or use one of the special sprouter caps now available in natural foods stores) and pour off the water the next morning. Shake the jar and turn it so that the seeds adhere to the sides; if they are clumped in a layer at the bottom the seeds on the bottom won't get any air and will rot. Wrap the jar in a towel to keep out the light and lay it on its side; place in a cool, dry place.

Rinse the seeds with water and drain twice a day for three days, making sure you shake and turn the jar after you do this. After three days your sprouts will be ready. Place them in the sun for an hour to bring out the chlorophyll, then refrigerate in a sealed plastic bag or container, or in a jar.

Sprouts will last for up to a week in the refrigerator if they are kept dry.

Redwood sprouters are now available in many natural foods stores. These are flat perforated trays in a redwood frame. They provide the sprouts with a little "plot" to grow on, so that they grow upward and don't pile on top of each other. If you eat a large amount of sprouts, these pieces of equipment are very worthwhile.

Thickening Soups and Sauces

Making a roux: A roux is a paste made with butter or oil and flour to which liquid is added to make a sauce. Melt the butter or heat the oil in a heavy-bottomed saucepan and stir in the flour. Cook together, stirring with a wooden spoon, for a few minutes, and just before the roux begins to brown slowly pour in the liquid, whisking all the time. When the mixture reaches the boiling point, it will thicken. Continue to cook and stir for a few minutes to obtain a smooth, even consistency. Use as a sauce or to thicken a soup.

Pureeing: This is a good method for thickening soups, especially leguminous ones; it makes it unnecessary to cook a soup for hours and hours to obtain a thick consistency. Cook the soup until the beans or vegetables are soft and the broth is flavorful and aromatic. Remove half the beans or vegetables and puree in a blender or food processor, then return to the soup and mix well. Heat through and serve (or chill for cold soups).

Enriching with eggs: Eggs are often used to enrich a soup or sauce. For a soup, bring the soup to a simmer just before serving. Beat the eggs in a bowl (with other ingredients if the recipe calls for them) and carefully stir them into the soup; they should bind—"scramble"—in a minute or two. Serve immediately. If you want the eggs to curdle, bring the soup to a rapid boil. A very slow simmer will result in a milky broth.

For sauces, beat the eggs and carefully stir into a barely simmering sauce.

Adding arrowroot and cornstarch: Always dissolve the arrowroot or cornstarch in a little liquid before adding it; otherwise it will lump. Add dissolved arrowroot or cornstarch to a hot sauce, soup, or other dish. It will thicken and glaze when it reaches the boiling point.

Miscellaneous Helpful Hints

Making cold blender soups: The most efficient way to make a cold blender soup is to separate your solid and liquid ingredients, placing all the solid ingredients in one bowl and adding them to the blender jar or food processor in batches, with enough of the liquid (and this includes tomatoes, since they liquefy immediately) to make a smooth puree. Pour the puree from the blender into a large bowl, and when all the solids are liquefied add the remaining stock or juice until your soup reaches the desired consistency, then correct the seasoning.

Making bread crumbs: I find that I don't even need dry bread when I use this efficient method. Just put one or two slices of bread, torn up into large chunks, in the blender jar or food processor and blend at high speed. You'll have bread crumbs in no time.

Storing herbs: To store herbs, freshly picked or bunches of them bought in the supermarket, place them in a jar with their stems in a little water. Cover with a plastic bag. Attach the plastic bag to the rim of the jar with a rubber band and refrigerate.

Covering prepared dishes for storage before baking: To ensure freshness, and to prevent foil from reacting with the acids in your food, cover first with plastic or waxed paper, then with foil. Always wrap tightly.

Whipping cream: Chill your bowl and beater. If you forget to chill the bowl, place it in a bowl of ice cubes. Add the sweetener or flavoring after the cream is whipped.

Separating eggs: This method presents no threat of jagged eggshell edges breaking the yolk. You have to get your hands slimy, but that usually happens anyway when you're separating eggs.

Have three clean, dry bowls. Break the egg carefully into a small bowl. Then carefully lift out the yolk with your hands, letting the white run through your fingers back into the bowl. Place the yolk in one bowl and pour the white into another. (By using three bowls instead of two you won't lose all the separated eggs if one refuses to separate correctly.)

In any recipe calling for eggs, as a matter of fact, you should break each egg into a separate small bowl, then add it to your recipe. Occasionally an egg is rotten; I once had to throw out an entire cake batter because I cracked a rotten egg into it.

Making casseroles: Take time with each element of your casserole. If every part tastes good on its own, your casserole will be outstanding.

Too often one gets overenthusiastic at the beginning of putting a casserole together, only to run out of cheese or tomato sauce before the top layer is reached. So be stingy at first, then be generous. Remember that you'll be serving from the top, and this must look lavish. The sauces on the top will sink down to the bottom—but nothing on the bottom will rise to the top.

THE ART OF ENTERTAINING

A caterer is a professional party giver. My job is to provide not only food (sometimes for hundreds of people) but also excitement; everything must look dazzling. My supper club and catering business have taught me much about orchestrating parties, so that when I give my own—and I do that as often as I can, because giving parties is a passion of mine—I am now quite relaxed.

I am even fairly relaxed now when I am responsible for something like an extravagant wedding reception for two hundred people, because I am *organized*—and that's the key to successfully hostessing (or hosting) a party of any size.

Here is the way I go about planning a private dinner party or a large catering job. First, I choose the menu. If it's a catering job, I meet with clients and we decide together. Often when it's my own dinner party there will be one dish I've been wanting to cook for some time, and I'll plan the menu around that; or I'll have a leftover from a cooking class that needs to be used up, and that gives me a good excuse for entertaining. There are several factors that go into planning a menu, such as the weather, the guests (if you don't know them well, you should choose reliable favorites), the amount of time you have, how to make it easiest on yourself. I think about the entirety of the meal or buffet. If guests eat some of everything, will they have eaten too much? Will they have eaten a preponderance of rich or starchy food? Or will they have gotten enough? Especially with a vegetarian spread, it's important for people to feel completely satisfied—without feeling stuffed. Variety and balance of textures, flavors, calories, and protein content, and food you can display beautifully are key factors.

Once my menu is planned, I make shopping lists. First I write down everything I have to buy, then the places I have to go to get them. Included on my lists are paper goods and rentals, and where I need to go to get them.

I then make a calendar for shopping and food preparation. The more I can get done in advance the better. This is especially true for large catering jobs, but I do this for small parties as well. If I have people helping me, their jobs are included on the lists. I now know that, no matter how far ahead of the clock I think I am, I will always do some racing at the last minute (I love that "show biz" aspect of entertaining and catering), and the more I've done in advance the less critical this rushing is. I post my lists in the kitchen so that I can check things off and actually see my progress. I try to leave a big space on the last day so that if I've fallen behind I can still get everything done.

Here is an example of a menu and schedule for a large wedding reception held on a Saturday.

Menu:

Assorted breads and cheeses
Herbed Cream Cheese (page 62)
Extraordinary Chalupas (page 147)
Marinated Vegetables Vinaigrette (page 74)
Vegetable Platter with Assorted Dips (page 77)
Oranges Grand Marnier (page 279)
Wedding cake (subcontracted out)

All the breads were baked on weekends beforehand and frozen; bread is so time consuming that I put it by whenever I can so I won't have to fit it into a tight catering schedule.

Monday:

Order cheese
Check on rentals (which have been ordered well in advance; try
    to find a rental service that delivers)
Buy paper goods
Start sprouts (I order large quantities from the co-op)

Tuesday:

Soak beans and refrigerate (can be done Wednesday as well)
Make hot sauce, freeze or refrigerate

Wednesday:

Pick up cheese
Buy onions, garlic, lemons, other nonperishables
Make yogurt, mayonnaise, other dips
Make radish roses and celery curls (the longer they soak in cold
    water, the more they will open up and curl)

Thursday:

Cook beans
Buy all produce except leaf lettuce
Pick up chalupa shells

Friday:

Make vinaigrette
Buy leaf lettuce, wash, dry, and refrigerate
Puree or refry beans
Herb cream cheese
Vegetable prep
Marinate vegetables for vinaigrette
Thaw bread

Saturday A.M.:

Chop tomatoes
Make Oranges Grand Marnier
Arrange vegetable platters
Slice and rewrap some of the bread
Make guacamole

I also make lists of equipment I will need, things I need to bring to the catering job, and the night before put them all in a box so I don't have to think about them during the final rush. The less you have to think about as "curtain time" approaches, the better. For large buffets I make blueprints of the table arrangements so my help can set them up quickly and easily.

A party in your home is seldom such a production, but I urge that you follow the same principles. Make lists and get as much done as you can ahead of time. One thing to get out of the way early, the night before if possible, is table setting. No matter how frantic things may be in the kitchen, you will at least be reassured to know that the guests will find an air of tranquility in the dining and living area.

I always try to have time to compose beautiful food arrangements. Presentation is one of the most important aspects of entertaining, as well as of good cooking, and the most fun part of the preparation. Entertaining becomes an art when you can give the food this flair (and hopefully maintain your composure). Surprise and delight your guests with unexpected touches—champagne with the hors d'oeuvres, a colorful assortment of vegetables judiciously arranged around a fondue (instead of the usual squares of bread) and garnished with bright, fresh herbs. Arrange your crackers or sliced bread in a nice pattern around cheese, and place radish roses, olives, herbs, and other raw vegetables or sliced apples (dipped in lemon juice so they won't discolor) here and there for color. Place a big wooden bowl of orange wedges on the coffee table to greet your guests in the winter. Mold your Hommos (page 57) or Mushroom Pâté (page 60) in a pretty bowl and garnish it with olives, pimientos, cherry tomatoes or radishes, and fresh herbs, or pipe your *hommos* or Baba Ganouch (page 61) onto squash and cucumber rounds from a pastry bag. Arrange marinated vegetables on a platter over a bright green bed of leaf or Boston lettuce and set them off with black olives. Remove the chokes from your artichokes, place mayonnaise in the middle, and stand asparagus up inside. Place scalloped lemons and more mayonnaise around the artichokes.

Surprise your guests again with beautifully garnished bowls of soup and pretty main dishes and salads. For a grand finale I once unmolded a strawberry sherbet into a punch bowl and floated strawberries in champagne (a semidry dessert champagne) around it; that was quite a sensation. Recently I delighted my guests by placing chilled *ratatouille* (left over from my cooking class and the excuse for the dinner party) in a ring on the edge of an elegant china platter, then placing soft Boston lettuce tossed with vinaigrette in the middle under a mound of marinated vegetables. The platter was further garnished with walnuts, sprouts, and herbs. Everything else was simple: artichokes and asparagus prepared as described above for hors d'oeuvres, white wine, cheese soufflé with the *ratatouille* platter, and a sherbet for dessert. I had had time to compose every part of the meal exactly as I wanted it to be; the soufflé was ready to pop into the preheated oven as soon as we were well into the hors d'oeuvres, and I could come to my party.

"Garnish," then, is the key word, and the best ones are leafy lettuce, fresh herbs, fruits, vegetables, and flowers. Below are some suggestions for garnishes; further suggestions accompany recipes.

For spreads and pâtés:

> Sliced olives
> Parsley and other fresh herbs
> Radishes and radish roses
> Pimiento
> Cherry tomatoes and cherry tomato wedges (seeded)
> Cucumber and squash rounds

For hors d'oeuvre platters and salads:

> Bright vegetables, such as briefly steamed broccoli florets and asparagus
> Cherry tomatoes, carrots, cucumber and squash rounds
> Fresh herbs
> Black olives
> Lemons and limes, sliced or scalloped
> Walnuts
> Almonds
> Leaf lettuce
> Alfalfa sprouts

For soups:

> Sprouts
> Croutons
> Sunflower seeds
> Slivered almonds
> Yogurt
> Raw vegetables, such as thinly sliced mushrooms
> Lemon slices
> Grated cheese
> Fresh herbs
> Sliced apples

For main dishes:

> Fresh herbs
> Vegetables of contrasting color
> Sauces and grated cheese
> Nuts

For desserts:

Mint leaves
Slivered almonds
Liqueurs for flambés
Whipped cream
Yogurt
Thinly sliced fruit

If final meal preparations do require that you be in the kitchen and not with your guests, good wine and beautiful, delicious hors d'oeuvres will relieve you of some of the duties of social director. While people are loosening up with a glass of wine and taking the edge off their hunger with your impressive appetizers, you can retreat to the kitchen and you'll hardly be missed.

Finally, try to work in at least an hour for yourself before your guests arrive. Take a long bath, have a nap, choose your clothes, pamper yourself. Your composure will be contagious.

THE FINAL TOUCH

The final taste of a dish is dependent upon you and your taste buds. No two tomatoes or green peppers are the same; every clove of garlic is a different size. The spices on my shelf may be more aromatic than those on yours, and you may like salt or honey more than I do. You can follow a recipe through to the end, but it is at this point that you must taste it. If the taste of a soup doesn't linger on your tongue, add a little more salt or perhaps a bit more garlic. Learn to recognize the flavors of herbs and spices; a touch more of oregano or nutmeg, or a dash of lemon juice is often exactly what you need. If you are afraid of overseasoning a dish but feel that it needs more of something, remove a cupful and add a very small amount of the seasoning to see. But a word of warning: take very small tastes, or even better (making sure that nobody is looking), spit out if you are doing a lot of tasting, and drink water between tastes. If I didn't do it this way I would have no appetite at the table, and I do like to eat with my guests. It is at the table, after all, where you will do the final tasting and make your mental notes on a recipe.

BREADS

Bread is miraculous. I've made it week after week for years, and the experience has never been the same, because the dough is alive. Of all cooking activities, bread baking is the most sensual (and bread *eating* may be the most sensual of all eating activities). Each type of dough feels and handles differently; some are heavy, some light, some sticky, some dense. And even the same kind will vary from week to week, because the dough responds to weather conditions, and the quality of your ingredients may vary. Baking is an exhilarating experience for me; I'm so aware of the fact that I'm working with living organisms, which are transforming the raw ingredients into the most basic food of mankind. Working with the dough means working with these ever-multiplying yeasts, and it's so satisfying to manipulate the dough, watch it grow, and make it into bread.

Not only do the breads in this section taste like no other breads in town, but they look divine. The first one, Mixed Grains Bread, is the one I always have on hand. The others are either variations of this or are my own versions of breads you may recognize; they should serve you for many occasions.

Depending on the size of your family and the amount of bread you consume, you may not have to bake too often. Bread freezes well. Wrap your extra loaves tightly in plastic, then seal in plastic bags or foil to freeze. The breads thaw at room temperature in 2 hours, or wrapped in foil in a 350-degree oven in 30 minutes.

37

MIXED GRAINS BREAD

For the sponge:
1 tablespoon (1 envelope) active dry yeast
3 cups lukewarm water
2 tablespoons mild honey
2 tablespoons molasses (or use ¼ cup honey in all)
2 cups unbleached white flour
2 cups whole-wheat flour

For the dough:
¼ cup safflower or vegetable oil
1 tablespoon salt, preferably sea salt
1 cup rolled or flaked oats
1 cup cracked wheat (you can crack your own by running wheat berries in the blender, ½ cup at a time, at high speed)
¼ cup chia seeds (optional)
1 cup finely cracked millet or millet meal (can be done in a blender the same way as cracked wheat)
1 cup soy flour
2 to 3 cups whole-wheat flour, more as necessary

For the topping:
1 egg
¼ cup water
Sesame seeds or poppy seeds

Step 1. Mixing up the sponge: In a large mixing bowl, dissolve the yeast in the water. Add the honey and molasses and stir to dissolve. Use water from the bowl to rinse the measuring spoons.

Add the flour, *a cup at a time,* stirring with a whisk or wooden spoon to incorporate the flour into the liquid. The mixture will gradually develop a mudlike consistency. Keep stirring in the flour until you have added all 4 cups.

Now stir the mudlike mixture a hundred times. This sounds like a lot of work, but it goes very fast. Make sure you are stirring the batter up from the bottom and center of the bowl. There should be no lumps when you are finished. If there are, stir a little while longer.

Cover the bowl with a damp towel or the lid of a large pot and set aside in a warm place—over a pilot light, on a heater, in an oven with a pilot light, or in an oven that has been turned on low heat for 10 minutes, then turned off. If your pilot light is very hot, place a baking pan between it and the bread bowl. In the summertime almost any place will suffice, and the pilot light will probably be too hot.

Let the sponge rise for 50 to 70 minutes. At the end of this time it should be bubbling, and you will actually be able to see the mixture expanding.

Step 2. Adding the remaining ingredients; kneading: Pour the oil onto the sponge and sprinkle on the salt. Incorporate into the sponge by folding the sponge over with a large wooden spoon, turning a quarter turn, folding again, and so on until you no longer see the oil.

Add the grains, a cup at a time, and fold in just as you folded in the oil and salt: sprinkle on a cup, fold, turn the bowl a quarter turn, fold again, turn, and so on. Each cup should take about four turns to be incorporated. Start with the oats, then the cracked wheat, then the chia, then the millet.

Add the soy flour, and fold in.

Now begin adding the whole-wheat flour, a cup at a time, and fold in. By the time you begin this the dough should be stiff enough for you to press some of the flour in with your hands from the top, then folding the dough over with the spoon. It should also be getting kind of hard to work with.

After the first cup of whole-wheat flour, the dough should begin to come away from the sides of the bowl and have some semblance of a lump, though a sticky, formless one. As soon as you see that the dough will stay in one piece, more or less, it is time to dump it out onto your kneading surface. Place a cup of whole-wheat flour on the board or table, spread it around, and turn out the dough. Part of the dough will adhere to the bowl; don't worry, just scrape it out onto the top of the dough that's already on the table.

Now you are ready to go. Your kneading surface should be low, about level with your hips or a little bit lower. *Take your rings off* and flour your hands. To knead, take the far end of the dough, fold it in half toward you; lean into the dough, letting your weight push through the palms of your hands and through your fingertips. Turn the dough a quarter turn, fold toward you, lean into it. Turn, fold, lean; turn, fold, lean. Each time the dough becomes sticky add a handful of whole-wheat flour to the board; you can also sprinkle some flour on top of the dough. Eventually add flour only to the board. As you continue this process the dough will become stiff and hard to work with, but keep kneading for at least 10 minutes, adding flour—but not too much—whenever it becomes sticky. After 10 to 15 minutes of kneading, the dough should be stiff, elastic, and heavy; the surface

Mixing up the sponge

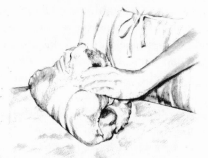

Stirring the sponge

Folding the sponge

Kneading the dough

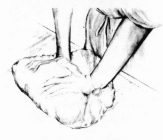

Kneading the dough

Punching down the risen dough

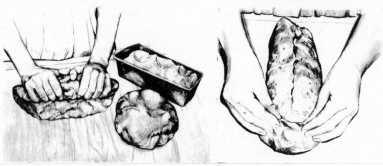

Forming the loaves

will be smooth but not necessarily glossy. If you knead for too long it will keep getting sticky, and you will end up adding too much flour. This will result in a heavy bread. Ten to 15 minutes of vigorous kneading is sufficient.

Now the dough is ready to rise. Fold each side toward you and turn without kneading. Pinch the folds together at the bottom so that the dough is formed into a ball. Wash out the bread bowl and oil it well; place the dough, round side down, in the bowl and roll it around to coat with the oil. (This will prevent it from getting a dry, crusty shell.) Turn the dough over and cover with a damp towel. Set in a warm place and let rise 50 to 60 minutes; it should almost double in bulk.

*Step 3. **Punching down; third rise:*** Punch down by gently pushing your fists into the puffed-up dough about thirty times. (This is the easiest and probably the most fun part of the whole process.) Let rise again for 45 minutes to an hour. The dough should be very puffed up, doubled in bulk but much lighter than after the previous rise.

*Step 4. **Forming the loaves; fourth and last rise:*** Remove the dough from the bowl and place it on your kneading surface. If the dough is sticky you will have to flour the surface lightly.

Shape the dough into a ball by folding all the way around in the same manner as in Step 2. Cut this ball into two equal pieces with a sharp knife and shape each of these into a ball. (You can weigh the pieces to make sure they're equal.)

Oil two bread pans. You can do this by pouring some oil into one pan and turning it upside down on top of another pan so the oil drips into the second one. It is important to oil the pans well so that the bread can be removed quickly and easily after baking. Use your hands or a pastry brush to spread the oil evenly, making sure you coat the corners of the pan, as well as the sides and bottom.

Preheat the oven to 350 degrees.

To make the loaves, take each ball, beginning with the one you made first, knead a few times for extra spring, then press out into a rectangle and roll up lengthwise into a "log" shape; or fold like a business letter. Pinch together firmly along the lengthwise crease; fold the ends over toward the crease and pinch the folds.

Place the loaf creased side up in an oiled loaf pan; gently push it into the pan with the backs of your hands to allow it to be oiled and shaped by the pan. The loaf at this point should be two thirds to three quarters the volume of the pan. Then turn the loaf so that the smooth side is up, gently press it into shape again, and set aside to rise (covered with a towel if the room is drafty) for 15 to 25 minutes, until the middle of each loaf is a little higher than the edge of the bread pan.

Step 5. Preparation for baking; baking, cooling, and storing: With a very sharp knife, make about three ½-inch deep slashes across each loaf. This allows air to escape as the bread bakes; otherwise the loaves will tear. (You can slash a design in the loaves, if you prefer.)

Make an egg wash by mixing together the egg and the. ¼ cup water. Brush each loaf generously to obtain a rich, shiny brown surface. Sprinkle with sesame seeds or poppy seeds and brush again with egg wash to paste on the seeds.

Bake in the preheated 350-degree oven for 50 to 60 minutes, for extra-shiny, rich brown loaves brushing again with the egg wash halfway through baking. The bread is ready when the surface of each loaf is golden brown and it responds with a hollow thumping sound when tapped with the tips of your fingers. Remove from the bread pans immediately and cool on racks. (Sometimes the egg wash will run down the sides of the loaf and cause it to stick to the bottom of the pan. Oiling the pan very well will help prevent this. If you have trouble removing the bread, run a butter knife around the edges of the loaf several times, turn upside down, and shake the pan or beat on the bottom of it.)

Let cool several hours. When *completely* cool, place the loaves in plastic bags and store in your bread box, or freeze the bread (wrapped first in plastic, tightly, then placed in plastic bags or wrapped in foil) and thaw out at a later date. After about three days in the bread box, the bread should be stored in the refrigerator to prevent spoilage.

2 loaves

BROWN RICE OR LEFTOVER GRAINS BREAD

In Step 2 of the preceding recipe, substitute 1 to 3 cups cooked brown rice or other cooked grains for the cracked wheat and millet. Because the cooked grains contain more water than the raw grains, the dough will be stickier and you will need more whole-wheat flour. The dough will also be lighter and will rise more than the mixed grain dough. Do not be alarmed if the dough is very sticky when you turn it out onto the board to make the loaves. Just sprinkle your board with a small amount of whole-wheat flour to prevent sticking, and handle carefully. Proceed as in the previous recipe.

2 loaves

BLACK BREAD

1 heaping tablespoon Postum dissolved in ½ cup hot water, or ½ cup strong coffee

2 tablespoons (2 envelopes) active dry yeast

2 cups lukewarm water

⅓ cup dark molasses

½ teaspoon ground ginger

2 cups dark or whole-wheat bread crumbs, or 1½ cups bread crumbs plus ½ cup wheat germ

3 cups unbleached white flour, plus more as necessary for kneading

¼ cup safflower oil

2 teaspoons salt, preferably sea salt

3 cups rye flour

1 cup soy flour

For the topping:

1 teaspoon Postum

¼ cup hot water

1 egg

Sesame seeds or poppy seeds (optional)

After dissolving the Postum, set the solution aside to cool to lukewarm.

In a large bowl, dissolve the yeast in the 2 cups lukewarm water. Add the molasses and ginger and stir together. When the Postum mixture has cooled to lukewarm, add it to the yeast mixture.

Now add the bread crumbs and wheat germ, if used, and 2 cups of the unbleached white flour, a cup at a time, to make a sponge. Stir a hundred times and set aside in a warm place, covered. Let rise 50 to 60 minutes.

At the end of the rising time, fold in the oil and salt. Add the rye flour and the soy flour, a cup at a time; the mixture will be very sticky.

As soon as the dough comes away from the sides of the bowl in one lump, place the remaining cup of unbleached white flour on your board and turn the mixture out onto it. Flour your hands generously and begin to knead. Knead very slowly and gently at first, and don't let the moistness of the dough discourage you. The dough will soon start to stiffen up and you can begin to knead more vigorously. Knead for at least 10 minutes, adding unbleached white flour as needed.

When the dough is stiff and smooth (or somewhat smooth; it may still be a little sticky), shape it into a ball. Wash out your bowl and oil it, then place the dough upside down in it first, then right side up. Cover and set in a warm place to rise until doubled in bulk, about 1½ hours.

(continued)

Preheat the oven to 400 degrees.

Punch the dough down and turn it out onto a lightly floured board. Divide into two or four equal pieces (weighing the pieces, if you wish, to be sure they're equal), and shape the pieces into two long or round loaves or four small long or round loaves. Make the loaves high, as the dough will spread out. Brush with oil and place on oiled cookie sheets, cover with a towel, and let rise again for 30 minutes, until nearly doubled in bulk.

Prepare an egg wash by dissolving 1 teaspoon Postum in ¼ cup hot water and then beating in an egg. Brush the loaves with the egg wash, then, using a sharp knife, make a few slashes across the top of each loaf. Sprinkle with sesame or poppy seeds, if you wish, and brush again.

Bake for 40 to 45 minutes, for extra-shiny loaves brushing again with egg wash halfway through the baking. Remove from the baking sheet and let cool completely on a rack.

2 large or 4 small loaves

RYE-OATMEAL BREAD

For the sponge:
2½ cups lukewarm water
1 tablespoon (1 envelope) active dry yeast
1 tablespoon Postum or instant coffee dissolved in ½ cup hot water and cooled to lukewarm
¼ cup molasses
2 cups unbleached white flour
2 cups whole-wheat flour

For the dough:
¼ cup safflower or vegetable oil
1 tablespoon salt, preferably sea salt
2 to 3 tablespoons caraway seeds
1 cup rolled or flaked oats
1 cup rye flakes or 1 more cup rolled or flaked oats
1 cup soy flour
2 cups rye flour
2 cups whole-wheat flour, approximately

For the topping:
egg wash (1 egg beaten with ¼ cup water)
Postum (optional)
Caraway seeds (optional)

Proceed as in Mixed Grains Bread (pages 38–42), adding the Postum mixture to the water and yeast in the sponge before you add the molasses and flour.

To make darker loaves, dissolve some Postum in the egg wash water before stirring in the egg.

Note: These loaves may be heavier than the first two breads in this section, since rye flour has less gluten than whole wheat.

2 loaves

FRENCH BREAD

These loaves are light and delicate. The wheat germ and whole-wheat flour add a nutty flavor but don't overwhelm the bread or make it "weighty"—and don't worry about this tasting like "health bread." The dough will be much more delicate than others in this section, and when you form the loaves after the final rise it may be sticky. If this is the case, lightly flour your work surface and your hands.

1 tablespoon (1 envelope) active dry yeast
1 tablespoon mild honey
3 cups lukewarm water
5 cups unbleached white flour, plus more as necessary for kneading
1 tablespoon melted butter or safflower oil
1 scant tablespoon salt, preferably sea salt
2 cups wheat germ
1 cup whole-wheat flour
  Egg wash (1 egg beaten with ¼ cup water)
  Yellow cornmeal

Dissolve the yeast and honey in the water. Mix in 3 cups of the unbleached white flour, a cup at a time. When the flour is mixed in, stir the batter a hundred times. Cover and set in a warm place for 30 minutes.

When the 30 minutes are up, fold in the melted butter or oil and the salt. Then fold in the wheat germ and the whole-wheat flour, a cup at a time. Add 1 cup unbleached flour and fold in. The dough should now be stiff enough to turn onto a board. Place a cup of unbleached white flour on the board and turn the dough out. Begin to knead, adding unbleached white flour as necessary. Knead until the dough is satiny smooth and very elastic, at least 10 minutes.

(continued)

Shape the dough into a ball and place in the oiled bowl, upside down first, then right side up. Cover with a towel and place in a warm spot until doubled in bulk, about 1 to 1½ hours.

Punch down and let rise again until doubled in bulk, about 1 hour. Meanwhile, butter or oil a baking sheet and sprinkle it lightly with cornmeal.

Turn the dough out onto a lightly floured board. It will be soft and may be sticky. Handle it carefully, but don't let its softness worry you. Add dustings of flour to the board to avoid sticking.

Divide the dough into three parts. Roll out each part into a long, wide rectangle, 12 to 14 inches long by about 8 inches wide. Roll this rectangle up tightly lengthwise until it is a long, thin loaf about 2 inches wide. Pinch together at the seam and the ends and place, crease down, on the baking sheet. Brush with the egg wash and slash three or four times across the top with a sharp knife; set the egg wash aside for use later.

Cover the loaves with a dry towel and let rise until nearly doubled in size, about 30 to 45 minutes.

Preheat the oven to 400 degrees.

Bake for 40 to 45 minutes, spraying the inside of the oven every 10 minutes or so with a fine mist from a spray bottle. Set your timer for 20 minutes at first and brush the loaves with the reserved egg wash. Set it then for 10 minutes, and brush the loaves again. Then set the timer for a final 10 minutes. If the bread is golden brown and responds to the tap of your fingertips with a hollow sound, remove from the oven and cool on a rack. Otherwise, bake another 5 minutes.

3 slender loaves

FRENCH HERB BREAD

This aromatic bread is especially nice for parties, with cheese. Of the three herbs I think it is the rosemary that contributes most to its special flavor. You will be following the recipe for my French bread here, and adding the herb-onion mixture to the sponge along with the oil or butter and salt.

To the ingredients for French Bread (see preceding recipe), add:

3 cloves garlic, put through a press
2 teaspoons fresh rosemary or ¾ teaspoon dried
1 tablespoon chopped fresh dill or 1 teaspoon dried
2 tablespoons chopped fresh parsley
1 onion, minced and sautéed in butter until tender

Make the sponge, following the recipe for French Bread. Let rise for 30 minutes.

Place the garlic, rosemary, dill, and parsley in a mortar and grind together into a paste.

Fold the oil or butter into the sponge. Add the salt, the sautéed onion, and the herb mixture and fold in. Proceed from here as for French Bread.

3 large or 4 small loaves

WHOLE WHEAT–SESAME PITA BREAD

Pita bread is Middle Eastern flatbread that puffs up during baking, leaving a nice pouch that you can fill for Fallafels (page 197) or with Baba Ganouch (page 61) or anything you would normally use for a sandwich. I love it for sandwiches because it contains the filling so nicely and is fairly light. Torn in strips, pitas make good dippers for Hommos (page 57) and *baba ganouch*.

The trick to making pita successfully is not to let it brown too much in the oven. Once it begins to brown it will get crisp, and what you want is a soft, flexible loaf that puffs up during baking, then deflates (sometimes you have to push it down gently, but if it's soft it won't tear). When you tear or cut it open the inside will be hollow.

When your pita has cooled (it cools quickly), wrap it well in plastic and foil, or put it in plastic bags. Pita freezes well.

2 tablespoons (2 envelopes) active dry yeast
¼ teaspoon mild honey
2 cups lukewarm water
¼ cup olive oil
  Scant 1 tablespoon salt
½ cup sesame seeds
2½ cups whole-wheat flour
3 cups unbleached white flour
  Cornmeal

Dissolve the yeast and honey in ½ cup of the lukewarm water in a mixing bowl and let sit for 10 minutes to proof (bubble up). Add the remaining water and mix well, then whisk in the oil, salt, and sesame seeds. Stir in the whole-wheat flour, a cup at a time; fold in 2 cups of the unbleached white flour, a cup at a time. Place the remaining cup of unbleached white flour on your board and turn out the dough. Knead vigorously for 10 to 15 minutes, until the dough is smooth and elastic, then shape into a ball and place in an oiled or buttered bowl, upside down first

48

to coat the dough, then right side up. Cover and let rise in a warm place for 1½ to 2 hours, until doubled in bulk.

Punch the dough down and turn it out onto your board. Knead three or four times and allow to rest for 10 minutes, then divide into eight or ten equal pieces (depending on how large you want the pitas to be) and shape each piece into a ball. Place the balls on a floured surface, cover with a towel, and let rise for 30 minutes.

Using a well-floured rolling pin, flatten each ball and roll it out into a circle approximately ⅛ inch thick and 8 inches in diameter. Dust two *unoiled* baking sheets with cornmeal and place two circles on each sheet. Leave the remaining ones on your lightly floured board. Cover and let rise again for 30 minutes. Meanwhile, preheat your oven to 500 degrees.

Place a filled baking sheet on the rack in the middle of your oven and bake for 5 minutes without opening the oven door. Check your loaves, and if they are beginning to brown, remove from the oven. If they still smell yeasty and not like baking bread, leave for another 2 to 5 minutes. (If this is the first time you're making pita, the first loaves will probably be experimental, so you can get an idea of the proper time for your oven.)

Bake all the rounds this way, cool on racks, and wrap well. Keep at room temperature if you're eating them soon, or refrigerate or freeze.

8 to 10 round loaves

CRANBERRY-ORANGE ANADAMA BREAD

This is a sweet bread that is very nice for breakfast or brunch. It's also a good holiday bread. It's dense, and won't rise as much as other breads in this section.

1⅔ cups orange juice
½ cup yellow cornmeal, preferably stone-ground
⅓ cup molasses
1 tablespoon (1 envelope) active dry yeast
½ cup warm water
2½ cups unbleached white flour, approximately
1½ cups whole raw cranberries
1 tablespoon grated orange rind
¼ cup mild honey
2 tablespoons vegetable or safflower oil
2 teaspoons salt, preferably sea salt
1½ cups wheat germ
2 cups whole-wheat flour
Egg wash (1 egg beaten with ¼ cup water), into which 1 teaspoon Postum can be dissolved, if desired)

Warm 1⅓ cups of the orange juice in a small, heavy-bottomed saucepan until bubbles form around the rim of the pan. Gradually add the cornmeal, stirring with a fork or wire whisk. Reduce the heat to a small flame and cook and stir with a wooden spoon, scraping the cornmeal up from the sides and bottom of the pan, until the mixture is thick; this will take a few minutes. Make sure to break up any lumps of cornmeal. Remove the pan from the heat and add the molasses. Allow to cool to lukewarm.

Dissolve the yeast in the warm water in a large bowl. When the cornmeal mixture has cooled, add it to the yeast and water. Then stir in 1 cup of the unbleached white flour. Stir a hundred times (the mixture will be thick and hard to stir, so be sure to use a wooden spoon), then cover and set aside in a warm place for 30 minutes.

Meanwhile, put the cranberries, orange rind, honey, and remaining orange juice in a blender or food processor and blend until the cranberries are coarsely chopped.

Fold the oil and salt into the sponge. Fold in the cranberry mixture, the wheat germ, and the whole-wheat flour, a cup at a time. Add enough unbleached white flour to make a soft dough.

Flour your kneading surface and turn the dough out onto it. Knead for 10 to 15 minutes, adding the remaining unbleached white flour as necessary. When your dough is smooth and elastic, wash out your bowl, oil it, return the dough to it, and let rise for 1 hour.

Punch the dough down and let rise again for 50 to 60 minutes. Meanwhile, oil two bread pans.

Turn the dough out onto the board and divide in half. Make two loaves, round or for loaf pans. Place them in the prepared pans or on the baking sheet and allow them to rise until the mounded tops are higher than the edges of the pans, if using, or for 45 minutes.

Toward the end of the rising time, preheat the oven to 350 degrees.

With a sharp knife, make several slashes across the tops of the loaves, and brush them with egg wash. Bake for 50 minutes at 350 degrees. Cool on a rack. Store in plastic bags, or wrap in plastic and then in foil and freeze.

2 loaves

CHALLAH

Challah is a traditional braided Jewish bread made with eggs. This version incorporates wheat germ and whole-wheat flour, like my French Bread (see page 44), and has a rich texture and flavor. This recipe makes two large braided loaves, or you can make a six-stranded braided loaf by placing a smaller braid on top of a large one, plus a smaller braided loaf.

    1 tablespoon (1 envelope) active dry yeast
1½ cups warm water
    3 tablespoons mild honey
    3 eggs
    4 to 5 cups unbleached white flour, plus more as necessary for kneading
    ¼ cup safflower oil or melted butter
    2 teaspoons salt, preferably sea salt
    1 cup wheat germ
    2 cups whole-wheat flour
      Egg wash (1 egg beaten with ¼ cup water)
      Poppy seeds

Dissolve the yeast in the water, then add the honey. Beat the eggs well and add them to the yeast mixture. Stir in 3 cups of the unbleached white flour, a cup at a time, to make a sponge. Stir a hundred times, then cover and set in a warm place for 1 hour.

When the hour is up, fold in the safflower oil and salt, then the wheat germ and the whole-wheat flour. When the dough comes away from the sides of the bowl, place a cup of unbleached white flour on your kneading surface and turn out the dough. Knead until the dough is stiff and elastic and somewhat silky, adding more unbleached white flour as necessary.

Wash out your bowl, oil it, and set the dough in it to rise for 1 to 1½ hours.

Punch the dough down and turn out onto your work surface, then divide into six equal pieces (for two braided loaves), weighing the pieces, if desired, to make sure they're equal. Roll each piece out into a rectangle about 9 inches long, then roll up into a tight cylinder. Roll each cylinder on the work surface until it is 12 to 14 inches long. Attach three cylinders by pinching the ends together. Fold the pinched part under and make a braid; pinch together at the other end and fold under. Place the braids on an oiled baking sheet and brush with oil. Let rise in a warm place for 30 minutes.

Toward the end of the rising time, preheat the oven to 375 degrees.

Brush the braids with the egg wash, sprinkle with poppy seeds, and brush with egg wash again. Bake for 40 minutes, brushing again with the egg wash halfway through. Cool on a rack.

2 loaves

BOSTON BROWN BREAD

This is one of my favorite breakfast breads, especially spread with a little ricotta cheese. It keeps for weeks if well sealed in the refrigerator, and is moist, rich, sweet, and wholesome. It's a steamed bread, and you can use coffee cans, juice cans, or pudding molds to steam it. Steaming a bread may sound strange to you, but it works, and that's what makes this bread so moist and contributes to its wonderful texture.

1 cup rye flour
1 cup yellow cornmeal, preferably stone-ground
⅔ cup whole-wheat flour
⅓ cup soy flour
2 teaspoons baking soda
1 teaspoon salt, preferably sea salt
¾ cup dark molasses
2 cups buttermilk
1 cup raisins

Sift together the rye flour, cornmeal, whole-wheat flour, soy flour, baking soda, and salt. Stir in the molasses and buttermilk and blend well, then stir in the raisins.

Butter two 1-pound coffee or juice cans, or several smaller cans, generously. Fill each can three-quarters full of batter. Butter pieces of foil and cover the cans, sealing well with tape if necessary.

Place the cans in a large pot and pour in water to the depth of 1 inch. Bring the water to a boil on top of the stove. Cover, then reduce the heat and simmer for 3 hours, checking once in a while to make sure the water hasn't boiled off. Remove the cans from the pan, unmold, and cool on a rack. If your bread seems too moist, place in a 375-degree oven for 10 minutes.

2 large or several small loaves

COFFEE CAKE

The dough for this is slightly sweet because of the orange juice. You can use whatever you have on hand for the filling. I first made it because I had several cups of Dried Fruit Compote (page 279) I needed to use up. You can make the dough the night before you wish to serve it, refrigerate it overnight, and bake the coffee cake the next morning. It reheats nicely too.

(*continued*)

For the dough:
  1 tablespoon (1 envelope) active dry yeast
  ½ cup warm water
  ½ cup orange juice
  3 tablespoons mild honey
  1 egg, beaten
  ⅓ cup spray-dried milk
  1 tablespoon lemon juice
  1 tablespoon grated orange rind
2½ cups unbleached white flour, plus more as necessary for kneading
  3 tablespoons melted butter or safflower oil
  1 teaspoon salt, preferably sea salt
1½ cups whole-wheat flour

For the filling:
  ¼ cup water, more if necessary
1½ cups chopped dried figs, prunes, dates, apricots, raisins, or a mixture
  ½ cup finely chopped almonds
  1 teaspoon ground cinnamon
  ¼ teaspoon freshly grated nutmeg
  1 tablespoon grated orange rind
  ¼ cup mild honey
  1 teaspoon vanilla extract
  1 teaspoon rum (optional)
    Pinch of salt, preferably sea salt

For the topping:
    Egg wash (1 egg beaten with ¼ cup water)
  ½ cup slivered almonds
  ¼ to ½ cup mild honey heated in ½ cup water

First prepare the dough. Dissolve the yeast in the water in a large bowl. Heat the orange juice in a small pan and stir in the honey, then remove from the heat and let cool to lukewarm. Add to the yeast mixture; stir in the egg, spray-dried milk, lemon juice, and orange rind. Stir in 1½ cups of the unbleached white flour and stir a hundred times for the sponge. Cover and set in a warm place for 1 hour.

When the hour is up, fold the butter or safflower oil and salt into the sponge; fold in the whole-wheat flour and remaining cup of unbleached white flour. Turn out onto a floured work surface and knead until smooth and elastic, adding more unbleached white flour as necessary. Wash out your bowl, oil it, and place the dough in it; let rise 1 hour.

Meanwhile, combine the ingredients for the filling in a saucepan. Simmer, adding a little more water if necessary, until the fruit is softened and the mixture thick.

Punch the dough down, turn out onto your work surface, and roll out to a rectangle about 12 x 14 inches. Spread with the fruit mixture and roll up lengthwise, like a jelly roll. Place on an oiled baking sheet and join the ends by pinching them together. Using kitchen shears or a sharp knife, cut slits halfway through the dough and 1 inch apart. If you wish, twist each slice to the left, so the inside of each slice is facing up. Let rise for 30 to 45 minutes.

Toward the end of the rising time, preheat the oven to 350 degrees.

Brush the dough with egg wash, sprinkle with the slivered almonds, and brush again with egg wash. Bake for 30 to 40 minutes, until golden brown.

Meanwhile, heat the ¼ to ½ cup honey in the ½ cup water. When you remove the coffee cake from the oven, dribble the syrup over the top.

Serve warm.

1 ring-shaped loaf

CORN BREAD

This is very moist and somewhat sweet. You can reduce the amount of honey to 1 tablespoon if you wish.

1 **cup stone-ground yellow cornmeal**
⅓ **cup soy flour**
¼ **cup whole-wheat flour**
2 **teaspoons double-acting baking powder**
1 **teaspoon salt, preferably sea salt**
1 **egg**
1 **cup milk, blended with 2½ tablespoons spray-dried milk or 3½ tablespoons instant, such as Carnation**
2 **tablespoons mild honey**

Preheat the oven to 375 degrees.

In a large bowl, mix together the cornmeal, soy flour, whole-wheat flour, baking powder, and salt.

In a separate bowl or blender blend together the wet ingredients—the egg, the enriched milk, and the honey.

Gradually add the liquid mixture to the dry mixture and stir together until the dry ingredients are moistened. Don't overbeat; the lumps, if any, will dissolve while baking.

(continued)

Either butter an 8- or 9-inch cast-iron skillet and heat it in the oven, or oil a 1-quart baking pan and heat it. Pour in the batter and bake for about 30 minutes, until just beginning to brown.

Serve hot from the pan, or cool and cover well.

16 squares

SESAME CRACKERS

These are always a hit at a party, with their rich, nutty flavor. There's something impressive about making your own crackers, too, and these are very easy. Make sure you roll them out thin enough, and don't overbake.

These crackers cut well with a cookie cutter. My catering logo is a crescent moon and star, and I've spent many an afternoon making dozens of lunar sesame crackers.

1½ cups whole-wheat flour
¼ cup soy flour
¼ cup sesame seeds
¾ teaspoon salt, preferably sea salt
¼ cup safflower or vegetable oil
½ cup cold water, approximately

Preheat the oven to 350 degrees.

Stir together the flours, seeds, and salt. Cut in the oil and blend well by rolling the mixture briskly between the palms of your hands. Add enough water to create a dough the consistency of pie pastry.

Gather the dough into a ball and roll it out to a thickness of ⅛ inch on a well-floured board, or between 2 pieces of waxed paper. Cut the dough into squares, rectangles, sticks, or cookie-cutter shapes and place on an oiled baking sheet.

Bake until crisp and golden, about 20 minutes. Be careful not to let them get too brown, or they will taste bitter.

3 to 4 dozen

CROUTONS

2 to 3 slices your choice of bread, each ¼ inch thick
1 to 2 tablespoons butter or Herb Butter (page 61)
1 clove garlic (optional)

Toast the bread in a toaster or under a broiler until brown and crisp. Cut into small (¼ to ½ inch) squares. Melt the butter in a skillet and add the optional garlic, or melt the herb butter in the skillet. Add the croutons and toss until saturated.

Remove from the heat, cool, and store in a sealed jar. Good with soups and salads.

1 cup

COCKTAIL SNACKS
AND HORS D'OEUVRES

The most gracious way to receive company is with a glass of good wine and a beautiful and tempting appetizer. No matter how elaborate the rest of my menu may be, I never leave out this course. James Beard calls it a "rite"; often the mere display of hors d'oeuvres will ensure an animated party. A bountiful platter of *crudités* around a piping hot chafing dish of fondue, a loaf of homemade bread on a board with a pâté or a nice cheese will dazzle your guests' eyes, then their palates, and will take the edge off their hunger. Pour the wine and relax with your guests. Once you see that people are eating you can retreat to the kitchen to tend to the soup. You needn't feel that you are abandoning your company. If they have nothing else in common, the food itself will stimulate conversation.

Cocktail snacks and hors d'oeuvres are what I do most as a caterer. At wedding receptions I set long skirted tables with colorful vegetable platters, aromatic chafing dishes, and elaborate boards of cheeses and homemade breads. Throughout the event we never stop refilling chafing dishes, slicing more bread, smoothing out pâtés, and replenishing cheeses. People congregate around the food, and the better it looks and tastes, the more successful the party.

My own dinner parties aren't quite as frenetic. Before a dinner party one or two, or at most three, items will suffice; my hors d'oeuvres are sometimes as simple as bread, butter, and cheese. But I always give myself time to decorate whatever I'm serving, whether it's simple or elaborate.

The choice of hors d'oeuvre and the amount of preparation time it demands should be determined by the remainder of the menu. If there's bread in your soup or if your main dish is heavy, don't offer bread before dinner; serve *crudités* or marinated vegetables. Sliced apples with fondue is a refreshing way to begin a light repast. Stuffed mushrooms are almost always appropriate. Cheese-y hors d'oeuvres can provide the protein you may fear is lacking in the rest of the meal, if it's a light one.

In any case, whatever the occasion, always have hors d'oeuvres ready and waiting when your guests arrive. They will feel well looked after, and you will all be put at ease.

Assorted Spreads and Pâtés

HOMMOS

Hommos, one of my very favorite foods, is a Middle Eastern garbanzo bean–sesame seed spread flavored with garlic, lemon juice, and olive oil. You can mold it into a bowl or onto a plate and garnish it with fresh parsley, cherry tomatoes cut in wedges, olives, and radishes; you can spread it on bread or crackers for canapes, or pipe it from a pastry bag onto sliced rounds of cucumbers, squash, or eggplant. It can be made up to two days in advance and stored, tightly covered, in the refrigerator. It makes a wonderful sandwich spread as well, on whole-wheat bread or pita (Middle Eastern flat bread), with mayonnaise, lettuce or sprouts, and tomatoes.

This recipe will feed from six to twelve people if you aren't serving a number of other hors d'oeuvres, and up to twenty people if it is one of many.

2¼ cups cooked garbanzo beans (1 cup dried; see page 25), drained (save some of the liquid), or 1 can (16 ounces) cooked garbanzos
¼ cup lemon juice
¼ cup olive oil, more if necessary
2 cloves garlic, or more to taste
⅓ cup sesame tahini
    Salt, preferably sea salt, to taste (you will need a generous amount)

If you want a textured *hommos*, keep out half the garbanzos and mash in a bowl with a potato masher.

Put the lemon juice, olive oil, and garlic in a blender or food processor. Turn it on and slowly pour in the remaining garbanzos. Puree until smooth, stopping the machine and stirring the mixture if necessary. If the mixture is very dry, add a bit of cooking liquid from the beans or more olive oil.

Remove the mixture from the blender and combine with the mashed garbanzos and the sesame tahini. Salt to taste, cover, and refrigerate. (If you are using a food processor add the sesame tahini to the mixture in the food processor after the garbanzos are pureed.)

If you want a smooth *hommos,* puree all the garbanzos. If you want it runny, use a little more olive oil; taste for lemon juice and add more if desired.

Serve either version as described in the beginning of the recipe.

3 cups

SOYA PÂTÉ

Soya pâté is one of the most popular dishes in my repertoire. It's a staple in my own home, as it lasts for up to a week in the refrigerator, is extremely high in protein and B vitamins, and is delicious. It's also cheap and easy to make, filling and low in calories. It's one of those dishes I'm famous for, because it's made from soybeans "but you'd never know it." I think it tastes like top-quality liverwurst.

The secret to this pâté is the Marmite or Savorex. It occurred to me one day that I could combine soya with the yeast extract to achieve a liverlike flavor. Then it was just a question of working out the seasonings, and a study of traditional liver pâté recipes helped me in this. A friend once remarked that this had all the attractive qualities of a pâté without the heavy, fat-laden sensations.

A little soya pâté goes a long way. It makes a tasty and attractive hors d'oeuvre and a fine sandwich spread. For hors d'oeuvres I mold it in a mound and cover it with sliced olives and pimientos, and surround it with deep-green parsley and other herbs. Hard-boiled eggs make a nice garnish, too. The pâté goes beautifully with mayonnaise or mustard, and on whole-grain bread it's a meal in itself.

As with *hommos,* you can cook the soybeans up to two days in advance and keep them in the refrigerator until you're ready to make the pâté. And you'll have to remember to soak the beans before you cook them.

2 eggs
¼ cup milk
2 tablespoons brandy

2 teaspoons Marmite or Savorex
2 teaspoons tamari
2 cloves garlic
½ teaspoon dried thyme
⅛ teaspoon ground allspice
⅛ teaspoon ground ginger
¼ teaspoon salt, preferably sea salt
¼ teaspoon freshly ground pepper
½ onion, sautéed in butter or vegetable oil until tender
2 cups cooked soybeans (¾ cup dried; see page 25) or 2 cups cooked soy flakes (1 cup raw; see page 25)

Preheat the oven to 350 degrees.

If you are using a blender, place all the ingredients except the onion and soybeans in the blender jar and turn on at low speed. Increase the speed and gradually pour in the cooked soybeans. Blend until the mixture is completely smooth, stopping and stirring occasionally if necessary. Stir in the onions. If using a food processor, grind the beans first with ten stops and starts of the machine, then add the remaining ingredients except the onion, turn on the machine, and blend until smooth. Stir in the onion. Make sure your mixture is completely smooth; it takes over a minute of grinding in the food processor.

Oil or butter a small casserole (1 quart size), a bread pan, a soufflé dish, or a pâté tureen. Pour in the pâté, cover tightly with foil or a lid, and bake in the preheated oven for 45 to 50 minutes. Remove from the oven, allow to cool, and refrigerate. Do not eat until completely chilled.

3 cups

MUSHROOM PÂTÉ

This is a wonderful combination of savory, aromatic mushrooms and crunchy ground almonds. Since these mushrooms will be cooked and blended, you needn't look for the most beautiful ones you can find (as you would for stuffed or marinated mushrooms). In fact, you can even use just stems, if you have enough. When I serve Marinated Vegetables Vinaigrette (page 74), I use the stems for mushroom pâté.

Mushroom pâté is easy to make and keeps for five days, well sealed, in the refrigerator.

(*continued*)

2 tablespoons butter

½ cup almonds (for a stiffer pàté use an additional ½ cup)

1 tablespoon olive oil

½ cup chopped onion

¾ pound fresh mushrooms

1 clove garlic, minced or put through a press

¼ teaspoon dried thyme

Salt, preferably sea salt, and freshly ground pepper to taste

2 tablespoons dry vermouth

1 teaspoon grated lemon rind (optional)

Chopped fresh parsley for garnish (optional)

Heat 2 teaspoons of the butter in a small skillet and sauté the almonds for 5 minutes or until they are toasted, shaking the pan. Watch them carefully, because they will begin to burn soon after they begin to toast. As soon as they begin to smell toasty, remove them from the heat and from the pan. Set aside 2 tablespoons for garnish and grind the rest in a blender or food processor. Place the ground almonds in a mixing bowl and set aside.

Heat the olive oil and remaining butter in a 9- or 10-inch skillet or a wok and sauté the onion gently until tender. Add the mushrooms, garlic, thyme, salt, and freshly ground pepper and cook over medium heat, uncovered, until the mushrooms are tender and aromatic, about 15 to 20 minutes. Add the vermouth and cook for 3 more minutes.

Puree the mushrooms in a blender or food processor. Pour into the bowl with the ground almonds and stir the mixture together. Taste and adjust salt, pepper, and garlic to taste. If you wish, add the finely grated lemon rind.

Place in a jar or mold, cover, and refrigerate for several hours. Serve garnished with the almonds you have set aside and, if you wish, with parsley.

2 cups

BABA GANOUCH

Middle Eastern Eggplant Spread

Baba ganouch is another garlic-flavored, lemony spread from the Middle East. It sometimes incorporates the charred skin of the baked or broiled eggplant, which gives it a roasted flavor. I myself like this somewhat "burnt" taste, but since I'm not sure everyone else will, I clean off the crisped edges when I make it for guests.

This dish can be made one or two days before you plan to serve it.

1½ pounds eggplant, prepared as on page 23, but "steamed" for 20 to 30 minutes, and cooled slightly
¼ to ½ cup lemon juice, to taste
3 to 4 tablespoons sesame tahini
2 cloves garlic
Salt, preferably sea salt, to taste
Garnish of your choice (chopped green pepper, fresh parsley or basil, chopped or sliced red pimiento, pitted, sliced black olives)

When the "steamed" eggplant is cool enough for you to handle, peel off the charred skin, if you wish, and puree the pulp in a blender or food processor (or mash with a fork or mortar and pestle) with the other ingredients. Add salt to taste and correct the seasonings.

Place in a serving bowl and garnish with your choice (or a combination) of chopped green pepper, fresh parsley or basil, red pimiento, and black olives.

Note: Baba ganouch can be somewhat runny. Spoon it onto bread, or use pita bread (Middle Eastern flat bread) or vegetables as dippers.

2 cups

HERB BUTTER

Herb butter can be made a day in advance and refrigerated, covered with plastic, but it is much better if served soon after it is made. The herbs will be very fresh, and the garlic and onions sweet. After a short time the garlic and onion will begin to sour and dominate the subtle herbal flavors.

Make sure that you let the butter soften before you make this. You will be able to proceed much faster if you do, whether you use a food processor, a wooden spoon, a whisk, or a hand mixer.

If you are using a food processor, use the steel blade only for chopping the garlic, onions, and herbs, and be very careful to chop them with a minimum of one-second bursts. The green from the herbs and onions (as well as the bitter juice from the onions) is quickly released by the steel blade, and if you aren't careful you'll have green herb butter. (I once had to serve some that my processor had made green, and guests piled it onto their bread, thinking it was guacamole. What a shock when they bit into all that butter!)

This can be molded and garnished with parsley and other herbs.

¼ pound (1 stick) butter, softened
1 clove garlic, minced or put through a press
1 green onion, both white part and green, finely minced, or 1 tablespoon chopped fresh chives or shallots
1 tablespoon chopped fresh parsley
1 teaspoon chopped fresh dill (omit if fresh is unavailable)

If you are not using a food processor, put the softened butter in a small bowl and whip with a whisk, a wooden spoon, or an electric mixer. Add the remaining ingredients and mix well. If you are using a food processor, insert the steel blade and chop the herbs with a very few one-second bursts. Remove them and wipe out the bowl, then replace the steel blade with the plastic blade. Make sure the butter is softened, and mix the herbs, onions, and garlic together with the butter, using the plastic blade.

Place the herb butter in a butter dish or mold, cover well, and chill until serving time.

Note: I use lightly salted butter for my herb butter. If you are using unsalted butter, you might want to add a little salt to taste.

About ½ cup

HERBED CREAM CHEESE

This is a glorious combination, bursting with the fragrance of fresh herbs.

I like to mold this in a ring, then shortly before serving unmold it onto a platter and garnish with herbs and fresh vegetables. To unmold, dip the mold in warm water for 10 seconds and invert onto your platter. Refrigerate immediately to stop the surface from melting.

This is easier to make with a mixer than with a food processor, since the juices of the herbs and onions are released by the action of the steel blade (see the note preceding the recipe for Herb Butter on page 61), and if you aren't careful to clean the bowl and replace the steel blade with the plastic one you'll have green herbed cream cheese.

8 ounces cream cheese, softened
3 to 4 green onions, both white part and green, chopped

2 small or medium cloves garlic, minced or put through a press
½ teaspoon dry mustard
½ teaspoon Worcestershire sauce
¼ cup chopped fresh parsley
¼ cup chopped fresh dill (omit if fresh is unavailable)
2 to 4 tablespoons chopped fresh basil (optional)
¼ cup chopped ripe olives
1 to 2 tablespoons lemon juice
  Salt, preferably sea salt, and freshly ground pepper to taste

In a large mixing bowl, whip the softened cream cheese and add the other ingredients. Mix well, add salt and pepper to taste. Mold in a bowl or ring, or in a mound on a platter. Cover and refrigerate, or serve immediately (although if it is runny or too soft, 15 minutes in the refrigerator will stiffen it up), garnished with fresh herbs and vegetables.

1½ cups

POTTED ROQUEFORT SPREAD

This spread makes a delightful gift, sealed in ceramic crocks. It is a somewhat runny mixture and can't be molded. It will keep for several days in the refrigerator, though it does get more pungent with each day—a thought you should use as a guideline for how far in advance you make it.

8 ounces sharp Cheddar cheese, grated
8 ounces Roquefort or blue cheese
8 ounces ricotta
¼ to ⅓ cup dry white wine
¼ cup dry sherry
1 teaspoon Worcestershire sauce
1 tablespoon finely chopped onion, green onion, or fresh chives
1 clove garlic, minced or put through a press (optional)
  Freshly ground pepper (optional)

Grate the Cheddar cheese into a mixing bowl and crumble in the Roquefort cheese. Stir in the ricotta and blend thoroughly, using either a wooden spoon, mixer, or food processor.

Stir in the wine, sherry, Worcestershire, and onion and blend thoroughly. Add garlic, if you wish, and freshly ground black pepper.

Place the mixture in a well-sealed crock or jar and refrigerate. Serve as a dip or a spread.

3 cups

QUICHETTES

There are two ways to make "quichettes." You can make little crusts in tart pans and fill them, or you can make a big quiche, allow it to cool, and cut it into neat little squares. I prefer the latter. The little tart pans are expensive, and you need a number of them, and making all those little pastries is very time consuming for me. It depends upon how much you like working with pastry. I usually assemble and bake my quiche several hours or a day in advance and allow it to cool and set; then I cover it with plastic wrap and refrigerate it. You can make your pie crust well in advance and freeze it, or up to three days in advance and refrigerate it, making sure it is well sealed.

See the recipe for Spinach and Onion Quiche in a Whole-Wheat Crust (page 150). Instead of a pie pan use an oblong pan (8 x 10 inches); you need only cover the bottom with your crust. Beat an egg and brush the crust with it before prebaking; this will keep the crust from getting soggy. Fill it with the spinach and onion filling, or onion alone, or onion and 2 cups sliced mushrooms, sautéed until soft and fragrant in a little butter and olive oil with 1 clove garlic, minced, and salt and pepper.

Proceed as in the quiche recipe. Allow to cool, cover and refrigerate. When you are sure it has set, cut into 2-inch squares. Warm in a 250-degree oven on buttered baking sheets, remove to a platter or plate, and serve. You can also keep these warm in a chafing dish. Garnish with tomato wedges or radish flowers, or parsley and sliced oranges.

If you are using little tart pans, you will need eight to ten of them. Brush the shells with egg and prebake, then fill with the quiche mixture but bake only 25 minutes (check then, and continue to bake if necessary until firm).

6 to 10 servings

TORTILLAS

These are not the Mexican flat bread here, but the flat Spanish omelet, made as described on pages 169–70. In the bars in Spain they are served cold or warm, cut into pie-shaped wedges or squares, as *tapas* (hors d'oeuvres). Make the omelet of your choice (see pages 169–72), for six people. Remove from the pan and allow to cool. Either serve on a plate, cut in wedges, or cut into 1- or 2-inch squares.

The *tortilla* lasts a day in the refrigerator, well wrapped, and is good cold.

6 to 10 servings

STUFFED MUSHROOMS

I have made the fillings for stuffed mushrooms a day in advance and stored them, tightly covered, in the refrigerator. The flavors mature and are actually more savory. I do think it is best, however, to do the step of preparing the mushrooms themselves and filling them on the day you wish to serve them. This way they will not lose their shape or become soggy.

Stuffed mushrooms also make an excellent side dish at a meal, and jumbo mushrooms can be filled and served as a main course, garnished with chopped fresh parsley.

1 **pound large, firm fresh mushrooms (or enough to allow 2 to 3 per person)**
2 **tablespoons olive oil**
1 **teaspoon butter**
1 **clove garlic, minced or put through a press**
  Salt and freshly ground pepper
  Pinch of dried thyme
  Filling of your choice (see below)

Thinking in terms of 2 to 3 mushrooms per person, choose the largest, firmest mushrooms you can find; they will shrink when cooked. A fresh mushroom is closed up to the stem on the underside; don't choose those whose caps are accordionlike on the underside.

Clean the mushrooms and carefully remove the stems by cutting or twisting them off at the cap; if you can twist them off, you will have a bigger space to fill. Set the stems aside to use in the filling.

Heat the olive oil in a large skillet or wok and add the butter and garlic. Add the mushrooms and sauté gently just until they begin to soften up and become aromatic. Add salt and freshly ground pepper, and a pinch of thyme. Give them another stir and drain on paper towels.

Preheat the oven to 325 degrees.

Stuff with the filling of your choice. Even the small mushrooms that look like they have no cavity to fill will hold a certain amount; they are soft, and by pressing the mixture in with the back of the spoon you will be surprised to see how much you can get in there. The filling should make a little mound over the top of the mushroom.

Place the mushrooms, filled side up, in an oiled baking dish, cover with foil to prevent drying out, and bake for 20 minutes. Serve hot.

6 to 8 servings

WILD RICE FILLING

1 cup Vegetable Stock (page 91) or water
⅓ cup wild rice
  Salt, preferably sea salt
½ cup chopped onion
1 clove garlic, minced or put through a press
1 tablespoon butter or vegetable oil
⅓ cup minced mushroom stems
¼ to ½ cup finely chopped almonds
2 tablespoons dry sherry
1 tablespoon chopped fresh parsley
¼ teaspoon dried thyme
  Freshly grated nutmeg
  Freshly ground pepper to taste
  Tamari to taste (optional)

Bring the stock or water to a boil in a saucepan. Wash the rice and slowly pour into the boiling liquid. Add ½ teaspoon salt, reduce the heat, and cover. Cook for 40 minutes, then remove the lid and cook for another 10 minutes, or until the rice is tender; pour off the excess liquid.

In a large frying pan, sauté the onion and garlic in butter or oil until the onion is soft. Add the mushroom stems and the almonds and sauté a few minutes more. Add the cooked wild rice, sherry, parsley, thyme, and seasonings and stir together. Cook over a low flame for 5 to 10 minutes, stirring occasionally, until the mushroom stems are cooked through and the mixture is nice and aromatic. Correct the seasoning, adding a little tamari if you wish, and perhaps more garlic. Remember, if you are making the filling for the next day, that the flavors will mature overnight.

Store, covered, in the refrigerator, or fill the mushrooms, bake, and serve.

Note: You may have more filling than you need for the mushrooms. In this case, surround the filled mushrooms with a ring of filling, or keep it in the refrigerator for up to three days and serve it as a side dish.

Enough to fill 30 mushrooms, or 1 pound

SAVORY ALMOND FILLING

½ small onion, chopped
1 clove garlic, minced or put through a press
  Stems from the mushrooms, chopped fine
1 tablespoon butter or vegetable oil
½ cup finely chopped almonds (you can do this quickly in a blender)
1 carrot, grated
¼ cup freshly grated Parmesan cheese
2 tablespoons chopped fresh parsley
  Salt, preferably sea salt, and freshly ground pepper to taste
  Tamari to taste (optional)

In a large frying pan, sauté the onion, garlic, and mushroom stems in the oil or butter until the onion is tender. Add the almonds and cook a few minutes longer. Add the remaining ingredients, stir together, and cook, uncovered, over a low flame for 5 more minutes, stirring occasionally. Check the seasoning and remove from the heat.

Store, covered, in the refrigerator, or fill the mushrooms, bake, and serve.

Enough to fill 30 mushrooms, or 1 pound

KASHA FILLING

1 egg
½ cup raw buckwheat groats
1¼ cups boiling Vegetable Stock (page 91) or water
½ onion, chopped
½ carrot, chopped
½ stalk celery, chopped
  Stems from the mushroom, chopped fine
½ teaspoon salt, preferably sea salt, or to taste
  Freshly ground pepper to taste

Beat the egg in a bowl. Combine with the buckwheat groats and stir together until all the grains are coated with egg.

Heat a heavy pan over moderate heat and pour in the groats/egg mixture. (You are pouring this into a dry pan, which may puzzle you, but the mixture will not stick if the heat is moderate and you continue to stir it.) Keep stirring the mixture with a wooden spoon until the egg is absorbed and the grains begin to toast; it's important that the egg be absorbed completely or you will have unattractive strings of cooked egg in the kasha. (This step gives the dish its toasty aroma.)

(continued)

Immediately pour in the boiling stock or water. Add the onion, carrot, celery, mushroom stems, and salt and bring to a second boil. Lower the heat, cover, and cook slowly for 35 minutes, then remove the lid and continue cooking until the liquid is absorbed. Season to taste with more salt, if desired, and pepper.

Cover, refrigerate, and store overnight, or fill the mushrooms, bake, and serve.

Enough to fill 30 mushrooms, or 1 pound

HERBED BREAD CRUMBS FILLING

4 green onions, both white part and green, minced
1 to 2 cloves garlic, minced or pureed
1 tablespoon butter or vegetable oil, more if necessary
1 cup bread crumbs, preferably whole wheat
¼ cup chopped fresh parsley
¼ teaspoon dried tarragon
¼ teaspoon oregano
¼ cup freshly grated Parmesan cheese

Sauté the green onions and garlic gently in butter or olive oil for 3 minutes. Add the bread crumbs and herbs and sauté, stirring, until the bread crumbs are toasted. Add more butter and olive oil if necessary. Add the Parmesan; stir together and remove from the heat. Correct the seasoning. Cover, refrigerate, and store overnight, or fill the mushrooms, bake, and serve.

Enough to fill 30 mushrooms, or 1 pound

TIROPITES

Greek Filo Turnovers

Tiropites are triangular turnovers made with filo dough. You can make the fillings and assemble the *tiropites* a day in advance, but bake them just before serving to assure their crispness. To store, place on an oiled baking sheet, cover with plastic, and refrigerate.

The little squares of filo may give you some trouble as you fold them into triangles and try to seal them. Don't overstuff them, and use plenty of butter or egg around the edges to seal. But don't worry: the last time I made them no matter what I did they didn't appear to be well sealed, but when they baked they stayed together.

You needn't restrict yourself to the fillings that follow. Use your imagination—and your leftovers—to fill the *tiropites* with anything you think would contrast nicely with the crisp, buttery filo.

1 **pound filo dough**
½ **cup melted butter**
　Filling of your choice (pages 70–71)
　Beaten egg (optional)

Preheat the oven to 375 degrees. Remove the filo dough from the package and unfold it carefully. Remove a sheet of the dough and brush it with some of the melted butter. Lay another sheet on this, and another sheet on the second one. Butter the third sheet and add two more sheets. Butter the fifth sheet and add two more. Now cut this seven-layer sheet into equal-sized squares, the size of which will depend on the size triangle you want and the number of them. Remember that you will be placing filling on each square and folding it in half like a triangle, and that the sheets are delicate, so you will need a certain amount of surface area to play with, but if you want small *tiropites* (which I prefer), you need only remember to place small amounts of filling (teaspoonfuls as opposed to tablespoonfuls) on the squares.

Butter the top sheet of filo and place a spoonful or two of filling (depending on how big your square is) in the center of each square. Butter the edges or brush with egg. Fold the square over on the diagonal to make a

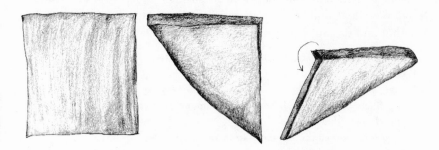

triangle and press the edges together. Brush the edges of the seal with butter or egg.

Place on a buttered baking sheet and bake for 30 minutes, or until golden.

2 dozen, depending on size

GREEK SPINACH FILLING

This filling may be made a day in advance and stored in a covered container in the refrigerator. Stir it up before you fill the *tiropites*.

1 small onion, minced
1 tablespoon butter or olive oil
2 eggs, beaten
4 ounces feta cheese
10 ounces spinach, blanched, drained and chopped, or 1 package (10 ounces) frozen spinach, thawed, squeezed dry, and chopped
¼ cup freshly grated Parmesan cheese
Pinch of freshly grated nutmeg
¼ teaspoon dried rosemary
¼ teaspoon oregano
Salt, preferably sea salt, and freshly ground pepper to taste (remember that the cheeses are very salty)

Sauté the onion in the butter or olive oil until tender. In a medium-sized mixing bowl, beat the eggs and crumble in the feta. Add the remaining ingredients and stir together.

Store, refrigerated, or use right away.

Enough to fill 2 dozen tiropites

MEXICAN FILLING

This filling should not be made in advance unless you are filling the *tiropites* with it and then storing them. Grated cheese tends to clump together and dry up, and it'll be hard to work with if kept too long.

12 ounces Monterey jack or Cheddar cheese, grated
1 cup ricotta
2 eggs, beaten
¼ cup finely chopped fresh or canned jalapeño peppers
½ cup chopped black olives
½ to ¾ teaspoon cumin, or more to taste
Salt, preferably sea salt, to taste

Combine all the ingredients and mix well.

Enough to fill 3 dozen tiropites

RICOTTA FILLING

This filling may be made a day in advance and stored in a covered container in the refrigerator. Stir it up before you fill the *tiropites*.

½ cup chopped onion
1 to 2 tablespoons butter or olive oil
2 eggs
4 ounces feta cheese
12 ounces ricotta
2 tablespoons chopped fresh parsley or dill
   Freshly ground pepper to taste
¼ cup grated Parmesan cheese

Sauté the onion in the butter or olive oil until tender. Set aside.

In a medium-sized bowl, beat the eggs, then crumble in the feta. Add the remaining ingredients and mix well.

Enough to fill 3 dozen tiropites

LITTLE SPANOKOPITAS, OR "SPINACH BAKLAVAS"

These can be assembled a day or two in advance, covered, and stored in the refrigerator before baking; or they can be baked, then cooled, wrapped, and frozen for up to two weeks. Prepare the recipe for Spanokopita on page 166, then proceed in either of the two following ways.

If serving right away: Remove the *spanokopita* from the oven and cut into diamond shapes about 2 inches long. To do this, cut diagonal strips across the *spanokopita,* then turn your pan and cut diagonal strips in the other direction. The filo dough will flake and the top layers may fall off, but don't get frustrated by this; just replace them if you can. Transfer the little diamonds to a platter and serve.

If freezing: The *spanokopita* shrinks from the sides of the pan when it bakes and is easy to remove in one piece. You can either wrap the entire *spanokopita* in one piece and cut it into diamonds right after it has thawed, or cut it into the diamond shapes after it has been baked and cooled, then wrap the pieces up in small packages. Whichever way you prefer, wrap the baked, cooled *spanokopita* in plastic wrap, then in foil, and freeze. The *spanokopita* will thaw in 2 hours. To reheat, unwrap and place on buttered baking sheets. Heat through at 300 degrees for 30 minutes.

The only drawback to storing the already baked *spanokopita* is that the filo loses its crispness and the pie its puffed-up quality. However, the savory spinach filling doesn't lose its rich flavor, and my guests have always found these mouthwatering.

Make sure you give yourself plenty of time to cut the pie and clean up the filo, which will undoubtedly flake all over your work surface.

10 servings

NACHOS WITH BLACK BEAN TOPPING

No matter where I am, the flavor of the black beans in this dish always carries me back to Mexico. The nachos are easy to assemble, and the beans can be soaked and cooked up to two days in advance; don't refry or puree more than one day in advance, or they may dry out. The amount of time this recipe takes will depend on whether or not you use prepared nacho crisps. Using the prepared ones, with my beans ready and cheese grated, I once assembled four hundred of these for a wedding, and did it in three hours!

There are two methods for making the bean topping. One involves refrying the beans and mashing while refrying, the other is a simple puree. The flavors will be almost the same. Do note that the beans have to be soaked overnight, or at least for a few hours, before you can prepare them—and that the preparation itself will take a couple of hours.

  1 cup dried black beans
    Safflower oil
  ½ onion, chopped
  2 cloves garlic, minced or put through a press
  3 cups water
  1 tablespoon coriander (*cilantro*) leaves
    Salt, preferably sea salt
  1 teaspoon ground cumin, more as necessary
  1 teaspoon chili powder
  1 package nacho chips, or 1½ dozen corn tortillas
  8 ounces white Cheddar cheese or Monterey jack, grated
  6 fresh jalapeño peppers or 1 small can (4 ounces) jalapeños, sliced in rounds

Cook the beans as in Black Bean Enchiladas (page 144), using 1 tablespoon safflower oil, the chopped onion, garlic, water, coriander, and 1½ teaspoons salt.

Method 1: Refrying the Beans: Pour off most of the liquid from the cooked beans. Heat some safflower oil in a large, heavy-bottomed skillet and add the beans. As they begin to bubble and fry, mash them with a potato masher or the back of a spoon. Add the cumin and chili powder and continue to cook and mash until the mixture is fairly dry. Remove from the heat and correct the seasoning.

Method 2: Refrying the Beans: I prefer this method to the refrying, because no additional oil is needed. Pour off almost all the liquid from the beans and puree with a minimum of liquid in a blender or food processor, adding the cumin and chili powder. Blend until the beans form a thick paste, but don't blend too much, as you want the beans to retain some texture.

Preheat the oven to 350 degrees.

If you are using tortillas, cut them into quarters. Heat ¼ inch of safflower oil in a skillet; add some salt and the tortilla quarters. Sauté on both sides until they are crisp, being very careful not to burn (once they begin to cook, they cook quickly), and drain on paper towels.

Spread a layer of the refried bean mixture on each nacho chip. Top with grated cheese, then with the sliced jalapeños. Place on baking sheets and heat through in the oven until the cheese melts, about 15 minutes.

Serve hot.

6 dozen nachos

CRUDITÉ SALAD

This salad makes an excellent hors d'oeuvre.

1 cup finely shredded green or red cabbage
1 cup finely grated carrot
1 cup finely grated beets
1 cup sliced fresh mushrooms
1 cup thinly sliced cucumber
2 tomatoes, sliced thin
1½ cups Brown Rice Salad (page 245)
1 recipe Vinaigrette (page 261)
   Leaf or Boston lettuce, leaves separated, washed and drained

Put each of the vegetables, and the rice salad, in separate bowls and toss separately with the dressing.

Line a platter with lettuce leaves and place each item in mounds on the lettuce, with tomatoes interspersed. (Alternatively, you can line individual salad plates with lettuce and place small amounts of each item on top.)

6 to 8 servings

MARINATED VEGETABLES VINAIGRETTE

This, always a crowd pleaser, makes a stunning platter. Don't feel compelled, however, always to serve all of these vegetables. One or two alone always work. For instance, you may just want to start a meal off with marinated mushrooms or cucumbers, or potatoes and cauliflower. Use your imagination for different combinations.

For the vegetable platter:

    4 tomatoes, cut in wedges, or ½-pint box cherry tomatoes, stems removed and halved, if desired
    2 green peppers, or 1 red pepper and 1 green pepper, sliced crosswise
    ½ pound fresh mushroom caps
    ½ head cauliflower, broken into florets and steamed for 5 minutes
    1 cucumber, peeled if waxed or bitter, and sliced (score the skin with a fork if not waxed or bitter)
    1 yellow squash, sliced
    1 cup alfalfa or mung bean sprouts (optional)
    3 red or new potatoes, steamed until crisp-tender and sliced
    1 head Boston or leaf lettuce
    Radish flowers for garnish (see page 78)
    ½ cup pitted ripe or Greek olives

For the marinade:

    Juice of 1 lemon
    ½ cup wine vinegar or cider vinegar
    1 clove garlic, minced or put through a press
    2 teaspoons prepared Dijon-style mustard
    ½ teaspoon dried tarragon
    ½ teaspoon dried marjoram
    1 teaspoon chopped fresh dill
    Salt, preferably sea salt, and freshly ground pepper to taste
1½ cups olive oil
    ½ Bermuda onion, sliced in thin rounds

Prepare all the vegetables; separate the leaves of lettuce and hold for garnish, along with the radish flowers and olives.

Make a marinade by combining the lemon juice, vinegar, garlic, mustard, herbs, and seasonings. Stir in the olive oil and blend well; stir in the Bermuda onion.

Toss the vegetables with the marinade either together or in separate bowls, and refrigerate for several hours or overnight, tossing them every once in a while to distribute the marinade evenly.

When ready to serve, cover a serving platter with the lettuce leaves. Arrange the vegetables in a nice design, perhaps with the mushrooms in a mound in the middle, surrounded by the cucumbers, squash, and onions. Here and there scatter tomatoes and clumps of sprouts. Place the green peppers over the other vegetables and scatter the olives and radishes throughout.

Serve with toothpicks, either stuck into the vegetables or in little cups near the platter. Have napkins close by.

Note: If you wish, you can substitute 2 to 3 tablespoons chopped fresh herbs—such as parsley, basil, marjoram, or fennel—for the dried herbs in the marinade.

6 to 10 servings

MARINATED BROCCOLI STEMS

Here is a brilliant way to use your trimmed broccoli stems. I always felt so wasteful throwing them away before. This serves as a tasty hors d'oeuvre, a side dish, a great addition to green salads, and can be a salad in itself.

You'll be pleased here to see how easy it is to peel the stems.

3 to 4 broccoli stems
½ teaspoon salt, preferably sea salt
1 clove garlic, crushed
1 tablespoon white wine vinegar or cider vinegar
1 tablespoon safflower or olive oil

Peel the broccoli stems, slice diagonally ⅛ inch thick, and place in a jar. Add the salt, then cover the jar, shake, and place in the refrigerator overnight, or for several hours at least.

In the morning, or after several hours, drain the water from the jar. Add the crushed garlic, vinegar, and oil, shake well, and refrigerate for several hours longer.

About 1 cup

MARINATED VEGETABLES À LA GRECQUE

The flavors of many different spices make this a sensational dish; fennel or anise adds an exceptional touch.

In addition to the vegetables I've mentioned here, squash, eggplant, and cucumber are nice for this dish. You will want to use different ones according to what's available. My favorite vegetables in this recipe are the carrots; they turn out delicate but still crunch.

This is a dish that *must* be made the day before you wish to serve it, or very early that morning. However, it keeps well in the refrigerator, so you can make it several days beforehand.

For the marinade:
  1 cup freshly drawn tap water, more if necessary
  ½ cup dry white wine, more if necessary
  ⅓ cup red wine vinegar or cider vinegar, more if necessary
  1 cup olive oil, more if necessary
  2 cloves garlic, minced or put through a press
  1 dozen whole black peppercorns
  2 bay leaves
  1 teaspoon whole fennel seed or ½ teaspoon aniseed
  1 teaspoon chopped fresh thyme or ½ teaspoon dried
  4 sprigs fresh parsley
  ½ teaspoon mustard seed
    Salt, preferably sea salt, to taste
  1 onion, sliced
  ¼ cup currants

For the vegetable platter:
  12 whole pearl onions, peeled
  1 pint Brussels sprouts, trimmed (optional)
  ½ head cauliflower, cut into small florets
  ½ pound carrots, quartered if very large or halved if small, and cut into 3-inch sticks
  12 medium-sized whole mushrooms, stems cut level with the caps
  ½ pound green beans, ends cut off
  1 small jar (6 ounces) artichoke hearts or bottoms
  ½ pint box cherry tomatoes
  1 tablespoon coriander seed, freshly cracked or ground
    Sprigs of fresh water cress, coriander (*cilantro*), or parsley for garnish

Combine all the ingredients for the marinade in a large, heavy saucepan. Bring to a simmer, cover, and continue to simmer for 10 to 15 minutes, to combine and bring out the flavors. You can be preparing the vegetables in the meantime.

Drop the little onions into the simmering liquid and cook for 10 minutes. Add the Brussels sprouts and cauliflower and cook for 5 minutes. Next add the carrots and cook 5 minutes. Add the mushrooms and cook 5 minutes, then add the green beans. Make sure all the vegetables are submerged in the liquid; if they are not, add more water, wine, vinegar, and olive oil in their original proportions. Now cook all the vegetables, uncovered, for 5 to 10 minutes, until tender but not too soft. Add the artichoke hearts and cherry tomatoes and simmer for another 5 minutes.

Remove from the heat and allow the vegetables to cool in the marinade. Then place the entire contents of the saucepan, the vegetables still covered with the marinade, in wide-mouthed jars or a bowl and cover tightly. Refrigerate overnight.

Serve these vegetables on a large platter with toothpicks, arranged to your fancy—the green beans and cauliflower in the middle, perhaps, surrounded by the rest of the vegetables. Crack the coriander seed over the vegetables and garnish with fresh water cress, coriander, or parsley.

Note: You may also serve these vegetables on individual salad plates, as a first course.

6 servings

VEGETABLE PLATTER WITH ASSORTED DIPS

For this dish you can use whatever vegetables are in season. The important thing to use is your imagination. The variety of colors you get from the different vegetables makes this a dramatic hors d'oeuvre. Give yourself enough time to make a nice arrangement; you'll be creating a garden on a platter. Be fanciful and have fun.

Your dips can be simple or elaborate. Plain homemade mayonnaise, always popular, is a good place to begin. Both mayonnaise and yogurt serve as the bases for many of the dips listed below.

The amount of servings will depend on the quantity of vegetables you use.

Suggested dips are:

Homemade Yogurt (page 259)
Blender Mayonnaise (page 259)
Tofu Mayonnaise (page 260)
Curry Dressing (page 262)

(continued)

Russian Dressing (page 79)
Green Dressing (page 262)
Sunflower Seed Dressing (page 263)
Avocado Dip (page 79)

Suggested vegetables are:

Broccoli
Asparagus
Cauliflower
Carrots
Celery
Cucumbers
Yellow squash
Red and green peppers
Cherry tomatoes
Radishes
Black olives

Break broccoli into florets and steam until bright green. Immediately run under cold water to stop the cooking.

Break the tough stems off asparagus and, as for broccoli, steam until bright green, immediately cooling under cold water.

Break the cauliflower into florets and either blanch them or leave raw (I leave them raw).

Cut carrots into sticks, or cut curls with a vegetable peeler (this is tedious work). Place in cold water in the refrigerator for at least a day.

You can either cut celery into sticks or, a few days beforehand, make celery curls. Cut off the leafy ends and carefully quarter the stalk lengthwise from the base. Slice each quarter into thin lengthwise sections, leaving them connected at the base. Submerge these sections in cold water and refrigerate for a few days; they will curl during this time.

Score and slice cucumbers and yellow squash.

Seed and slice bell peppers crosswise.

Remove the stems from the cherry tomatoes; if the tomatoes are very large, cut them in half.

Make radish flowers a few days beforehand. Cut four "petals" by running the knife down from the top just on the inside of the skin on all four sides, stopping just short of the base of the radish. Place the radishes in cold water and refrigerate for a few days; the "petals" will curl out. If you are able to get the tiny French radishes, leave them whole.

Black olives should, of course, be pitted.

You can prepare the vegetables and dips a day in advance if you refrigerate them tightly covered or sealed well in plastic bags. Submerge carrots and celery in water to prevent them from drying out.

Preparing the platter: After you have prepared your vegetables and made your dip, comes the fun part. Choose a large round or oval platter. Make a circle of broccoli and cauliflower, leaving a space inside; in this space stand the asparagus upright in a wide-mouthed glass jar or ceramic container. Surround the broccoli and cauliflower with alternating rounds of cucumber and yellow squash, and surround these in turn with carrots and celery. Scatter sliced peppers here and there, and place tomatoes inside the pepper rounds; scatter radishes and olives throughout. Garnish with parsley.

Of course, this is just a suggestion. You may want to incorporate the dip into the arrangement, and you may want to create other designs. Have fun with it; you can't lose, as the materials with which you are working are so beautiful.

RUSSIAN DRESSING DIP

1 cup Blender Mayonnaise (page 259)
1 to 2 teaspoons prepared horseradish
2 green onions, both white part and green, minced
¼ cup chili sauce

Stir all the ingredients together. Store, refrigerated, in a well-sealed jar.

About 1½ cups

AVOCADO DIP

1 avocado
½ cup plain yogurt, homemade (see page 259) or commercial, more if desired
Juice of ½ lemon
Salt, preferably sea salt, to taste
Ground cumin and chili powder to taste (optional)

Peel and seed the avocado and puree with the yogurt in a blender. Add the lemon juice and salt to taste, and the optional spices. Add more yogurt, if you wish. Chill, if desired, before serving, or serve immediately.

About 1½ cups

FRESH FRUIT AND NUTS

This is a refreshing appetite whetter. Choose fruits in season—in the fall and winter, pears, oranges, and apples (toss the pears and apples with lemon juice to prevent discoloration), in the spring and summer, melon, pineapple, strawberries, berries, and peaches. Cut melon and pineapple into bite-sized chunks and serve with toothpicks. Arrange all the fruit on a platter, paying attention to color, and garnish with wedges of fresh lime. Or fill a large bowl with the cut fruit and scatter lime wedges throughout.

Fill bowls with nuts—almonds, cashews, brazil nuts, hazelnuts, walnuts, pecans—or place them on the platter with the fruit.

EGG ROLLS

I've taught egg rolls in my classes for years, and my students are always pleased to see that there is no great mystery to them. Egg rolls make a wonderful hors d'oeuvre, first course, or side dish. These are especially bounteous, and the filling, seasoned with tamari, is crunchy and saladlike. The *hiziki* seaweed, available in Oriental food stores, has a distinctive Oriental and "seafoody" flavor that enhances the authenticity of these egg rolls.

This recipe makes a large amount of filling—enough for an entire 1-pound package of egg roll wrappers (twenty to twenty-five or so, and available in Oriental food stores). If you don't plan to make this many, freeze the extra egg roll skins (wrapped tightly in plastic, then placed in bags or wrapped in foil) and cut the recipe in half. If you still have leftover filling, it makes a great salad.

You can assemble these several hours before you deep-fry them, but they should be cooked shortly before serving or they'll become soggy. If you are holding the assembled egg rolls, keep them on lightly floured waxed paper.

½ cup *hiziki* seaweed
   Peanut or safflower oil as needed
½ pound carrots, shredded
½ head green cabbage, shredded
1½ cups chopped green onion, both white part and green
1 cup chopped mung bean sprouts
1 green pepper, seeded and minced
1 cup sesame seeds
1 cup sunflower seeds
2 cloves garlic, minced or put through a press

¼ cup tamari, or to taste
1 package egg roll wrappers
1 tablespoon arrowroot or cornstarch

Soak the *hiziki* in water for 5 minutes. Squeeze out the water and sauté in the oil with the remaining vegetables, seeds, and garlic until the chopped green onion is tender and the vegetables begin to change color; this should take 5 minutes. Add tamari and stir together.

To make a neat egg roll, place a wrapper on your work surface diagonally, so it appears diamond-shaped rather than square. Place two or three tablespoons of the filling in the center. Fold the sides in over the filling about an inch from the corners (see illustration 1), then fold the bottom or top edge over this and roll up tightly (see illustrations 2 and 3). This makes a compact egg roll that will fry quickly without absorbing too much oil. Seal each egg roll with arrowroot or cornstarch dissolved in a little water.

Heat peanut or safflower oil to a depth of 4 to 6 inches in a wok or deep-fryer to 370 degrees. Deep-fry the egg rolls until golden brown and drain on paper towels.

Serve with Sweet and Sour Sauce (page 258).

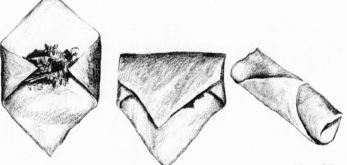

20 to 25 egg rolls

TEMPURA'D VEGETABLES WITH ASSORTED DIPS

Be prepared to get your fingers full of this fritter batter. It's thick, but it's the best I've tried. The beaten egg white makes it nice and light, and your tempura will have a shell that's crisp on the outside and fluffy on the inside.

The dips that follow on pages 83–84 may be made a day in advance and refrigerated in sealed jars. Another nice dip to use is the Sweet and Sour Sauce on page 258.

(continued)

For the batter:
- 1 teaspoon salt, preferably sea salt
- 1 cup sifted flour (whole-wheat or a combination of unbleached white and whole-wheat)
- 2 tablespoons safflower, sesame, or vegetable oil or melted butter
- 2 eggs, separated
- 1 cup water

For the vegetables:
- ½ head broccoli, cut into florets
- ½ head cauliflower, cut into florets
- 1 onion, cut in rings
- ½ pound green beans, ends snapped off
- 1 carrot, grated, cut in sticks, or sliced
- ½ cup flour (whole-wheat or a combination of unbleached white and whole-wheat), more as necessary
- 1 zucchini or yellow squash, grated or sliced
- 1 quart oil (safflower, sesame, soy, or corn), more as necessary

First make the batter. Combine the salt, flour, oil or butter, egg yolks, and water. Stir together but don't beat. Let stand for 20 minutes, then whip the egg whites until fluffy and fold them into the batter.

Blanch the broccoli and cauliflower and drain well.

Toss the cauliflower, broccoli, onion, and green beans and carrots (if you've cut or sliced them) in the additional ½ cup flour. (If you've grated the carrots, take them up, along with the squash, in clumps, and dip them in the flour. You will have to hold them together with your fingers as you then dip them into the batter, which is why you should be prepared to get the batter all over your hands. Some of the shredded vegetables will fall apart, but enough will stay together to give you a crisp, shoestringlike tempura.) Dip the other vegetables into the batter and roll around to coat evenly.

Heat the oil in a wok or deep-fryer to 370 degrees. When it is hot enough, carefully drop in the coated vegetables, a few at a time. They should float to the top and turn a golden brown very quickly. When they are evenly cooked and golden, remove them with a slotted spoon, allowing the excess oil to drip into the pan. Drain on paper towels and serve plain or with assorted dips.

6 to 10 servings

DIPPING SAUCE

½ cup Vegetable Stock (page 91) or water
¼ cup tamari
3 to 4 tablespoons sake or dry sherry
4 teaspoons freshly grated gingerroot

Combine the stock, tamari, and sake or sherry in a small saucepan. Heat just to the boiling point and add the ginger. Remove from the heat and allow to cool.

1 cup

TERIYAKI

¼ cup tamari
¼ cup sake or dry sherry
2 tablespoons mild honey
1 tablespoon freshly grated gingerroot or 1½ teaspoons ground ginger
2 cloves garlic, minced or put through a press
1 tablespoon vegetable oil
¼ teaspoon dry mustard

Combine all the ingredients in a small bowl.

¾ cup

TAHINI-TAMARI SAUCE

¼ cup tamari
½ cup sesame tahini
1 teaspoon freshly grated gingerroot
2 teaspoons dry sherry
Hot water

Combine the tamari, tahini, ginger, and sherry. Thin out to the desired consistency with hot water.

¾ to 1 cup

TEMPURA'D TOFU WITH DIPPING SAUCES

1 **pound tofu**
¼ **cup tamari**
½ **cup unbleached white flour**
   **Batter and deep-frying oil as for Tempura'd Vegetables with Dipping Sauce
   (page 82)**

Cut the tofu into slices and sprinkle with or dip into the tamari, then dip carefully into the flour and the batter. (You will have trouble with the tofu falling apart in some cases, in the same way that you had trouble with shredded vegetables falling apart. It depends on the tofu. Bear with it and get your fingers into the batter. Even if the pieces of tofu end up very small, the tofu in this deep-fried batter is a delicious combination, so it will be well worth your trouble.)

Deep-fry as for Tempura'd Vegetables; drain on paper towels.

Use the dipping sauces for Tempura'd Vegetables on pages 83–84.

6 to 8 servings

CHEESE FONDUE

Cheese fondue is traditionally served with cubes of French bread, but there is really a world of possibilities for dippers—anything you like to eat with cheese that will hold up will do. I prefer apples or raw vegetables because of the contrast in texture. Besides, they are lower in calories, and the fondue is rich. A carefully arranged platter of crisp, raw vegetables surrounding cheese fondue in a chafing dish makes a truly exquisite hors d'oeuvre.

Temperature control is very important here. Once the fondue cools, the cheese will harden and the fondue will become a rubbery mass; if the flame beneath it is too hot, on the other hand, the cheese will burn and its smell will permeate the room. So you should either make the fondue in a chafing dish or in a very heavy pot above a low flame and then transfer it to a chafing dish for serving. Be sure to maintain a sufficient level of water in the water pan, and to have enough Sterno or fuel to keep your flame going for as long as you and your guests may need it. Once you lose your heat source that will be the end of the fondue.

The ingredients for the fondue can be prepared well in advance. The cheese can be grated and tossed with the flour, then covered and stored in the refrigerator for up to 4 hours. The raw vegetable dippers can be prepared and chilled a few hours in advance. But the fondue itself should be begun only 15 to 20 minutes before serving. It is a quick and easy process.

For the fondue:
   1 pound Swiss Gruyère cheese
   2 tablespoons whole-wheat pastry flour or unbleached white flour
   1 clove garlic, halved
1½ cups dry white wine
   3 to 4 tablespoons kirsch
      Freshly ground pepper (optional)

For the dippers (choice or combination of):
   1 loaf French bread, cubed
   3 apples, cubed or sliced and tossed with lemon juice to prevent from turning brown
   ½ head cauliflower, cut into florets
   ½ head broccoli, cut into florets and steamed until bright green
   4 small zucchini, cut in half crosswise and then into lengthwise spears
   4 small yellow squash, cut like the zucchini
   ½ pound carrots, cut in 3-inch sticks
   1 bunch radishes, trimmed

Grate the cheese and toss together with the flour in a large bowl; set aside.

Rub the inside of a chafing dish or heavy-bottomed pan with the cut garlic. Heat the dish and pour in the wine. Bring it *just* to the boiling point, then turn down the heat and add the cheese, a little at a time. Stir constantly with a wooden spoon, a fork, or a whisk, and as each portion of cheese melts add another; continue to stir until all the cheese is melted and bubbling and the mixture is homogenous. Add the kirsch, and if you wish grind in some black pepper.

Serve the fondue immediately, keeping it over a medium flame, with the dippers of your choice. Your guests can use small fondue skewers or toothpicks to dip the vegetables or bread cubes into the fondue.

6 to 10 servings

SESAME EGGPLANT ROUNDS WITH HOMMOS

These provide a marvelous contrast of flavors and textures: eggplant in a nutty, crunchy shell of sesame seeds, deep-fried to a savory crispness and topped with *hommos*. (The eggplant rounds are also quite good served plain, without the *hommos*.)

1 eggplant
Salt, preferably sea salt, and freshly ground pepper to taste
1 cup sesame seeds, slightly ground
2 eggs, beaten
1 cup safflower oil
1 cup olive oil
1 cup Hommos (page 57)
Parsley sprigs and tomato slices for garnish

Leaving the skin on the eggplant, slice it very thin, about ⅛ inch thick. Cut the larger slices in half. Sprinkle liberally with salt and let sit for 30 minutes, then rinse and pat dry. Salt lightly again and sprinkle with freshly ground pepper.

Place the sesame seeds in one bowl and beat the eggs in another. Heat the two oils together in a large frying pan, wok, or deep-fryer to 370 degrees. Dip the eggplant rounds into the egg, then coat with sesame seeds and drop, a few at a time, into the hot oil. They should float to the surface and then brown immediately. Turn the rounds over to make sure both sides fry to a golden brown and remove from the oil with a slotted spoon. Drain on paper towels.

Spread a thin layer of *hommos* on each round and place on a platter. Garnish with parsley and sliced tomatoes and serve. Or serve plain.

6 to 8 servings

GARBANZO BEAN CROQUETTES

These are Middle Eastern *hommos* croquettes, crisp and crusty on the outside and magically light and flavorful on the inside. You can have the croquettes rolled and refrigerated several hours in advance, ready to deep-fry (the *hommos* can be made up to 3 days ahead); you can deep-fry the croquettes up to an hour in advance and keep them warm in the oven.

For this dish you should be careful not to make a very runny *hommos*, as it will be very hard to manipulate. Use a minimum of olive oil and don't run too long in the food processor.

The croquettes are also used in this book as part of a main dish (see the recipe for Fallafels on page 197).

2 cups Hommos (page 57)
½ teaspoon ground coriander
½ teaspoon ground cumin
¼ teaspoon dried marjoram
½ cup whole-wheat pastry flour
½ cup sesame seeds
½ teaspoon salt, preferably sea salt
2 eggs
1 quart safflower, sesame, or vegetable oil
   Chopped fresh parsley and tomato slices for garnish

Mix together the *hommos,* coriander, cumin, and marjoram. Roll into small balls.

Combine the flour, sesame seeds, and the salt in one bowl; beat the eggs in another. Dip the croquettes in the beaten egg, then roll them in the flour–sesame seeds mixture.

Heat the oil to 370 degrees in a deep-fryer. Carefully drop in the croquettes, a few at a time, and deep-fry to a golden brown. Drain on paper towels.

Serve warm or at room temperature, garnished with chopped fresh parsley and sliced tomatoes.

6 to 8 servings

ROASTED SOYBEANS

A good way to introduce soybeans into your diet, and to use up extra cooked soybeans, these make a terrific crunchy snack or party nibble. Unlike commercially roasted soybeans, they are not oily and need not be salty. Crack them in a blender and use them as you would bacon bits; they make a great sandwich with tomato, lettuce, and your own homemade mayonnaise (see Blender Mayonnaise, page 259).

One cup dried soybeans makes 1 cup roasted.

1 cup dried soybeans
3 cups water
   Salt, preferably sea salt

Soak the soybeans overnight or for several hours. Cook as directed on page 25, just in the water with 1 teaspoon salt, making sure your pot is at least twice the volume of the beans to allow for expansion. Cook for 1 hour and drain.

Preheat the oven to 325 degrees.

Spread the beans on a cookie sheet or in a baking pan and salt them, then place in the oven and bake for about 1 to 1½ hours, turning every 15 minutes and checking carefully when the soybeans begin to smell toasty; they will sometimes smell done before they are crunchy all the way through, but be careful not to remove them from the oven prematurely. To test for doneness, remove one from the pan, let cool, and bite through to see. If it is not crunchy, leave the beans in about 10 to 15 minutes longer. (Be careful at this stage, because the roasted soybeans will burn quickly once they are done.) Remove from the oven when they are ready and allow to cool in the pan. Store in a covered jar (these keep very well if covered tightly).

1 cup

SOUPS

⸎

When I ran my "supper club," the soups were always the most talked-about part of the menu. In the wintertime a hot, soothing bowl of nourishing Pistou (page 96), a thick Puree of White Bean Soup (page 97), or a creamy Raw and Cooked Mushroom Soup (page 101)—and in the summer a serving of crisp, cool Blender Gazpacho (page 135), tangy Egg-Lemon Soup (page 111), or fruity Puree of Strawberry (page 140)—along with a bread and salad, will often suffice for a meal.

Garnish can turn a good bowl of soup into a brilliant one. For me, part of the ritual of giving dinner parties is the serving and garnishing of this course. We used to have a "soup assembly line" at the club. When enough people had arrived, I would call upon some friends to help. One person would ladle the soup out into bowls, another might add a dollop of yogurt, another sprinkle on croutons or sunflower seeds, while the next might top it with alfalfa sprouts. The last person in the line would deliver the bowls to the table.

There are so many food items you can sprinkle or spread over a soup to give it body, texture, creaminess, or "zip." A savory cheese soup served with dark, buttered Croutons (page 54) is like a splendid fondue, as the bread becomes coated with the soup but stays crisp. Croutons also add a great touch to Puree of White Bean Soup (page 97), with its luscious enrichment of herb butter. Sprouts and sunflower seeds always surprise and please my guests; the seeds become coated with soup and the sprouts become enmeshed in it. Sunflower seeds provide a welcome crunch to purees like Chilled Avocado-Tomato Soup (page 137). Yogurt and tofu not only enliven a soup, but also add to the protein content.

If soup is to be a first course, ladle out small servings so you and your guests won't get full right off the bat. You can vary the richness of a cream soup by varying the thickness of your roux. A thin, light soup will require only two tablespoons of butter and two of flour; a medium-thick cream soup will use three each; and a rich one will take four. Most of the recipes in this section call for three tablespoons of each in the roux; try it this way first, then experiment. I have found that the richness of the vegetable puree is often enough; others like a thicker soup.

Most of the recipes here call for Vegetable Stock (page 91) or Tamari-Bouillon Broth (page 91). Use the Tamari-Bouillon Broth whenever you're short on time; it's perfectly acceptable. And always have tamari and vegetable bouillon cubes on hand.

Many of these soups are quite substantial when served with a salad and bread. Pistou (page 96), Puree of White Bean (page 97), Cheese and Black Bread (page 106), Potato-Cheese (page 114), Noodle-Bean (page 125), Cabbage-Cheese (page 116), Minestrone (page 118), Cream of Wheat Berry (page 109), Black Bean (page 128), and the two Lentil Soups (pages 129 and 130) all have enough richness and body to stand as a main course. The menu suggestions listed here are just a few possibilities. Use your imagination to combine hors d'oeuvres, breads and soups, salads and desserts for some outstanding meals. And remember that a simple meal—soup, salad, bread—is often the best.

The recipes in this section feed six to eight people.

Stocks and Broths

Most people set aside at least a day for making traditional meat-based stocks so they can make huge amounts. But the stocks and broths here are easy; there is no endless simmering of soup bones and skimming off of fat. In fact, it rarely takes me longer than 10 minutes to do the preparation for any of these. The recipe for Garlic Broth (page 92) may look tedious, but if you use the garlic-peeling trick mentioned on page 23 it will go quickly.

These can all be made up to three days in advance and kept refrigerated. They may also be frozen.

VEGETABLE STOCK

2½ quarts freshly drawn tap water
2 medium onions, quartered
2 carrots, coarsely chopped
2 stalks celery, coarsely chopped
2 to 3 potatoes, unpeeled and cut in large pieces
2 leeks, white part only, washed well and coarsely chopped
6 cloves garlic
4 sprigs fresh parsley
1 bay leaf
½ teaspoon dried thyme
4 whole black peppercorns
1 tablespoon tamari
2 teaspoons Marmite or Savorex
   Salt, preferably sea salt, to taste
3 vegetable bouillon cubes (optional)

Combine all the ingredients in a large stock pot. Bring slowly to a gentle boil, then reduce the heat and simmer, uncovered, for 1 to 2 hours, until you have a nice, aromatic broth. Correct the seasoning.

Strain and discard the vegetables and whole seasonings. Use this stock for soups (you may have to add more water to get the amount called for) and sauces.

This stock freezes well.

7 cups

TAMARI-BOUILLON BROTH

6 cups water
4 vegetable bouillon cubes
3 cloves garlic, minced or put through a press
⅓ cup tamari
   Salt, preferably sea salt, and freshly ground pepper to taste

Combine all the ingredients in a stock pot. Bring to a boil, then reduce the heat and simmer gently for 30 minutes. Make sure bouillon is dissolved.

6 cups

GARLIC BROTH

This has the rich, soothing flavor of a chicken broth with none of the fat. Guests sometimes don't believe it doesn't contain meat.

2 heads garlic, separated into cloves and peeled (see page 23)
2 quarts water or Vegetable Stock (page 91)
4 vegetable bouillon cubes (if using water)
2 tablespoons olive oil
1 bay leaf
 Pinch of dried thyme
4 sprigs fresh parsley
 Pinch of dried leaf sage
2 teaspoons salt, preferably sea salt, or to taste

Combine all the ingredients in a stock pot. Bring to a gentle boil, then cover and reduce the heat. Simmer for 1 to 2 hours. Strain and discard the garlic, bay leaf, and parsley.

This is excellent as a starting stock for soups and some sauces, and it can be frozen.

7 cups

RATATOUILLE

Ratatouille is actually a vegetable stew, but I usually serve it as a first course, in a bowl, so I'm including it here. It goes beautifully with cheese dishes such as quiche or soufflé, and as a filling it makes an omelet or crêpe truly distinctive. It is wonderful hot or cold, and if you make it the day before you serve it, the flavors will have a chance to ripen and mature.

1 eggplant, prepared as directed on page 23, but "steamed" for only 5 to 10 minutes
¼ cup olive oil, more as necessary
2 onions, sliced
3 large cloves garlic, minced or put through a press
2 green peppers, seeded and sliced
1 pound zucchini, sliced ¼ inch thick (or use half zucchini, half yellow squash)
½ cup Vegetable Stock (page 91) or dry white wine
½ cup tomato paste
1 cucumber, peeled, seeded, and chunked (optional)
4 tomatoes, peeled and sliced
1 to 2 teaspoons oregano, or to taste

1 tablespoon chopped fresh basil or 1 teaspoon dried
Salt, preferably sea salt, and freshly ground pepper to taste

After the eggplant has been "steamed" and is cool enough to handle, dice it, skin and all, with a sharp knife and set it aside.

Heat the olive oil in a heavy stock pot or wok and sauté the sliced onion, along with the garlic. When it is transparent and beginning to soften, add the green peppers. Sauté until they are saturated and beginning to cook through, then add half the eggplant and zucchini. Sauté for a few minutes, stirring and tossing gently until all the vegetables are beginning to cook through, then add the rest of the eggplant and zucchini (or yellow squash). Gently stir and toss well.

Combine the stock or white wine and tomato paste and add to the vegetable mixture, along with the cucumber. Toss the mixture together, then cover and cook over low heat, stirring occasionally, for 30 to 45 minutes. Add the tomatoes, herbs, and seasonings and cook, uncovered, for 15 minutes more, or until the eggplant is cooked through and the *ratatouille* is thick. Correct the seasoning, then remove from the heat and serve, or cool and chill. (If you're serving it hot the next day, reheat *gently*.)

Note: You may top with sprouts and a douse of Vinaigrette (page 261) if serving chilled. Hot *ratatouille* is delicious topped with a little freshly grated Parmesan cheese.

6 to 8 servings

Suggested Menus

Vegetable Platter (page 77) with Tofu Mayonnaise (page 260)
Ratatouille (see above)
Spinach and Onion Quiche (page 150)
Marinated Vegetables Vinaigrette (page 74)
Pears Poached in Red Wine with a Touch of Cassis (page 277)

Stuffed Mushrooms (page 65) *or* Marinated Vegetables Vinaigrette (page 74)
Ratatouille (see above)
Cheese Soufflé (page 157)
Mixed Green Salad (page 238)
Bananas Poached in White Wine (page 277)

EGG DROP SOUP WITH BEAN SPROUTS

This easy soup has a delicate, silky texture and a warming, chicken-souplike broth. The "egg drops" aren't really drops, they're fluffy wisps of batter that float on the surface of the broth.

It's important to serve this soup right after the eggs bind or the vegetables will cook too much and lose their bright green color.

    2 tablespoons safflower or vegetable oil
    1 bunch green onions, both white part and green, chopped separately
    1 clove garlic, minced or put through a press
    8 fresh mushrooms, sliced
    1½ quarts Vegetable Stock (page 91)
    ¼ cup tamari
    3 tablespoons chopped fresh parsley
    ½ pound snow peas, stringed
    2 tablespoons melted butter
    2 tablespoons whole-wheat flour
    2 eggs, beaten
      Salt, preferably sea salt, and freshly ground pepper
    1½ cups mung bean sprouts

Heat the oil in a stock pot and sauté the chopped white part of the green onions, the garlic, and the mushrooms until the mushrooms are just beginning to be tender. Add the stock, tamari, 1 tablespoon of the chopped parsley, and the chopped green part of the green onions and bring to a simmer. Add the snow peas and cook for 3 minutes.

Meanwhile, in a medium-sized bowl, combine the melted butter, flour, eggs, salt, pepper, and remaining chopped parsley and mix into a smooth batter. Bring the soup to a boil and pour in the egg mixture in a slow stream, while gently stirring the soup with a fork to whisk the egg through. Work rapidly. As soon as the egg drops have floated to the surface, remove from the heat and serve by placing ¼ cup bean sprouts in each of six soup bowls and ladling the soup over them. Should the egg drops fall apart, take a fork and stir the egg mixture through the soup gently.

6 servings

Suggested Menus

Tempura'd Vegetables (page 81) and Tempura'd Tofu (page 84) with Dipping Sauces (pages 83–84)
Egg Drop Soup with Bean Sprouts (see above)
Crêpes Florentine (page 177)

Tomatoes and Fresh Herbs (page 247)
Apple Pie (page 294) *or* Peaches Marsala (page 282)

Sesame Eggplant Rounds with (or without) Hommos (page 86)
Egg Drop Soup with Bean Sprouts (see above)
Brown Rice Salad (page 245)
Marinated Lentil Salad (page 252)
Fresh fruit (see page 276)

STRACCIATELLA

This is a light, delicate soup, so it's perfect with heavy Italian dishes such as Eggplant Parmesan (page 178) or Lasagne (page 187). It's really an Italian version of egg drop soup.

You can prepare all the ingredients beforehand, have the stock made and the spinach stemmed and washed, the cheese grated and the bread crumbs ready. But the final steps are a last-minute operation, and the soup must be served immediately.

3 cloves garlic, minced or put through a press
1½ quarts Tamari-Bouillon Broth (page 91) or Vegetable Stock (page 91)
   Salt, preferably sea salt, to taste
½ pound fresh spinach, washed and stems removed
2 eggs, beaten
¼ cup whole-wheat bread crumbs
¼ cup freshly grated Parmesan cheese

Combine the garlic and broth or stock in a stock pot and simmer for 30 minutes. Season with salt to taste, then add the spinach and simmer for 30 seconds.

In a medium-sized bowl, mix together the beaten eggs, bread crumbs, and cheese. Bring the stock to a boil and stir in the egg mixture; the eggs should bind in a few seconds.

Serve immediately.

6 to 8 servings

Suggested Menus

Orange wedges in a bowl
Stracciatella (see above)
Eggplant Parmesan (page 178)
Mixed Green Salad (page 238)
Italian Fruit Compote (page 278)

(*continued*)

Marinated Vegetables Vinaigrette (page 76)
Stracciatella (see above)
Lasagne (page 187)
Tender Lettuce with Oranges (page 242)
Fresh fruit (see page 276) *or* Bavarian Crème au Café (page 286)

PISTOU

Provençal Vegetable Soup

Pistou is a hearty soup, and it's a favorite with both my students and my catering clients. There are many versions, some "green" and some with tomatoes, of which this is one. Like *ratatouille*, it goes well with cheese dishes, but it's substantial enough to be served with just a nice salad and bread.

The stock can be done in advance, as can the "pesto." You will also have to remember to soak and cook the white beans, which are an important ingredient. The other vegetables may be prepared in advance, but don't add them to the stock until shortly before serving. This will give the soup a nice variety of textures, and the vegetables will still be very much alive.

For the soup:
    2 medium onions, chopped
    2 carrots, sliced
    1 potato, unpeeled and diced
    4 cloves garlic, peeled and left whole
    3 vegetable bouillon cubes (optional)
    1 teaspoon salt, preferably sea salt, or to taste
      Freshly ground pepper to taste
    ¼ teaspoon saffron threads (optional)
    2 quarts water
    1 small zucchini, sliced
    1 cup fresh or frozen green peas
    1 cup cooked white beans (⅓ cup dried; see page 25)
    ½ cup broken dry spaghetti

For the "pesto":
    4 cloves garlic, minced or put through a press
    ½ to 1 cup chopped fresh basil or 2 to 4 tablespoons dried
    ½ cup tomato paste
    ½ cup freshly grated Parmesan cheese
    ¼ to ½ cup good-quality olive oil, to taste

For the garnish:
 ¼ **cup chopped fresh parsley**
 ¼ **cup freshly grated Parmesan cheese**

Combine the onion, carrots, potato, garlic, bouillon cubes, salt, pepper, saffron, and water in a large stock pot and bring to a boil. Reduce the heat and simmer, uncovered, for 1 hour. Meanwhile, prepare the remaining vegetables and set them aside, along with the white beans and broken spaghetti.

With a fork and small bowl, or preferably with a mortar and pestle, mix the garlic thoroughly with the basil, tomato paste, and Parmesan. Beat in the olive oil by droplets, stirring well to get it completely incorporated. (You may use a food processor for this, too: place the garlic, basil, and cheese in the bowl of the processor and blend together; add the tomato paste and blend, then slowly add the olive oil.) Set the "pesto" aside.

About 20 minutes before serving, have the stock at a gentle simmer and add the white beans and spaghetti. Stir well so the spaghetti doesn't stick together. Wait for 10 minutes, and then add the reserved green vegetables; taste to correct the seasoning.

Now check to see that the spaghetti is tender and the green vegetables are cooked through and bright green, then carefully stir in the "pesto." Blend thoroughly to dissolve the "pesto" and serve, topping each serving with Parmesan and chopped parsley.

Alternatively, you can place a teaspoonful of "pesto" in each bowl of soup, ladle the soup over it, and either stir to dissolve or have your guests stir to dissolve. This method makes a more intense bowl of soup, but it can be time consuming and messy.

6 to 8 servings

Suggested Menus
The same as for Ratatouille (page 57).

PUREE OF WHITE BEAN SOUP

This is an elegant soup. Bay leaf is essential—it brings out the delicate flavor of the white beans—but it's the lemon–herb butter enrichment which makes this soup absolutely sublime.

There are two methods for the first part of this soup, the cooking of the beans. You can soak the beans and cook them according to Method 1, or if you don't have time for soaking you can use Method 2. Whichever method you use, this part of the recipe can be done a day in advance and kept in the refrigerator. The herb butter may also be done a day or two in advance, though it's always best made fresh. But the beans should be pureed on the day you are serving the soup, and the final enrichment should be done shortly before serving.

2 cups dried white beans, washed
6 cups Vegetable Stock (page 91) or water, more if necessary
3 tablespoons oil (safflower, olive, or vegetable) or butter
2 medium onions, chopped
2 to 3 cloves garlic, minced or put through a press
1 bay leaf
2 teaspoons salt, preferably sea salt, more if necessary
  Milk
2 egg yolks
  Freshly ground pepper
4 to 6 tablespoons Herb Butter (page 61)
  Juice of 1 lemon
2 tablespoons chopped fresh parsley
  Croutons (page 54)

Method 1: Wash the beans and soak them overnight or for several hours in the 6 cups water or vegetable stock. When ready to cook, heat the oil or butter in a large stock pot or Dutch oven and sauté the onion and one of the garlic cloves gently until the onion is tender. Add the beans and their liquid and bring to a boil. Add the remaining garlic, bay leaf, and salt, then reduce the heat, cover, and simmer for 1 to 2 hours, until the beans are tender.

Method 2: If you haven't soaked the beans, heat the oil or butter in a large stock pot or Dutch oven and gently sauté the onion and one of the garlic cloves until the onion is tender. Add the beans, water or stock, the remaining garlic, and bay leaf and bring to a boil. Add the salt and boil for 2 minutes, then cover tightly and turn off the heat. Allow to sit 1 hour, covered. Bring to a boil again, then reduce the heat and simmer, covered, for 1 to 2 hours, until the beans are tender. (You may have to add more liquid during this time.)

When the beans are tender and the broth is aromatic, place a colander over a bowl or pot and drain the beans, saving the liquid. Discard the bay leaf, return the liquid to the soup pot, and puree the beans, in batches, in a blender or through a food mill (use some stock if necessary). Return the puree to the soup pot and simmer over low heat while you prepare the egg yolk–milk and lemon–herb butter enrichments. Thin out with some milk if it's too thick.

In a small bowl, beat together the egg yolks and ½ cup milk. Ladle a few spoonfuls of the simmering soup into this to heat the egg yolks through, then pour it all back into the soup pot. (Be careful not to let it boil.) Stir and adjust the seasoning, adding salt and pepper as desired.

Now comes the final touch. Mix together the herb butter and lemon juice and stir into the soup, or stir in the herb butter and then the lemon juice. Heat through until all the butter is melted. Serve immediately, garnishing each bowl with crisp croutons (black bread croutons are especially good) and freshly chopped parsley.

6 to 8 servings

Suggested Menu

Spinach Gnocchi (page 192)
Puree of White Bean Soup (see above), with black bread Croutons (page 55)
Mixed Green Salad (page 238) *or* Beet and Endive Salad (page 248)
Fruit and cheese *or* Oranges Grand Marnier (page 279) *or* Mince Pie (page 273)

FRUIT SOUP

Served hot in the winter, this is a very warming soup. It's also one of the most refreshing *cold* soups you can make in the summer. I usually eat the leftovers for breakfast.

Fruit soup gets sweeter every day in the refrigerator; but the fruit will retain its lovely appearance for only a day or two.

1 pound mixed dried fruit
2 quarts water
1 tablespoon rose hips (optional)
2 pounds mixed fresh fruit (apples, bananas, pears, peaches, berries)
⅓ cup lemon juice
  Mild honey to taste
  Freshly grated nutmeg
1 tablespoon brandy
  Plain yogurt, homemade (see page 259) or commercial, for topping
2 tablespoons sunflower seeds or slivered almonds

Combine the dried fruits and the water in a stock pot. Put the rose hips in a tea ball and add to the pot. Bring to a boil and simmer over low heat until tender, about 30 minutes.

(continued)

Add the fresh fruit, except for the berries, and cook for 5 minutes. Add the berries and cook for 5 minutes more.

Remove from the heat and remove the tea ball; add the lemon juice, honey, nutmeg, and brandy and stir well.

Adjust the sweetness to taste, then serve hot or well chilled, topped with a dollop of yogurt and a sprinkling of sunflower seeds or sliced almonds.

6 to 8 servings

Menu Suggestions
Hommos (page 57)
Fruit Soup (see above)
Vegetable Shish Kebab (page 199)
Couscous
World of Sprouts Salad (page 239)
Any dessert soufflé (see pages 288–91)

Egg Rolls (page 80)
Fruit Soup (see above)
Curried Tofu and Vegetables over Millet (page 208)
Cucumber Raita (page 235)
Banana Raita (page 235)
Pecan Pie (page 295)

TORTILLA SOUP

This is a hearty, warming soup, good on a cold night. Serve it with a light main course and a salad. The tasty tomato-garlic broth is enriched with tortillas fried in oil, and the combination is unforgettable.

The garlic broth may be made in advance, but the rest of the soup is best made on the day you are to serve it.

  6 cups Garlic Broth (page 92)
  ½ onion, minced
  1 clove garlic, minced or put through a press
  1 to 2 tablespoons olive oil
  2 tomatoes, peeled, seeded, and pureed
  ¼ cup tomato paste
    Safflower or vegetable oil
  12 corn tortillas, cut in strips

2 to 3 tablespoons chopped fresh coriander (*cilantro*), plus additional for garnish, if desired
Salt and freshly ground pepper to taste
½ cup grated Gruyère cheese
3 eggs, beaten

After preparing the garlic broth as directed on page 91, strain and discard the garlic, bay leaf, and parsley.

In a stock pot, sauté the onion and garlic in a little olive oil until tender. Add the tomato puree and tomato paste and cook over a low flame for 8 to 10 minutes. Add the garlic broth and stir well, then cover and let simmer for 30 minutes over very low heat.

Meanwhile, heat ¼ inch of safflower oil in a frying pan and sauté the tortilla strips in batches (do not crowd the pan), stirring or turning, for about 3 minutes; do not allow them to get too crisp. Drain on paper towels, then add to the soup and cook for 3 minutes, until soft. Add the coriander and cook for 1 minute. Taste the broth and season to taste with salt and pepper.

Put some grated Gruyère in each soup bowl.

Bring the soup to a boil and stir in the eggs; they should cook at once. Immediately spoon the soup into the bowls, over the cheese, and serve garnished, if desired, with more coriander.

6 to 8 servings

Suggested Menus

Tortilla Soup (see above)
Marinated White Beans with Pasta (page 195)
Avocado and Citrus Salad (page 239)
Strawberry and Cassis Sherbet (page 301)

Nachos with Black Bean Topping (page 72)
Tortilla Soup (see above)
Mixed Green Salad (page 238) *or* Spinach Salad (page 238)
Pineapple with Kirsch (page 282)

CREAM OF RAW AND COOKED MUSHROOM SOUP

Mushrooms become very aromatic as they cook and make an exceptional broth, so it's no wonder that mushroom soup is so popular. This lovely version adds the fresh, unique texture of raw mushrooms as garnish.

If you use a food processor to puree the mushrooms for this soup, the puree will have a somewhat grainy texture. I like this (and so do my guests), but you may want a creamy texture. If so, use a blender or sieve for the puree.

The stock can be made in advance.

1½ pounds fresh mushrooms
 1 quart Vegetable Stock (page 91)
 3 tablespoons butter
 ½ small onion, finely minced or grated
 3 tablespoons whole-wheat pastry flour or unbleached white flour
 2 cups milk
 3 to 4 tablespoons dry sherry, to taste
 1 teaspoon salt, preferably sea salt, or to taste
 Freshly ground pepper to taste
 Freshly grated nutmeg to taste (optional)
 Chopped fresh parsley to taste

Wash all the mushrooms and set aside about six to be used as garnish. (That's the "raw" part of this soup.) Cut the rest in half, or if they are very large quarter them, and combine with the stock in a large saucepan. Bring to a boil, then reduce the heat and simmer gently, uncovered, for about 45 minutes, until the mushrooms are very tender and the broth is aromatic. Pour off the broth and reserve in a bowl.

Liquefy the mushrooms in a blender or food processor, using a little broth to moisten.

In a heavy-bottomed saucepan or stock pot, melt the butter. When it begins to bubble, add the onion and cook a few minutes over very low heat, but do not brown. Add the flour and stir together with a wooden spoon to make a roux. Let cook a few minutes without browning, stirring all the while. Now slowly add 2 cups of the mushroom broth, stirring all the while with a wire whisk, and continue to stir until you have a smooth sauce. Pour back into the soup pot and simmer very gently for 10 to 15 minutes.

Meanwhile, heat the milk and carefully add it, along with the sherry. Season with the salt, freshly ground pepper, freshly grated nutmeg, if you wish, and some parsley.

Add the liquefied mushrooms and heat through; do not boil. Adjust the seasoning.

Slice the reserved raw mushrooms and garnish each bowl of the hot soup with a few of the slices, some chopped fresh parsley, and a sprinkling of freshly grated nutmeg.

6 to 8 servings

Suggested Menus

Black Bread (page 43), Brie, and raw vegetables
Cream of Raw and Cooked Mushroom Soup (see above)
Stir-Fry Chinese Tofu and Vegetables No. 1 (page 200)
Couscous or millet
Bavarian Crème au Café (page 286)

Tiropites (page 68) with Greek Spinach Filling (page 70)
Cream of Raw and Cooked Mushroom Soup (see above)
Potato Pancakes (page 218) with Homemade Applesauce (page 258) and
     yogurt
Beet and Endive Salad (page 248)
Light Cheesecake (page 291)

SOPA DE AJO

Garlic Soup

This is a good soup for a cold, as garlic is reputed to be a curative. Restorative powers or not, your kitchen will certainly smell heavenly as it simmers. Float a poached egg in it and you have a soup-and-main-dish, or a very hearty first course.

  2 heads garlic, separated into cloves and peeled (see page 23)
  2 quarts Vegetable Stock (page 91) or Tamari-Bouillon Broth (page 91)
  2 teaspoons salt, preferably sea salt
    Freshly ground pepper to taste
  2 whole cloves
  ¼ teaspoon dried leaf sage
  ¼ teaspoon dried thyme
  4 sprigs fresh parsley
  2 tablespoons olive oil
  ½ cup whole-wheat macaroni shells
  3 egg yolks
  2 tablespoons melted butter
  6 to 8 slices whole-wheat bread, buttered
  ½ cup grated Swiss cheese
  6 to 8 poached eggs (optional)

Drop the peeled cloves of garlic into the stock with the salt, pepper, cloves, sage, thyme, parsley, and oil. Bring to a gentle boil, then cover and simmer for 1 hour. Strain and discard the garlic, cloves, and parsley.

(continued)

About 20 minutes before serving, add the macaroni shells. When the shells are soft, beat together the egg yolks and butter and slowly add to the soup; do not let it boil.

Place a slice of bread in each bowl and sprinkle with some of the grated Swiss cheese. Ladle the soup over this and serve.

For a heartier meal, place a poached egg in each bowl of soup.

6 to 8 servings

Suggested Menus

Sopa de Ajo (see above)
Extraordinary Chalupas (page 147)
Guacamole (page 242)
Strawberry and Cassis Sherbet (page 301) *or* Pineapple Boats (page 281)

Cheese Fondue (page 84) with raw vegetables and apples as dippers
Sopa de Ajo (see above)
Black Bean Enchiladas (page 144)
Spinach Salad (page 238)
Oranges Grand Marnier (page 279)

Soya Pâté (page 58)
Sopa de Ajo (see above), with poached egg
Spinach and Citrus Salad (page 249)
Strawberry and Cassis Sherbet (page 301)

A RICH TOMATO SOUP

This smooth, warming soup is enriched with a roux-thickened sauce like Cream of Raw and Cooked Mushroom Soup (page 101). It's a versatile accompaniment, especially good with cheese-y main dishes. It may look like that famous brand of tomato soup, but it certainly doesn't taste like it; a hint of Cognac gives it a tantalizing flavor.

You can make the garlic broth and tomato stock and go through the step of combining them a day in advance. The final enrichments, which should be done shortly before serving, are not very time consuming.

1 quart Garlic Broth (page 92)
6 tomatoes, peeled
1 onion, chopped
2 tablespoons safflower or olive oil
1 teaspoon chopped fresh basil or ½ teaspoon dried

1 can (6 ounces) tomato paste
2 to 3 tablespoons Cognac
1 tablespoon lemon juice
  Salt, preferably sea salt, to taste
3 tablespoons butter
3 tablespoons flour (whole-wheat pastry flour or unbleached white, or a combination)
2 cups milk
  Freshly ground pepper to taste
  Chopped fresh parsley or basil for garnish

Have the garlic broth simmering in a stock pot when you begin.

Puree the tomatoes quickly in a blender or food processor, but don't liquefy; or you can chop them very fine. Set aside.

In a medium-sized saucepan, sauté the onion in oil until tender. Add the tomato puree or pulp and basil and simmer, uncovered, for 30 minutes, then press the mixture through a sieve, obtaining as much liquid as possible and leaving a dry pulp. Discard the pulp and add the sieved tomato stock to the garlic broth.

Stir the tomato paste into this mixture, then add the Cognac; blend together well. Simmer over very low heat, being careful not to boil (the surface of the soup should be "just smiling," trembling ever so slightly but not bubbling), for 20 to 30 minutes. Season with lemon juice and salt.

Meanwhile, in a medium-sized, heavy-bottomed skillet or saucepan, melt the butter. When it begins to bubble, stir in the flour to make a roux. Cook over low heat for a few minutes, stirring; do not brown. Slowly add 2 cups of the hot stock, stirring constantly. Continue to stir until you have a smooth sauce. Pour this back into the soup pot and blend well. Stir in the milk; correct the seasoning.

Just before serving, heat through, without boiling. Garnish with fresh parsley or basil and serve.

6 to 8 servings

Suggested Menus

Marinated Vegetables à la Grecque (page 76)
A Rich Tomato Soup (see above)
Oeufs Pochés en Soufflé à la Florentine (page 160)
Mixed Green Salad (page 238)
Raspberries in Red Wine (page 282)

(continued)

Baba Ganouch (page 61) and Sesame Crackers (page 54)
A Rich Tomato Soup (see above)
Mixed Grains Bread (page 38)
Potato-Egg Salad with Chilled Broccoli (page 251)
Fruit and cheese

CHEESE AND BLACK BREAD SOUP

Cheese and Black Bread Soup is a sumptuous soup, very high in protein. It may not be as thick as other cheese soups you may have had, but the wine, thyme, abundance of cheeses, and the eggs make it luxuriously rich.

Make sure the cheese is completely melted before you add it to the soup, and be careful not to boil the soup once the cheese has been added along with the eggs, or else the mixture will curdle.

The stock can be made in advance, the cheese grated and the croutons prepared. You may also do the sauce part of the soup the day before serving and refrigerate it, covered.

This is a great dish for a cold evening.

1½ quarts Vegetable Stock (page 91)
  3 tablespoons butter
  3 leeks, white part only, cleaned well and then sliced
  3 tablespoons whole-wheat pastry flour or unbleached white flour
  1 cup dry white wine
  1 teaspoon dried thyme
   Salt, preferably sea salt, and freshly ground pepper to taste
  1 teaspoon Worcestershire sauce
  5 eggs, beaten
  1 cup freshly grated Parmesan cheese
1½ cups grated Cheddar cheese
  2 cups black bread Croutons (page 54)
 ¼ cup melted Herb Butter (page 61)
   Chopped fresh parsley for garnish

When you begin, have the stock simmering in a stock pot over low heat.

Heat the butter in a heavy-bottomed saucepan and sauté the leeks. When they are tender, add the flour and stir together to make a roux. Stir in 2 cups of the hot stock and continue to stir with a whisk until you have a smooth sauce. Return this to the stock in the pot, then add the wine, thyme, salt, pepper, and Worcestershire. Cover and simmer over very low heat for 30 minutes.

Combine the eggs and cheeses in a large bowl. To this mixture add about 3 cups of the soup; stir vigorously to melt the cheese. Carefully pour back into the pot, stirring all the while; *do not boil.* Taste and adjust the seasoning.

Brush the croutons with the herb butter, or toss them in it, and place a handful in each soup bowl; ladle the hot soup over the croutons. If you have extra croutons, garnish the top of each bowl with them, along with chopped fresh parsley, and serve.

6 to 8 servings

Suggested Menus

Sliced apples *or* Cucumber Salad (page 243)
Cheese and Black Bread Soup (see above)
Stir-Fry Chinese Tofu and Vegetables No. 2 (page 203), with millet
Mixed Green Salad (page 238)
Moist Carrot Cake (page 298)

Cheese and Black Bread Soup (see above)
Sprout-Stuffed Artichokes (page 231) *or* Spinach Salad (page 238)
Beets Moutarde (page 233)
Peaches Marsala (page 282) *or* Peach Pie (page 294)

FRESH PEA SOUP

This soup is completely different from the split-pea soup with which you're probably familiar. It's a beautiful spring-green color—one of the most beautiful soups I've ever seen—and has the overwhelming sweetness of fresh garden peas (even if you use frozen ones!). You can make it as rich or as light as you wish by varying the amount of butter and flour you use in the roux for the cream sauce. For me the taste of the peas is rich enough, but some like it thicker.

Fresh pea soup can be made a day in advance and kept in the refrigerator. Reheat over a low flame and serve piping hot, or serve cold.

(continued)

4 cups fresh shelled peas (about 4 pounds unshelled), or 1 pound frozen peas
3½ cups Vegetable Stock (page 9) or water
   Salt, preferably sea salt, to taste
½ cup Rhine wine
2 to 4 tablespoons butter
2 to 4 tablespoons flour (whole-wheat pastry flour or unbleached white, or a combination)
2 cups hot milk
   Chopped fresh mint for garnish

Place the peas and stock or water in a stock pot or Dutch oven; salt lightly and bring to a simmer. Cook, covered, for 10 minutes, until the peas are cooked through but still bright green. Puree in a blender or food processor, or put through a sieve, and strain back into the pot with the stock. Stir in the wine.

If you want a light soup, very low in calories, use only 2 tablespoons butter and flour in the roux. For a medium soup use three, and for a very rich soup use four.

Melt the butter in a medium-sized saucepan and stir in the flour. Cook a few minutes over low heat, stirring. Slowly pour in the hot milk, stirring all the while with a whisk. Continue to stir until the mixture reaches the boiling point and a smooth sauce is achieved. (Don't boil hard, just simmer). Season with salt and pepper, then whisk the sauce into the pea puree.

Heat the soup through, making sure the sauce and soup are well blended, and serve, garnishing each bowl with chopped fresh mint. Or cool and chill and serve cold, garnished with mint.

6 to 8 servings

Suggested Menus

Fresh Pea Soup (see above)
Squash Soufflé (page 165) *or* Cheese Soufflé (page 157) *or* Pipérade (page 168)
Tomatoes and Fresh Herbs (page 247)
Mixed Green Salad (page 238)
Pineapple with Kirsch (page 282)

Fresh Pea Soup (see above), chilled
Fallafels (page 197)
Tabouli (page 240)
Bananas Poached in White Wine (page 277)

CREAM OF WHEAT BERRY SOUP

Occasionally I make an exception and succumb to a rich, creamy dish because it's so fabulous. That's the case with this soup. Simmering the béchamel with tiny diced vegetables and herbs makes it far more delicious than a plain white sauce, and enriches the wholesome, chewy wheat berries in their broth.

You can make the béchamel sauce a day in advance and keep it covered in the refrigerator. Warm it just before adding to the wheat berries and stock.

This soup is especially satisfying in the wintertime.

For the soup:
  6 cups Vegetable Stock (page 91) or Tamari-Bouillon Broth (page 91)
  1 cup wheat berries
  ½ teaspoon salt, preferably sea salt, or to taste
     Freshly ground pepper
  ⅛ teaspoon ground cardamom
  ⅛ teaspoon ground coriander
  ⅛ teaspoon freshly grated nutmeg
  3 tablespoons dry sherry
     Milk as necessary

For the béchamel:
  3 tablespoons butter
  ½ small onion, minced
  ½ small carrot, minced
  ½ rib celery, minced
  3 tablespoons flour (whole-wheat pastry flour or unbleached white, or a combination)
2½ cups milk, scalded
     Salt, preferably sea salt, and freshly ground pepper to taste
     Freshly grated nutmeg to taste
  2 sprigs fresh parsley
  ¼ teaspoon dried thyme
  1 small bay leaf

Combine the stock and wheat berries and bring to a boil. Add the salt, pepper, cardamom, coriander, and nutmeg and simmer for 1 hour, covered, until the wheat berries are tender and some of the stock has been absorbed. Meanwhile, prepare the béchamel.

Heat the butter in a medium-sized saucepan and sauté the vegetables until the onion is translucent. Add the flour and cook for 5 minutes, over a low flame, stirring; take care that the mixture doesn't brown. Slowly whisk in the scalded milk and bring to a gentle boil, stirring all the while. When the sauce begins to thicken, add the salt, pepper, and nutmeg, and the herbs. Turn down the heat and simmer gently, uncovered, for 30 minutes, skimming when necessary. Remove the parsley and the bay leaf, then set the béchamel aside.

When the wheat berries are tender, stir in the béchamel and add the sherry, then correct the seasoning and, if the soup is very thick, thin out with milk.

Serve piping hot.

6 to 8 servings

Suggested Menus

Cream of Wheat Berry Soup (see above)
Won Tons with Spinach and Tofu Filling (page 204)
Grated Carrot Salad (page 253)
Moist Carrot Cake (page 298)

Soya Pâté (page 58)
Cream of Wheat Berry Soup (see above)
Yorkshire Puddings with Cornmeal (page 229)
Water Cress and Mushroom Salad (page 247)
Fresh fruit (see page 276)

PUREE OF ASPARAGUS SOUP

Asparagus is practically all you need for this "cream soup." Actually there's no cream at all in it (unless you want to indulge in a little for garnish); the thickness comes from the puree itself. I love the subtle lightness of this soup—and it's hard to beat the taste of asparagus.

1 pound asparagus
1½ quarts Vegetable Stock (page 91) or water
  Salt, preferably sea salt, and freshly ground pepper to taste
1 to 2 tablespoons dry vermouth
  Cream or whipped ricotta (optional)

Trim the asparagus and cut it into 2-inch pieces. Set ½ cup of the tips aside and simmer the remainder gently in the water or stock, uncovered, for 30 minutes. Puree both cooked asparagus and stock in a food mill or food processor, or through a sieve. Return to the heat.

Five minutes before serving, drop in the remaining asparagus and season to taste with salt, pepper, and a little vermouth. If you wish, spoon a little cream or whipped ricotta (prepared with whisk, mixer, or food processor) into each bowl to enrich and garnish.

Note: This soup may also be served cold. In this case, do not drop the asparagus tips into the simmering soup but steam separately for 5 minutes and rinse under cold water to stop the cooking; otherwise they will continue to cook and will lose both their nice green color and their crunch. Add to the soup just before you serve.

6 to 8 servings

Suggested Menus

Puree of Asparagus Soup (see above)
Vegetable Paella (page 196)
Mixed Green Salad (page 238)
Watermelon-Fruit Extravaganza (page 280)

Potted Roquefort Spread (page 63)
Sesame Crackers (page 54) *or* Mixed Grains Bread (page 38)
Puree of Asparagus Soup (see above)
Garbanzo Bean Salad (page 254)
Raspberries in Red Wine (page 282)

EGG-LEMON SOUP

This remarkable soup, which can be served hot or chilled, comes from the Middle East. It's a favorite among my students and catering clients, whose eyes light up when they taste the delicate, lemony broth. The broccoli adds a nice touch of color.

3 eggs
½ cup lemon juice, or more to taste
1½ quarts Garlic Broth (page 92)
1½ to 2 cups broccoli florets
1½ cups cooked long-grained brown rice (¾ cup raw; see page 24)
  Salt, preferably sea salt, and freshly ground pepper to taste
  Paper-thin lemon slices for garnish

Beat together the eggs and lemon juice; bring the garlic broth to a simmer in a stock pot or large saucepan.

If serving hot: About 3 minutes before serving, add the broccoli to the broth. Then remove 1 cup of the broth and stir into the egg-lemon mixture.

(continued)

Have the broth just barely simmering, or "just smiling" (barely trembling at the surface but not bubbling). Slowly pour the egg-lemon-broth mixture into the soup pot, stirring constantly. When the eggs are bound—it should only take a minute or so—spoon 2 or 3 tablespoons of rice into each bowl and pour the soup over. Add a bit more lemon juice if it isn't lemony enough for you, and season to taste.

Serve, garnishing each bowl with a thin slice of lemon.

If serving cold: Steam the broccoli separately, until bright green, cool and hold. Follow the directions for the hot egg-lemon soup, but chill after the eggs are set, and add the broccoli and rice to each bowl or to the soup just before serving.

6 to 8 servings

Suggested Menus

Egg-Lemon Soup (see above)
Spanokopita (page 166)
Mixed Green Salad (page 238) *or* Tomatoes and Fresh Herbs (page 247)
Pears Poached in Red Wine with a Touch of Cassis (page 277)

Hommos (page 57) and Baba Ganouch (page 61), and bread of your choice (see pages 38–47)
Egg-Lemon Soup (see above)
Mixed Green Salad (page 238)
Fruit and cheese

A DIFFERENT ONION SOUP

Tomato juice makes this sweeter than the classic dark brown onion soup. It's very soothing—good for a cold.

4 large yellow or Spanish onions, quartered and sliced
1 clove garlic, minced or put through a press
2 to 3 tablespoons butter or safflower oil
1 quart Vegetable Stock (page 91) or Tamari-Bouillon Broth (page 91)
2 cups tomato or V-8 juice
½ teaspoon dried tarragon
Pinch of dried thyme
2 teaspoons lemon juice
1 tablespoon brandy, more as necessary
Salt, preferably sea salt and freshly ground pepper to taste
6 to 8 slices French Bread (page 45)
½ cup grated Gruyère or Parmesan cheese

Sauté the onions and garlic gently in butter or oil in a large, heavy-bottomed stock pot until the onion is tender. Add the stock and all the remaining ingredients except for the French bread and grated cheese. Cover and simmer for 1 hour; correct the seasoning.

Toast the slices of bread and sprinkle with the cheese. Pour the hot soup into soup bowls and float a slice of the toasted bread in each one.

Serve immediately.

Note: If you are serving bread with another part of your meal (see the second menu below), omit the croutons and simply place cheese in each bowl and ladle in hot soup.

6 to 8 servings

Suggested Menus

Crudité Salad (page 73)
A Different Onion Soup (see above)
Soufflé Roll with Mushroom and Broccoli Filling (page 162)
Mixed Green Salad (page 238)
Pears Poached in Red Wine with a Touch of Cassis (page 277)

Soya Pâté (page 58) and Mixed Grains Bread (page 38)
A Different Onion Soup (see above), omitting the croutons
Almond-Cheese Stuffed Crêpes (page 174)
Tomatoes and Fresh Herbs (page 247)
Fresh fruit (see page 276) *or* Gingerbread Soufflé (page 289)

LEEK SOUP

I first had this elegant soup while living in a little Mexican weaving village near Oaxaca. The Indian family I lived with thought that Americans were unable to digest anything other than soups or eggs, so they fed me many different wonderful soups for breakfast, lunch, and dinner. This soup is so simple that you will be amazed at how rich and soothing it is.

3 to 4 leeks, white part only, cleaned well and then sliced
3 tablespoons butter or safflower oil
1½ quarts Vegetable Stock (page 91) or Tamari-Bouillon Broth (page 91)
   Salt, preferably sea salt, and freshly ground pepper to taste
½ teaspoon dried tarragon (optional)
½ teaspoon Worcestershire sauce
2 tablespoons red wine (optional)
6 to 8 tablespoons freshly grated Parmesan cheese (optional)

In a Dutch oven or large stock pot, sauté the leeks in butter or oil for 5 to 10 minutes, until tender. Add the stock, salt, pepper, tarragon, and

Worcestershire, then cover and simmer for 1 hour. Stir in the red wine and correct the seasoning.

Pour the soup into bowls, sprinkle each serving with a tablespoon of the grated cheese, if desired, and serve.

6 to 8 servings

Suggested Menus

Leek Soup (see above)
Italian Soybean-Grains Casserole (page 181)
Spinach and Citrus Salad (page 249)
Bavarian Crème au Café (page 285)

Tiropites (page 68), with the filling of your choice
Leek Soup (see above)
Garbanzo Bean Salad (page 254) *or* Spicy Tofu Salad (page 243)
Broccoli Moutarde (page 233)
Mixed Grains Bread (page 38)
Fruit and cheese

POTATO-CHEESE SOUP

During the winter I get many requests for this thick, hearty soup. It's good with a salad and black bread, or with a vegetable-oriented main dish.

2 tablespoons butter
3 to 4 leeks, white part only, cleaned well and then sliced
5 large russet potatoes, unpeeled and diced
1 quart Vegetable Stock (page 91) or Tamari-Bouillon Broth (page 91)
Salt, preferably sea salt, to taste
2 cups milk
½ teaspoon caraway seeds
2 tablespoons fresh dill or 1 tablespoon dried
Freshly ground pepper to taste
1 cup grated Swiss cheese
¼ cup freshly grated Parmesan cheese
3 tablespoons plain yogurt, homemade (see page 259) or commercial
Chopped fresh parsley for garnish

In a large stock pot, melt the butter and sauté the leeks for 3 minutes. Add the potatoes, stock, and salt and bring to a boil. Reduce the heat, cover, and simmer for 30 minutes, until the potatoes are tender.

Add the milk, caraway seeds, dill, and pepper. Let simmer another 15 to 20 minutes; the soup should become thick and the potatoes should begin to fall apart. Stir in the cheeses and allow them to melt, then stir in the yogurt and heat through, but do not boil. Adjust the seasoning and serve piping hot, topped with parsley.

6 to 8 servings

Suggested Menus

Potato-Cheese Soup (see above)
Black Bread (page 43)
Mixed Green Salad (page 238) *or* Water Cress and Mushroom Salad (page 247)
Apple Pie (page 294) *or* Baked Apples (page 283)

Potato-Cheese Soup (see above)
Sprout-Stuffed Artichokes (page 231)
Chinese-Style Snow Peas and Water Chestnuts (page 230)
Carob Marble Cake (page 300)

POTATO-TOMATO SOUP

I make this smooth, comforting soup often in the wintertime; its familiar, good flavors make it a lovely choice for lunch along with a salad, and it also makes an elegant first course. It's quite easy, and you can vary the texture by pureeing all the potatoes or leaving some whole.

  2 onions, sliced
  2 to 3 tablespoons butter or safflower oil
  2 potatoes, peels left on and sliced
  ½ teaspoon caraway seeds (optional)
  1 quart boiling Vegetable Stock (page 91)
  5 cups peeled, sliced tomatoes
  2 teaspoons mild honey (optional)
     Salt, preferably sea salt, to taste
  ⅛ teaspoon paprika
  1 cup hot milk

In a stock pot or Dutch oven, sauté the sliced onion gently in the butter or oil until tender. Add the potatoes, optional caraway seeds, and the boiling stock. Cover and simmer for 30 minutes. Add the tomatoes, honey, salt, and paprika and simmer for 30 minutes longer.

Put the soup through a sieve or puree in a blender. Or puree half the soup and pour it back into the pot with the unpureed part (I think a few potato and tomato slices are nice). Reheat and correct the seasoning.

Carefully stir in the hot milk. Heat through, but do not boil; correct the seasoning and serve.

6 to 8 servings

Suggested Menus

Potato-Tomato Soup (see above)
Won Tons with Spinach and Tofu Filling (page 204)
Cole Slaw (page 256)
Fruit and cheese *or* Dried Fruit Compote (page 279)

Potato-Tomato Soup (see above)
Black Bread (page 43) *or* French Bread (page 45)
Herb Butter (page 61)
Mixed Green Salad (page 238) *or* Spinach Salad (page 238)
Orange Dessert Crêpes (page 285)

CABBAGE-CHEESE SOUP

This is a rich, creamy, heavenly soup. With bread and salad it suffices for a meal. Make sure that your potatoes are cooked through before you add the remaining ingredients, and don't worry if a thin crusty layer forms on the bottom of the pan while you are cooking them. It's difficult to avoid this no matter how much oil or butter you use, but the layer will wash off readily with a little soaking, and as long as you keep stirring the potatoes while they're cooking they won't burn and ruin the soup.

    2 tablespoons butter, more as necessary
    1 tablespoon safflower oil, more as necessary
    1 large potato, unpeeled and grated
    ½ pound white cabbage, shredded
    1 quart milk
    ½ teaspoon salt, preferably sea salt, or to taste
    2 cups Vegetable Stock (page 91)
    1 cup grated Swiss Gruyère cheese
    ½ cup freshly grated Parmesan cheese
      Freshly ground pepper

Heat the butter and oil in a stock pot or Dutch oven and sauté the potato for 15 minutes, or until tender. The grated potato will begin to stick to the bottom of the pan, but it won't burn if you keep tossing it with a wooden spoon. Add more oil or butter as you feel is necessary, and don't stir the layer that sticks to the bottom up into the potatoes. Add the cabbage and cook, tossing, until it begins to cook through, about 5 minutes.

Gradually add the milk, salt, and stock, stirring. Bring to a very slow simmer; do not boil. Cover and let cook slowly for 20 minutes, stirring occasionally.

About 5 minutes before serving, add the cheeses and grind in some black pepper. Stir until the cheeses melt, adjust the seasoning, and serve.

6 to 8 servings

Suggested Menu

Cabbage-Cheese Soup (see above)
Marinated White Beans (page 195) *or* Tempura'd Vegetables with Assorted
    Dips (page 81).
Brown rice, bulgur, *or* couscous
Tomatoes and Fresh Herbs (page 247)
Mince Pie (page 273)

DILL SOUP

Don't let the amount of potato in this lead you to believe it's a heavy soup. Yogurt and dill are added just before serving, making it light and refreshing.

This is a marvelous soup, hot or cold. Make it a day in advance if you plan to serve it chilled. If you're serving it hot and wish to prepare it ahead, you should make it only through the puree step and add the egg, yogurt, and dill just before you heat it through before serving.

1½ quarts water
  1 teaspoon salt, preferably sea salt, or to taste
  3 vegetable bouillon cubes
  5 potatoes, peeled and diced (peels reserved)
  2 carrots, coarsely sliced
  1 onion, quartered
  2 ribs celery, coarsely sliced
    Freshly ground pepper
  2 eggs
  ½ cup fresh dill, or ¼ cup dried (fresh is preferable)
  1 cup plain yogurt, homemade (see page 259) or commercial
    Alfalfa sprouts, sunflower seeds, yogurt, and cucumber slices (optional) for
    garnish

Pour the water into a stock pot and add the salt, bouillon cubes, potatoes and their peels (wrapped in cheesecloth for easy removal), carrots,

118

onion, and celery. Bring to a boil, then reduce the heat, cover, and simmer for 1 to 2 hours; the vegetables should be very tender.

Strain, retaining the stock. Discard half the vegetables and all of the potato peels. Press the rest through a sieve or food mill, or puree in a food processor, using the grater blade, not the steel blade (otherwise you'll get a very sticky paste), leaving some texture. Stir back into the stock and season with salt and pepper to taste.

In a bowl, beat the eggs and mix with the dill and yogurt. Pour some soup into the bowl and mix well, then pour the mixture back into the soup. Heat through gently, stirring; do not allow to boil.

Serve hot, garnished with alfalfa sprouts, sunflower seeds, and additional yogurt. Or on a hot day heat through, cool, and chill. Serve garnished with sliced cucumbers, sprouts, sunflower seeds, and yogurt.

6 to 8 servings

Suggested Menus

Dill Soup (see above)
Fallafels (page 197)
Cucumber Salad (page 243)
Fruit and cheese

Steamed asparagus, chilled
Dill Soup (see above)
Tomato Quiche (page 157)
Water Cress and Mushroom Salad (page 247)
Watermelon-Fruit Extravaganza (page 280)

MINESTRONE

Minestrone means "big soup." Irma Goodrich Mazza, in her delightful *Herbs for the Kitchen*, says it's closest to the heart of her household: "A plate of this pottage topped with grated Romano cheese, served with crisped and garlicked French bread, a salad and a glass of wine, and *we have dined.*" [1] Mine is tomato-y and thick, full of fresh vegetables, rich with beans and pasta and Parmesan cheese. Serve piping hot for a hearty winter meal; in the summer, serve it at room temperature in smaller bowls.

For this soup you will need the garlic broth and the stock, if you're using it, done in advance, and you'll need to remember to soak the beans.

[1] New York: Arco Publishing Co., 1973, p. 82.

Use vegetables in season; if you can find no fresh green beans or peas, use frozen.

This soup is even better one day after it's made. If you make it ahead, hold the fresh vegetables. The next day, bring the soup to a simmer and proceed as in the recipe, adding the vegetables 15 minutes before serving the soup and simmering until they are cooked through but still colorful and crisp.

½ cup dried navy beans, kidney beans, or garbanzo beans (navy beans rec-
    ommended)
2 cups Vegetable Stock (page 91) or water
2 tablespoons olive oil
1 large onion, chopped
2 to 3 or more cloves garlic, minced or put through a press
2 leeks, white part only, cleaned well and then sliced thin
1 teaspoon salt, preferably sea salt, or to taste
1 quart Garlic Broth (page 92)
2 carrots, sliced
4 tomatoes, peeled and sliced
1 can (6 ounces) tomato paste
1 potato, unpeeled and diced
¼ teaspoon celery seed
    Freshly ground pepper to taste
1 tablespoon chopped fresh basil or ¼ teaspoon dried
1 teaspoon oregano
¼ teaspoon dried marjoram
2 tablespoons chopped fresh parsley, plus additional for garnish
1 cup broken dry spaghetti
1 to 2 zucchini, sliced thin
⅔ cup fresh green beans, ends cut off and halved, or 1 cup fresh or frozen peas
1 cup shredded cabbage
⅔ cup freshly grated Romano or Parmesan cheese

Soak the beans in the stock or water overnight or for several hours.

In a large stock pot or Dutch oven, heat the olive oil and sauté the onion and garlic until the onion is tender. Add the leeks and sauté until they begin to soften, about 2 minutes; add the beans and their liquid. Bring to a boil, add the salt, then reduce the heat, cover, and simmer until tender, 1 to 2 hours. Check occasionally to see that the beans remain immersed in liquid, and add more liquid if necessary.

When the beans are tender, add the garlic broth, one of the carrots, the tomatoes, tomato paste, potato, celery seeds, pepper, and herbs. Bring to a simmer, then cover and cook for 45 minutes to an hour. Adjust the seasoning, adding more salt and pepper and garlic if you wish.

About 20 minutes before serving, add the spaghetti. Five minutes later, add the remaining vegetables and simmer until they are cooked through but still bright, with some texture.

Place a tablespoonful of grated Romano or Parmesan in each bowl. Spoon the soup in over this, and top with chopped fresh parsley. Sprinkle the remaining cheese into the soup and serve either hot or at room temperature.

6 to 8 servings

Suggested Menus

Stuffed Mushrooms (page 65)
Minestrone (see above)
Spinach Gnocchi (page 192)
Tender Lettuce and Orange Salad (page 242)
Fresh fruit (see page 276)

Minestrone (see above)
French Bread (page 45) *or* French Herb Bread (page 46)
Herb Butter (page 61)
Mixed Green Salad (page 238)
Light Cheesecake (page 291)

ESCAROLE SOUP

Here is another classic Italian egg drop-type soup, velvety, soothing, and light. A good accompaniment to a heavy meal.

6 cups Vegetable Stock (page 91) or Garlic Broth (page 92)
2 tablespoons tamari
1 pound escarole, chopped
2 eggs, beaten
¼ cup freshly grated Parmesan cheese
   Salt, preferably sea salt, and freshly ground pepper to taste
   Whole-wheat or black bread Croutons (page 54) (optional)

Bring the stock to a simmer in a large saucepan or stock pot and add the tamari.

About 5 minutes before serving, stir in the escarole.

Beat the eggs and combine with the Parmesan. Just before serving, carefully stir into the stock. Stir until the eggs set, about 1 to 3 minutes; do not allow the soup to boil. Add salt and pepper to taste and serve, garnished with toasted whole-wheat or black bread croutons, if you wish.

6 to 8 servings

Suggested Menu

Escarole Soup (see above)
Pasta with Soybean Spaghetti Sauce (page 215) *or* Lasagne (page 187) *or* Eggplant Parmesan (page 178)
Mixed Green Salad (page 238)
Italian Fruit Compote (page 278) *or* Orange Dessert Crêpes (page 285)

VICHYSSOISE

This isn't as rich as the traditional vichyssoise because it calls for milk enriched with spray-dried skimmed milk instead of cream, and yogurt instead of sour cream. It still has a very rich and satisfying flavor.

Remember to allow the soup to cool before you add the yogurt, or the yogurt will sour. Chill well.

3 tablespoons butter or safflower oil
3 leeks, white part only, cleaned well and then sliced
1 onion, chopped
3 potatoes, peeled and diced
  Salt, preferably sea salt, to taste
1 quart Vegetable Stock (page 91)
2 cups milk
½ cup spray-dried skimmed milk
1 tablespoon soy flour (optional)
1 cup plain yogurt, homemade (see page 259) or commercial
¼ cup chopped fresh chives
½ cup chopped fresh parsley

Heat the butter or oil in a stock pot and sauté the leeks and onion until tender. Add the potatoes, salt, and stock. Bring to a boil, then reduce the heat, cover, and simmer 30 minutes to 1 hour, until the potatoes are tender and beginning to fall apart. Purée in a blender or put through a sieve. Return to the pot.

Blend together the milk and milk powder and, if you are using it, the soy flour. Add to the soup and heat to the boiling point, stirring often to prevent sticking. Correct the seasonings, remove from the heat, and chill well.

When you are sure the soup is cold, stir in the yogurt.

Serve garnished with chives and chopped fresh parsley.

6 to 8 servings

Suggested Menus

Vichyssoise (see above)
Shredded Fruit and Vegetable Salad (page 255)
Curried Tofu and Vegetables over Millet (page 208)
Fresh fruit (see page 276) *or* Bavarian Crème au Café (page 286)

Sesame Eggplant Rounds (without Hommos) (page 86)
Vichyssoise (see above)
Any omelet (pages 169–72)
Spinach Salad (page 238) *or* Mixed Green Salad (page 238)
Pears Poached in Red Wine with a Touch of Cassis (page 277)

TOMATO-RICE SOUP

A crisp tossed salad, a good loaf of bread, and tomato-rice soup can make a marvelous meal. This soup can be made a day in advance up to the point at which you add the milk. Do that shortly before serving.

2 to 3 tablespoons safflower or olive oil
1 onion, chopped
2 cloves garlic, minced or put through a press
1 rib celery, sliced
1 carrot, sliced
2 tablespoons whole-wheat pastry flour or unbleached white flour
¾ cup raw brown rice
2 pounds fresh tomatoes, peeled, chopped, and mashed, or 1 can (28 ounces) tomatoes, chopped and mashed
   Salt, preferably sea salt, to taste
   Freshly ground black pepper to taste
1 to 3 teaspoons mild honey
1 teaspoon oregano
2 teaspoons chopped fresh basil or 1 teaspoon dried
3 cups Vegetable Stock (page 91)
3 cups hot milk

Heat the oil in a stock pot and sauté the onion and garlic until the onion is tender. Add the celery and carrot and sauté for another 5 minutes.

Add the flour and the rice and sauté, stirring, until the rice is toasty, about 5 to 10 minutes. Add the tomatoes, salt, pepper, honey, oregano, and basil and stir in the stock. Cover and simmer for 1 hour, or until the rice is done.

Add the hot milk and correct the seasoning. Heat through, being careful not to boil, and serve.

Note: Before adding the milk, you can, if you wish, puree part or all of the soup or put it through a sieve.

6 to 8 servings

Suggested Menu

Tomato-Rice Soup (see above)
Squash Soufflé (page 165) *or* Stuffed Eggplant (page 180)
Mixed Green Salad (page 238)
Pecan Pie (page 295) *or* Fruit and Spice Cake (page 299)

SESAME-SPINACH SOUP

Ginger, tamari, and sherry give this soup its Chinese character. It's quick and easy, yet elegant. You can have the stock simmering and the spinach stemmed in advance; then it's a last-minute operation.

 2 tablespoons oil (peanut, safflower, sesame, or vegetable)
 2 teaspoons freshly grated gingerroot
 ¼ to ½ cup sesame seeds, plus additional for garnish, if desired
 6 cups Vegetable Stock (page 91)
 5 tablespoons tamari
 ¼ cup dry sherry or sake
 2 cloves garlic, minced or put through a press
 ¼ teaspoon dry mustard
 1 tablespoon arrowroot or cornstarch
 10 ounces fresh spinach, washed well and stemmed
 ¼ cup chopped fresh chives for garnish

In a stock pot, heat the oil and sauté 1 teaspoon of the ginger and the sesame seeds for 3 minutes, or until the sesame seeds begin to smell toasty. Add the stock and bring to a simmer.

Combine the tamari and sherry with the remaining ginger and the garlic, mustard, and arrowroot. Add to the stock and simmer for 15 to 30 minutes.

Five minutes before serving, or less, add the spinach and stir until it is just cooked through. Serve immediately, topping each serving, if you wish, with more sesame seeds and chopped fresh chives.

6 to 8 servings

Suggested Menus

Sesame-Spinach Soup (see above)
Couscous with Vegetables (page 219) *or* Couscous with Fruit (page 221)
Mixed Green Salad (page 238)
Soufflé Grand Marnier (page 290)

Egg Rolls (page 80)
Sesame-Spinach Soup (see above)
Fruited Baked Beans with Chutney (page 216)
Mixed Green Salad (page 238)
Assorted cookies (see pages 303–305) *or* Millet-Raisin Pudding (page 292)

TAMARI-NOODLE SOUP WITH GREEN BEANS

Simple, light, and very pleasing.

6 cups Vegetable Stock (page 91)
½ cup tamari
½ pound buckwheat noodles
½ pound green beans, ends snapped off and washed, then sliced if desired

Bring the stock and tamari to a simmer in a large saucepan or stock pot. About 15 minutes before serving, add the noodles and green beans to the stock. Serve when the noodles are tender.

6 to 8 servings

Suggested Menus

Tamari-Noodle Soup with Green Beans (see above)
Fruited Baked Beans with Chutney (page 216) *or* Soufflé Roll (page 162)
Mixed Green Salad (page 238)
Millet-Raisin Pudding (page 292) *or* Bananas Poached in White Wine (page 277)

Tamari-Noodle Soup with Green Beans (see above)
Soyburgers (page 213)
Mixed Green Salad (page 238)
Tomatoes and Fresh Herbs (page 247)
Apricot Soufflé (page 289)

Quichettes (page 64)
Tamari-Noodle Soup with Green Beans (see above)
Brown Rice Salad (page 245)
Marinated Lentil Salad (page 252)
Melon au Porto (page 280)

NOODLE-BEAN SOUP

The combination of whole-grain noodles, beans, and *miso* not only give this delightful soup an Oriental character—they also make this an exemplary complementary soup. You must remember to soak and cook the beans in advance—they will keep for two days in the refrigerator with no problem. You can also make the stock a day in advance.

⅔ cup dried kidney beans
⅔ cup dried black beans or 1⅓ total cups dried kidney beans
 1 quart water
¼ cup safflower or vegetable oil
 2 onions, chopped
 3 cloves garlic, minced or put through a press
 1 teaspoon salt, preferably sea salt, to taste
 1 quart Vegetable Stock (page 91) or Tamari-Bouillon Broth (page 91), approximately
 3 tablespoons sesame seeds
 3 green onions, both white part and green, chopped separately
 1 cup tofu, cut in slivers
 1 cup matchstick-cut carrots
 1 cup matchstick-cut turnips
 1 tablespoon cider vinegar
 2 tablespoons tamari (omit if using tamari-bouillon broth)
¼ teaspoon chili powder
¼ teaspoon freshly ground pepper
 8 ounces flat buckwheat or other whole-grain noodles
 1 tablespoon *miso* paste
 1 cup lettuce, torn in pieces

Wash the beans and soak overnight or for several hours in the water.

In a stock pot or Dutch oven, heat 2 tablespoons of the oil and sauté half the onion and two of the garlic cloves until the onion is tender. Add the beans, in their liquid, and bring to a boil. Add the salt, then reduce the heat, cover, and simmer for 1 to 2 hours, until the beans are tender but not mushy and the broth is aromatic; add more salt as desired.

Place a colander or strainer over a large bowl or another pot and drain the beans. Measure out the liquid and add enough vegetable stock or tamari-bouillon broth to make 7 cups.

Wash out your stock pot and dry it, then heat the rest of the oil in it and sauté the remaining onion and garlic and the sesame seeds until the onion is tender. Add the chopped white part of the green onions, the tofu, ¼ cup each of the carrots and turnips, the beans and their liquid, vinegar, tamari, chili powder, freshly ground pepper, and a little salt. Bring to a gentle boil, then cover, reduce the heat, and simmer for 30 minutes.

Fifteen minutes before serving, add the noodles, and 5 minutes later add the remaining turnips and carrots.

Remove a cup of liquid from the pot and add the *miso* paste; stir well to dissolve. Pour back into the pot and add the lettuce and chopped green part of the green onions. Heat through, without boiling, for 3 to 4 minutes, then correct the seasonings. Make sure the noodles are cooked through and serve.

6 to 8 servings

Suggested Menus

Egg Rolls (page 80)
Noodle-Bean Soup (see above)
Stir-fry Chinese Tofu and Vegetables No. 1 or 2 (pages 200 and 203), with
     bulgur, millet, or rice
Salade Mimosa (page 248)
Apricot Soufflé (page 289) *or* Gingerbread Soufflé (page 289)

Noodle-Bean Soup (see above)
Spicy Tofu Salad (page 243)
Gingered Broccoli (page 231) *or* Baked Acorn Squash (page 234)
Fresh fruit (see page 276)

THICK CABBAGE SOUP

A wonderful, easy soup, one of my favorites. Sesame seeds are a nice touch, adding texture and nuttiness to a thick soup with a dark and fragrant broth. A little bit of cayenne goes a long way here; it's an important ingredient that enhances the character of the soup.

2 to 3 tablespoons safflower or corn oil
1 onion, chopped
3 tablespoons sesame seeds

7 cups shredded cabbage (about ½ large head)
2 tomatoes, chopped
2 slices whole-wheat or rye bread, diced
6 cups Vegetable Stock (page 91) or Tamari-Bouillon Broth (page 91)
  Salt, preferably sea salt, to taste
3 tablespoons soy sauce, or to taste
⅛ teaspoon cayenne pepper
½ teaspoon caraway seeds (optional)

In a heavy-bottomed stock pot, heat the safflower oil and sauté the onion, sesame seeds, and cabbage, over low heat, for about 10 minutes.

Stir in the remaining ingredients and simmer, covered, for 45 minutes. Serve hot.

6 to 8 servings

Suggested Menu
Crudité Salad (page 73)
Thick Cabbage Soup (see above)
Couscous with Vegetables (page 219)
Baked Acorn Squash (page 234)
Orange Dessert Crêpes (page 285)

MISO-VEGETABLE SOUP

Miso is fermented soybean paste, very concentrated and high in protein. Some of the first meatless dishes I cooked were *miso* soups. They're easy, light, and energizing. This one is full of vegetables cooked in a delicate stock.

1 onion, sliced
1 clove garlic, minced or put through a press
2 tablespoons safflower oil
2 carrots, sliced
1 rib celery, sliced
1 cup broccoli florets
2 quarts Vegetable Stock (page 91)
½ teaspoon salt, preferably sea salt
¼ cup tamari
1 cup fresh or frozen peas
1 heaping tablespoon *miso* paste
1 cup mung bean sprouts

In a stock pot, sauté the onion and garlic in the safflower oil until the onion is tender. Add all the other ingredients except the peas, the *miso* paste, and the bean sprouts and allow to simmer for 20 minutes. Add the peas, and when the peas are tender, remove a cup of liquid from the pot and dissolve the *miso* paste in it. Return to the pot and stir well; do not allow the soup to boil. Add the mung bean sprouts and cook for a few minutes longer, then serve.

6 to 8 servings

Suggested Menu
Miso-Vegetable Soup (see above)
Fettucine con Funghi (page 190)
Sprout-Stuffed Artichokes (page 231)
Mixed Green Salad (page 238)
Assorted cookies (see pages 303–305)

BLACK BEAN SOUP

Black bean soup is a Cuban dish traditionally made with lots of meat. But this is not just a pot of beans. What distinguishes it is the sherry and the lemon juice, which give it a nice tartness.

You must remember to soak the beans in advance. The soup can be made a day before serving; store it, covered, in the refrigerator.

2 cups dried black beans,
6 cups Vegetable Stock (page 91) or water
2 tablespoons safflower oil
1 onion, chopped
4 cloves garlic, minced or put through a press
1 rib celery, with leaves, chopped
2 teaspoons salt, preferably sea salt, or to taste
Freshly ground pepper to taste
1 teaspoon celery seed
Juice of 1½ lemons
3 to 4 tablespoons dry sherry
Paper-thin lemon slices
1 hard-boiled egg, chopped (optional)

Wash the beans and soak in the stock or water overnight or for severa hours.

In a large, heavy-bottomed stock pot or Dutch oven, heat the oil an sauté the onion, garlic, and celery until tender. Add the beans and thei liquid and bring to a boil. Add the salt, reduce the heat, cover, and simmer for 2 hours, or until the beans are tender.

Remove half the beans from the pot and puree in a blender, with soup liquid to cover, adding the pepper and celery seeds.

Return the puree to the pot and reheat, stirring, until it thickens slightly. Stir in the lemon juice and sherry.

Serve garnished with lemon slices and, if desired, chopped hard-boiled egg.

6 to 8 servings

Suggested Menus

Black Bean Soup (see above)
Any omelet (see pages 169–72)
Mixed Green Salad (page 238)
Almond Gems (page 303)

Marinated Vegetables Vinaigrette (page 74)
Black Bean Soup (see above)
Brown Rice Salad (page 245) *or* Yorkshire Puddings with Cornmeal (page 229)
Steamed green vegetables
Oranges Grand Marnier (page 279)

LENTIL SOUP

Bay leaves are a key herb here; they bring out the best in lentils. This easy recipe makes a rich but not heavy pot of soup.

    1 onion, chopped
    2 to 3 cloves garlic, minced or put through a press
    ¼ teaspoon chili powder or ⅛ teaspoon cayenne pepper
    ½ teaspoon cuminseed
    1 tablespoon safflower or peanut oil
    1 tablespoon butter
    2 quarts water or Vegetable Stock (page 91)
    2 cups dried lentils, washed
    1 carrot, sliced
    2 ribs celery, sliced
    1 bay leaf
    2 teaspoons salt, preferably sea salt, or to taste

In a stock pot or Dutch oven, sauté the onion, garlic, and spices in the oil and butter until the onion is soft. Add the remaining ingredients and bring to a boil, then reduce the heat, cover, and simmer for 1 to 2 hours. Correct the seasoning and serve.

6 to 8 servings

Suggested Menu

Lentil Soup (see above)

Vegetable Tempura with Tahini-Tamari Sauce, Served with Buckwheat Noodles (page 206) *or* any omelet (pages 169–72)

World of Sprouts Salad (page 239) *or* Spinach Salad (page 238)

Peach Pie (page 294)

CURRY-FLAVORED LENTIL SOUP

This is one of my favorites. It has a subtle delicacy unlike most lentil soups, which are usually heavy. Only half the lentils are pureed, so you'll have a thick soup with lots of whole lentils to bite into.

2 tablespoons peanut or safflower oil
1 onion, chopped
2 cloves garlic, minced or put through a press
¼ teaspoon chili powder
1 teaspoon turmeric
2 teaspoons curry powder (more to taste)
½ teaspoon cuminseed
½ teaspoon ground coriander
2 cups dried lentils, washed
2 teaspoons salt, preferably sea salt, or to taste
2 quarts water or Vegetable Stock (page 91)
2 tablespoons butter

In a large, heavy-bottomed stock pot, heat the oil and sauté the onion, garlic, and spices until the onion is tender. Add the lentils, salt, and water or stock and bring to a boil, then cover, reduce the heat, and simmer until the lentils are tender, about 1 to 1½ hours.

Remove half the lentils from the pot and mash. Return them to the pot, add the butter, and heat through. Correct the seasoning and serve.

6 to 8 servings

Suggested Menus

Vegetable Platter (page 77) with Curry Dressing (page 262)
Curry-Flavored Lentil Soup (see above)
Indonesian Rice (page 227)
Waldorf Salad (page 272)
Strawberry and Cassis Sherbet (page 301)

Curry-Flavored Lentil Soup (see above)
Fruit Curry (page 211)
Saffron Brown Rice (page 227)
Cheese

ALMOND SOUP

The idea of an almond soup may sound strange to you, and the ingredients in this recipe may look strange. But when you try the soup it won't *taste* strange. The seasonings here—cardamom, caraway, and nutmeg—are very distinctive. And the textures of the ground almonds and the rice are sublime. It's fabulous hot or cold, and will keep for a day refrigerated.

Give yourself plenty of time to remove the skins from the almonds, a step that is easy but rather tedious. (If you wish you can use packaged almonds that have already been blanched, though the almonds probably won't be as fresh and tasty as those you buy with skins.)

1 quart Vegetable Stock (page 91) or Tamari-Bouillon Broth (page 91)
2 cups whole almonds, blanched as directed on page 23
1 medium onion, chopped
1 tablespoon butter
Grated peel of 1 to 2 lemons
½ teaspoon ground cardamom
½ teaspoon caraway seeds (optional)
Salt, preferably sea salt, and freshly ground pepper to taste
2 cups milk
1 teaspoon lemon juice
1 cup cooked long-grain brown rice (½ cup raw; see page 24)
⅓ cup currants
Freshly grated nutmeg

Using enough stock to cover, puree the blanched almonds, a cup at a time, in a blender or food processor, allowing them to retain some texture. Add the almond puree to the remaining stock.

(*continued*)

132

In a stock pot, sauté the onion in the butter until tender. Add the a
mond-stock mixture, the grated lemon peel, the cardamom, optional cara
way seeds, salt, and pepper. Cover and simmer gently for 30 minutes, sti
ring occasionally.

Carefully add the milk and lemon juice and correct the seasoning. Ad
the rice and currants and simmer very gently for another 10 minutes.

Grate some nutmeg over the top and serve, or chill and serve colc
grating additional nutmeg over each serving.

6 to 8 serving

Suggested Menus

Almond Soup (see above)
Fruited Baked Beans with Chutney (page 216)
Grated Carrot Salad (page 253)
Soufflé Grand Marnier (page 290)

Almond Soup (see above)
Marinated White Beans (page 193)
Avocado and Citrus Salad (page 239)
Orange Dessert Crêpes (page 285)

CURRY OF EGGPLANT SOUP

A perfect marriage of eggplant and curry. This surprising soup is ele
gant served hot or cold.

3 tablespoons butter, more as needed
1 onion, chopped
2 cloves garlic, minced or put through a press
½ teaspoon crushed cuminseed or ground cumin
½ teaspoon ground coriander
1 teaspoon freshly grated gingerroot or ½ teaspoon ground ginger
2 teaspoons curry powder, or to taste
2 pounds eggplant, peeled and diced
6 cups Vegetable Stock (page 91) or Tamari-Bouillon Broth (page 91)
   Salt, preferably sea salt, to taste
1 cup milk or half-and-half
   Grated orange peel and sunflower seeds, or chopped fresh coriander (*cilan
   tro*) for garnish

Melt the butter in a heavy-bottomed stock pot and sauté the onion and garlic gently, along with the spices, until the onion is tender. Add the eggplant and more butter if necessary and continue to cook, stirring gently with a wooden spoon, until the eggplant begins to cook through. If the eggplant sticks, add more butter.

Pour in the stock and bring to a simmer. Cook, covered, for 1 hour; add salt to taste.

Puree the soup in batches in a blender or food processor. Return to the pot or a bowl and stir in the milk or half-and-half. Adjust the seasoning and chill for several hours, or serve hot.

Garnish with a sprinkling of grated orange peel and sunflower seeds, or with chopped fresh coriander.

6 to 8 servings

Suggested Menus

Curry of Eggplant Soup (see above)
Fallafels (page 197) *or* Omelet with Curried Orange Filling (page 172)
Tabouli (page 240)
Bavarian Crème au Café (page 286) *or* Pears Poached in Red Wine with a
   Touch of Cassis (page 277)

Curry of Eggplant Soup (see above)
Curry Salad (page 209)
Watermelon-Fruit Extravaganza (page 280)

MEATLESS MULLIGATAWNY

Mulligatawny is a curried soup from the East Indies; the name comes from *miḷakutaṇṇi* (Tamil), which means "pepper water." I've seen recipes in Indian cookbooks for lamb, chicken, lentil and mutton, almond and lamb, and apple and chicken mulligatawnies. This version, a mild curry that thickens as it cooks, uses ingredients from all these recipes and provides an unbelievable combination of tastes and textures—apple, vegetables, peanuts, ground almonds, raisins, coconut. Be prepared for many requests for seconds.

The traditional way to serve mulligatawny is to pass a bowl of rice after the soup is ladled out and have guests spoon their own into their bowls.

This hearty soup can be prepared up to a day in advance; the flavors will mature overnight.

(continued)

3 tablespoons butter
1 tablespoon curry powder
1 onion, minced
2 tart apples, green or red, peeled and diced
2 carrots, chopped fine
½ cup raw peanuts
2 green peppers, seeded and chopped
2 tablespoons whole-wheat pastry flour or unbleached white flour
2 quarts Vegetable Stock (page 91) or water
4 whole cloves
½ cup almonds, coarsely ground in a blender
2 teaspoons mild honey
¼ cup shredded coconut
½ cup raisins
1 teaspoon ground mace
Salt, preferably sea salt, and freshly ground black pepper to taste
3 tomatoes, peeled and pounded
Thin slices of apple for garnish
1 to 1½ cups cooked long-grain brown rice (see page 24), kept warm in a serving bowl

Melt the butter in a stock pot and stir in the curry powder. Add the onion, diced apple, carrot, raw peanuts, and green pepper and sauté until the onion is just about tender. Stir in the flour and blend well. Cook, stirring, for 5 minutes; do not brown.

Slowly add the stock, stirring constantly in order to blend in the flour. Add all the other ingredients except the apple slices and rice and simmer for 20 minutes over low heat.

Puree half the soup in a blender or put through a sieve. Pour back into the pot, heat through, and serve topped with thinly sliced apple. Pass the bowl of rice and have your guests spoon some rice into their soup.

Or place a large spoonful of rice in each bowl and pour the soup over it, then garnish with the apple.

6 to 8 servings

Suggested Menus

Meatless Mulligatawny (see above)
Sweet and Sour Cabbage (page 207) *or* Bean Sprout Omelet (page 172)
Mixed Green Salad (page 238) with Cucumber-Cream Dressing (page 261)
Orange Dessert Crêpes (page 285) *or* Moist Carrot Cake (page 298)

Quichettes (page 64)
Meatless Mulligatawny (see above)
Mixed Green Salad (page 238)
Peaches Marsala (page 282)

BLENDER GAZPACHO

There are probably as many recipes for gazpacho as there are villages in Spain. I prefer this one because it's so easy. It's like a liquid salad with an array of garnishes.

This gazpacho keeps for about four days. It's a convenient item to have on hand for a quick, healthy, and delicious meal.

For the soup:
    4 ripe tomatoes, peeled
    2 cloves garlic, peeled
    1 small onion, chunked
    1 carrot, coarsely chopped
    1 cucumber, peeled and coarsely chopped
    1 green pepper, seeded and quartered
    2 sprigs fresh parsley
    ¼ cup chopped fresh basil or 2 tablespoons dried
    ¼ to ½ cup lemon juice, or to taste
    ¼ cup olive oil
    3 cups cold Vegetable Stock (page 91) or V-8 juice
       Salt, preferably sea salt, and freshly ground pepper to taste
       V-8 juice as necessary

For the garnish:
    1 cup cubed tofu
    ½ cup grated carrot
    ¼ cup minced green pepper
    ¼ cup minced cucumber
    1 tomato, chopped
    ½ cup alfalfa or mung bean sprouts
    ¼ cup sunflower seeds
       Plain yogurt, homemade (see page 259) or commercial

Place tomatoes in one bowl, all the other vegetables and herbs in another bowl, the lemon juice and olive oil together in another bowl, and the stock in another (or have the V-8 in its can).

Puree the vegetables in a blender or food processor with the stock, lemon juice, and olive oil, according to the directions for cold blender soups on pages 27–28. Pour each batch off into a large container, and then, when all the vegetables have been pureed, stir together well and adjust the seasoning. For a richer tomato taste, and to thin out to desired consistency, add some V-8, then cover and chill for several hours.

For the garnish, mix together the cubed tofu, grated carrot, green pepper, cucumber, and chopped tomato in one bowl; have the sprouts and sunflower seeds in separate bowls. Place a spoonful of the vegetables and tofu in each serving bowl; spoon in the soup. Top with a dollop of yogurt, a clump of sprouts, and a sprinkling of sunflower seeds and serve.

6 to 8 servings

Suggested Menus

Blender Gazpacho (see above)
Almond-Cheese Stuffed Crêpes (page 175)
Spinach Salad (page 238)
Strawberry and Cassis Sherbet (page 301)

Blender Gazpacho (see above)
Any omelet (pages 169–72) *or* Spinach and Onion Quiche (page 150) *or*
    Black Bean Enchiladas (page 144)
Beet and Endive Salad (page 248)
Peaches Marsala (page 282)

APPLE-SPICE SOUP

This sweet, spicy soup tastes best when served hot, preferably prepared on the day you serve it. But it's delicious cold, too, and it does make a good leftover. Topped with yogurt, it makes a lovely dish for breakfast or brunch.

If, upon final tasting, it doesn't have quite enough character for you, add some more freshly grated nutmeg. You may think that honey or lemon juice is what it needs, but nutmeg is a magical spice and will enhance all the other flavors.

1½ quarts water
 4 large, tart apples, unpeeled, cored and sliced
 ⅔ cup raisins
 1 teaspoon freshly grated nutmeg, more if desired
1½ teaspoons ground cinnamon
 ¼ teaspoon ground cloves

½ teaspoon ground allspice
3 to 4 tablespoons mild honey, or to taste
3 slices Mixed Grains Bread (page 38) or whole-wheat bread, in 1-inch chunks
1 to 2 tablespoons lemon juice, or to taste
2 tablespoons brandy
½ to 1 cup plain yogurt, homemade (see page 259) or commercial

Combine the water, apples, raisins, spices, and honey in a stock pot or Dutch oven and bring to a boil. Add the bread, then cover, reduce the heat, and simmer for 45 minutes to 1 hour.

Remove from the heat and add the lemon juice, brandy, and ½ cup yogurt. Correct the seasoning, adding more honey, lemon juice, or nutmeg.

Top each bowl with a dollop of yogurt; sprinkle with nutmeg and serve.

6 to 8 servings

Suggested Menu

Apple-Spice Soup (see above)
Curried Tofu and Vegetables over Millet (page 208)
Cucumber Raita (page 235) *or* Banana Raita (page 235) or both
Chutney (page 235)
Lentil Dahl (page 229)
Bavarian Crème au Café (page 285) *or* Gingerbread Soufflé (page 289)

CHILLED AVOCADO-TOMATO SOUP

This soup tastes like a cross between gazpacho and guacamole and is very rich; it also keeps well in the refrigerator for up to three days. It's been a cooking-class favorite for years.

1 quart V-8 juice or tomato juice, preferably V-8
1 tomato, peeled and quartered
1 small onion, quartered
1 green pepper, seeded and coarsely chopped
2 to 3 ripe avocados, peeled, pitted, and sliced thick
¼ cup lemon juice
Salt, preferably sea salt, to taste
1½ cups plain yogurt, homemade (see page 259) or commercial
Sunflower seeds and alfalfa sprouts for garnish

Liquefy all the ingredients except the yogurt and garnishes in a blender or food processor until smooth, following the directions for cold blended

138

soups on pages 27–28. Stir in 1 cup of the yogurt; chill well.

Serve topped with a dollop of yogurt, and sprinkled with sunflower seeds and alfalfa sprouts.

6 to 8 servings

Suggested Menu

Chilled Tomato-Avocado Soup (see above)
Black Bean Enchiladas (page 144) *or* Extraordinary Chalupas (page 147)
Spinach Salad (page 238)
Oranges Grand Marnier (page 279)

BULGARIAN CUCUMBER SOUP

This soup is almost a salad, bursting as it is with cucumbers steeped in a vinaigrette-like marinade with an abundance of dill, and then tempered with creamy-rich yogurt. It's a terrifically refreshing and exciting summer soup.

Juice of 1 lemon
¼ cup vinegar
1 clove garlic, minced or put through a press
½ teaspoon salt, preferably sea salt
¼ teaspoon freshly ground pepper
¼ cup chopped fresh dill
¼ cup olive oil
1 Bermuda onion, sliced thin
¼ to 1 cup finely chopped walnuts, to taste
3 cucumbers, peeled and diced
1 quart or more plain yogurt, homemade (see page 259) or commercial
6 to 8 ice cubes
Mung bean or alfalfa sprouts for garnish (optional)

Combine the lemon juice and vinegar in a 2- or 3-quart bowl. Stir in the garlic, salt, pepper, and dill. Whisk in the olive oil. Add the onion, walnuts, and cucumber, then toss and let marinate, covered, in the refrigerator, for several hours.

Pour off some of the liquid and add the quart of yogurt. Toss well; add more yogurt, if you desire. Place an ice cube in each soup bowl, ladle in the soup, and serve, if you wish, topped with sprouts.

6 to 8 servings

Suggested Menus
Bulgarian Cucumber Soup (see above)
Curry Salad (page 209)
Watermelon-Fruit Extravaganza (page 280)

Bulgarian Cucumber Soup (see above)
Stuffed Zucchini (page 223)
Fig and Mint Salad (page 248)
Strawberry and Cassis Sherbet (page 301)

TURKISH CUCUMBER SOUP

A cooling, subtle soup, high in protein and very easy to make. This is different from the Bulgarian soup on page 138; all the ingredients are liquefied.

1 to 1½ quarts plain yogurt, homemade (see page 259) or commercial
3 cucumbers, peeled and coarsely chopped
   Juice and grated rind of 1 to 2 lemons, to taste
1 teaspoon chopped fresh dill
1 to 2 cloves garlic
1 teaspoon dill seeds
1 teaspoon chopped fresh mint leaves, plus additional for garnish
½ teaspoon salt, preferably sea salt, more if necessary
   Paper-thin lemon and cucumber slices for garnish

Liquefy all the ingredients except the garnishes in a blender or food processor, until smooth, following the directions for cold blended soups on pages 27–28.

Correct the seasoning, then chill and serve garnished with mint, lemon slices, and cucumber slices.

6 to 8 servings

Suggested Menus
Turkish Cucumber Soup (see above)
Fallafels (page 197)
Tabouli (page 240)
Baklava (page 296)

Turkish Cucumber Soup (see above)
Curry Salad (page 209)
Watermelon-Fruit Extravaganza (page 280)

PUREE OF STRAWBERRY SOUP

This is a sweet and refreshing summer soup. It's a wonderful starter for a brunch or luncheon, and even makes a good dessert. It can be made a day in advance.

2 pint boxes fresh strawberries in season, washed and stemmed
1½ cups freshly squeezed orange juice
¼ cup fresh mint leaves
⅛ teaspoon ground cinnamon
⅛ teaspoon ground allspice
   Mild honey to taste (optional)
1¼ teaspoons grated lemon peel
1 tablespoon lemon juice, or to taste
1 tablespoon lime juice, or to taste
2 cups buttermilk
   Thin slices of lemon or lime, fresh mint leaves, and sliced strawberries for garnish

Set aside six of the strawberries for garnish. Puree the rest in a blender or food processor along with the orange juice, mint, cinnamon, and allspice. Taste for sweetness, and if you wish add a little honey.

Pour the strawberry puree into a bowl or other container and add the grated lemon peel, lemon and lime juice, and buttermilk; stir together well. Taste and add more lemon and lime juice, if desired. Chill for a few hours or serve immediately, garnished with the reserved strawberries, sliced, and with mint leaves and thin slices of lime or lemon.

Note: An exciting way to serve this is to cut cantaloupes in half, scoop out some of the fruit, scallop the edges, and serve the strawberry soup in the cantaloupe "bowls." You can serve the scooped-out melon along with the soup, or as part of the dessert. This will make a more filling soup.

6 to 8 servings

Suggested Menu

Puree of Strawberry Soup (see above)
Cheese Soufflé (page 157)
Sprout-Stuffed Artichokes (page 231)
Mixed Green Salad (page 238)
Peaches Marsala (page 282) *or* Millet-Raisin Pudding (page 292)

ROSE HIPS SOUP

This is an excellent soup, hot or cold. It's like a rich, rich tea, and almost has the quality of a dessert. Rose hips are high in vitamin C.

    2 cups (½ pound) dried rose hips
 1½ quarts water
       Juice of 1 lemon, or to taste
    ½ cup mild honey, or to taste
    ½ cup raisins
 1½ tablespoons arrowroot, dissolved in ¼ cup water
       Freshly grated nutmeg to taste
    1 cup plain yogurt, homemade (see page 259) or commercial
    ½ cup slivered almonds

Crush or grind the rose hips and combine with the water in a large saucepan. Bring to a boil, then reduce the heat, cover, and simmer for 45 minutes, stirring occasionally. Strain and discard the rose hips.

Add enough water to the saucepan to bring the amount of liquid back to 1½ quarts. Add the lemon juice, honey, and raisins; taste for sweetness and tartness, then simmer for 5 minutes.

Bring the soup to a boil and stir in the arrowroot-water mixture. Stir until the mixture thickens, then sprinkle with freshly grated nutmeg.

Serve hot or chilled, garnished with yogurt and slivered almonds.

6 to 8 servings

Suggested Menus

Rose Hips Soup (see above)
Brown Rice Salad (page 245)
Mixed Bean Salad (page 252)
Peach Pie (page 294)

Rose Hips Soup (see above)
Almond-Cheese Stuffed Crêpes (page 175)
Mixed Green Salad (page 239)
Fresh fruit (see page 276) *or* Baked Apples (page 283)

MADRILÈNE

A light, refreshing summer soup.

1 quart strong Vegetable Stock (page 91)
4 cups peeled stewed tomatoes
1 onion, chopped
1 cup chopped carrots
½ cup diced turnips
½ cup chopped celery
2 sprigs fresh parsley
½ teaspoon dried thyme
2 teaspoons tamari
1 teaspoon Worcestershire sauce
  Salt, preferably sea salt, to taste
  Mung bean or alfalfa sprouts, or chopped fresh herbs and sunflower seeds, for
    garnish.

Combine all the ingredients except the garnishes and simmer for 1½ to 2 hours, until all the flavors have mingled. Press through a sieve, then correct the seasoning, cool, and chill.

Serve garnished with sprouts or fresh herbs and sunflower seeds.

6 to 8 servings

Suggested Menus

Madrilène (see above)
Potato-Egg Salad with Chilled Broccoli (page 251)
Sprout-Stuffed Artichokes (page 231) *or* Broccoli Moutarde (page 233)
Any fruit pie (see pages 293–95)

Madrilène (see above)
Marinated Lentil Salad (page 252)
Yorkshire Puddings with Cornmeal (page 229)
Tomatoes and Fresh Herbs (page 247)
Any fruit pie (see pages 293–95)

MAIN DISHES

When I was once in Brazil, where there are few vegetarians, I gave a dinner party. Later I found out that the guests had come reluctantly, expecting bread and water, or at best boiled vegetables, beans, and rice. Imagine their surprise when they were served a glorious *ratatouille* and big, beautiful slices of savory spinach and onion quiche.

Actually, I haven't had to try hard to avoid the predictable repertoire of typically vegetarian dishes, that "hair shirt" fare that seems to apologize for its absence of meat by masking vegetables with thick sauces and cheese or by employing meat "substitutes." You won't find that every dish here tastes like tamari; nor will every one contain nuts and raisins.

There's something for everybody in this chapter. When I give a dinner party and don't know all of my guests well, and certainly when I cater, I choose dishes that I know everyone will like. Some people are averse to sweet foods in a main dish, for instance, or don't like nuts or certain spices like caraway or ginger. So, when I suspect that there might be a few of these people at my table, I avoid dishes like Adzuki Bean Cobbler (page 153), Fruit Curry (page 211), or Fruited Baked Beans with Chutney (page 216).

The most reliable dishes for skeptical dinner guests and large crowds are cheese-y, eggy ones (there are at least twenty here) like quiches and soufflés, omelets and crêpes; or Italian and Mexican food—Eggplant Parmesan (page 178), Lasagne (page 187), or Black Bean Enchiladas (page 144). Potato dishes are also easy for everyone to "understand," dishes like Potatoes Gruyère (page 217) or Potato Pancakes (page 218).

If you or your guests prefer light dishes there are plenty to choose from: Chinese and Japanese vegetable dishes with marvelous sauces, Indian curries with chutneys and *raitas,* satiny couscous with vegetables or with fruits.

Some of these entrees are visually quite spectacular; they make great party fare. Soufflés puff up dramatically, as does Spanokopita (page 166), the Greek spinach strudel, which also bakes to the most beautiful golden brown. Vegetable Shish Kebab (page 199) displays a kaleidoscope of colors, the vegetables skewered over saffron-colored rice. Vegetable Paella (page 196), especially when served in a wok or paella pan, is another gorgeous one, with bright green peas, red pimientos, and black olives on saffron rice.

Some entrees here are perfect for cold winter nights—bean dishes, crêpes with rich fillings, grain dishes. Airy soufflés, curries, marinades, and stir-fries are good in the summertime. Complement rich soups with light main dishes, and prepare something more substantial if you plan to serve thin soup, or if the main dish is your only course.

These recipes serve six to eight.

BLACK BEAN ENCHILADAS

Black bean enchiladas are one of my favorites for entertaining a crowd; I often make them for catered dinners. The first of the casserole-type dishes in this section, they are a perfect model for my first casserole rule, which is this: If every part of a casserole tastes great alone, the casserole will be smashing.

In this recipe we start with a very tasty pot of beans, season it with chili powder and cumin, and use top-quality Cheddar cheese. A far cry from the ordinary bland tortillas, these are first sautéed in oil and a piquant tomato sauce. Delicious!

My other casserole rule is to start skimpy and end generous. That is, don't be overenthusiastic in the beginning with your cheese and black bean filling, or you'll run out of it before you've filled the last enchiladas. Remember that you'll begin serving from the top. That's the part everyone will see, and it should look lavish.

You'll have to start thinking about this dish a bit in advance, as you first have to soak and cook the beans. The cooked beans will last up to three days in the refrigerator. Putting the enchiladas together will go smoothly if you are organized: have your ingredients next to each other in bowls, the beans in the pot, and the tortillas on their paper towels. As with any casserole, this stage is "assembly line" work, and the less distance you and your hands have to move, the better it will go.

If you make the enchiladas a day in advance, be sure to cover them well, or they will dry out. After baking, keep them well covered until you're ready to serve.

Tortillas may be frozen, wrapped in plastic. Even if they're kept for a long time, they will be revitalized when you prepare them for the enchiladas.

For the black bean sauce:
  2 cups dried black beans, washed
  6 cups water
  2 tablespoons safflower or vegetable oil
  1 onion, chopped
  4 cloves or more garlic, minced or put through a press
  1 tablespoon salt, preferably sea salt, or to taste
  2 tablespoons chopped fresh coriander (*cilantro*)
  1 tablespoon cumin powder, or to taste
  1 tablespoon chili powder, or to taste

For the enchiladas:
     Safflower or vegetable oil as needed
  1 cup tomato sauce, approximately
     Salt, cumin, and chili powder as needed
1½ dozen corn tortillas
 12 ounces medium or sharp Cheddar cheese, grated
  ½ to ¾ cup very finely minced onion
  ½ cup chopped walnuts or pecans
  2 tablespoons chopped fresh coriander (*cilantro*)

Soak the beans in the 6 cups water overnight, or for several hours.

Heat the oil in a large, heavy-bottomed saucepan or flameproof bean pot and sauté the chopped onion and garlic until the onion is tender. Add the beans and their water and bring to a boil. Add the salt and cover, then reduce the heat and simmer for 2 hours, until the beans are soft and their liquid is thick and soupy. Add the coriander after the first hour, and more garlic and salt to taste.

Pour off half the liquid from the beans, then puree half the beans along with the cumin and chili, in some of their liquid. (This will thicken the sauce, while leaving half the beans whole, and will provide texture.) Return to the pot, and heat through over low heat, stirring occasionally to prevent sticking. You are now ready to start assembling the enchiladas.

In a heavy-bottomed skillet, heat 3 tablespoons oil, 3 tablespoons tomato sauce, and a dash each of salt, cumin, and chili powder. Taking a few at a time, heat the tortillas through on both sides, until soft and saturated with the flavor; do not cook too long or they will become crisp. Set aside on paper towels and continue until all the tortillas have been taken care of, adding oil, tomato sauce, and seasonings as needed. (This step is the key to flavorful enchiladas.)

Preheat the oven to 325 degrees.

Set aside 1 cup black bean sauce, ½ cup of the grated cheese, and ¼ cup of the minced onion.

To assemble the enchiladas, spread a large spoonful of black bean sauce over each tortilla, then a layer of grated Cheddar and a thin layer of minced onion. Roll up and place, seam side down, in an oiled 2½- or 3-quart baking dish or pan. (You can seal the enchilada by "pasting" it with sauce i the tortilla has gotten crisp and won't stay closed.) When all the tortillas have been filled, pour on the reserved sauce and sprinkle with the remaining cheese and onion and the nuts.

If you fill up the pan and need to make a second layer of enchiladas, top the first layer with some of the reserved sauce, cheese, onion, and nuts (save some for the second layer); oil some foil on both sides and place it on top of the first layer, then proceed with the second layer, topping it with the remaining sauce, cheese, onion, and nuts.

Cover tightly with foil and bake in the preheated oven for 30 minutes, until the cheese is bubbling. Remove the foil, garnish with the chopped coriander, and serve (see note below), passing a bowl of hot sauce for those who like their Mexican food more *picante*.

Note: The enchiladas become very soft when they bake, and you will need to use two spatulas to prevent them from falling apart when you serve. If they *should* fall apart, don't worry. Your guests, already overwhelmed by the aroma, will be impatient to cut into them and won't even notice.

6 to 8 servings

Menu Suggestions

Hors d'oeuvres: Guacamole (page 242) with tortilla chips, Cheese Fondue (page 84), with raw vegetables as dippers, Marinated Vegetables Vinaigrette (page 74)

Soups: Sopa de Ajo (page 103), Chilled Avocado-Tomato (page 137), Blender Gazpacho (page 135)

Salads: Spinach (page 238), Spinach and Citrus (page 249), Guacamole (page 242)

Desserts: Oranges Grand Marnier (page 279), Pineapple Boats (page 281), Pineapple with Kirsch (page 282)

EXTRAORDINARY CHALUPAS

The standard "Tex-Mex" *chalupa* consists of a crisp tortilla, refried pinto beans, shredded iceberg lettuce, guacamole, grated longhorn cheese, and chopped tomatoes. These "extraordinary" *chalupas* are a departure from the "Tex-Mex" variety. They consist of layer upon layer of delight, with some special surprises: I use black beans, sprouts doused with vinaigrette, good Cheddar cheese, yogurt enriched with ricotta, and—to set off the luscious guacamole and tomatoes—crunchy sunflower seeds.

These *chalupas* are always a great hit at large catered events. Scores of people move through the buffet lines, remarking that they've never seen some of these foods before, "but they sure are good, and they sure are pretty!"

If you don't want to make your own tortilla crisps, *chalupa* shells are now available in many supermarkets.

2 cups dried black beans, washed
1 onion, chopped
4 cloves or more garlic, minced or put through a press
1 tablespoon salt, preferably sea salt, more as necessary
2 tablespoons chopped fresh coriander (*cilantro*)
   Safflower or vegetable oil as needed
1 tablespoon ground cumin
1 tablespoon chili powder
1 to 2 avocados, depending on size
3 tomatoes
   Juice of ½ lemon
½ cup ricotta
½ cup plain yogurt, homemade (see page 259) or commercial
2 cups sprouts (alfalfa, mung bean, or lentil, or a mixture)
1 small can pitted ripe olives, sliced (optional)
¼ cup Mary's Basic Salad Dressing (page 260) or Vinaigrette (page 261)
   Safflower or vegetable oil as needed
1 dozen corn tortillas or prepared *chalupa* crisps
8 ounces Cheddar cheese, grated
½ cup sunflower seeds

Cook the black beans with the onion, garlic, salt, and 2 tablespoons of the chopped coriander as described in the recipe for Black Bean Enchiladas (page 145), through the point where you pour off half the liquid; here, however, pour off about three-fourths of the liquid (hold in a bowl) and then proceed as follows:

148

Heat 2 tablespoons safflower or vegetable oil in a skillet and refry the beans in their liquid, adding the cumin and chili powder. As you fry the beans, mash them with a potato masher or with the back of a spoon and stir often. (If the beans become too dry, add some of their liquid.) The refried beans should have the consistency of a very thick paste, with some of the beans remaining solid.

(You can also refry *without* oil. Follow these instructions but omit the oil. Or simply puree the beans: pour off most of the liquid from the beans; retain only what you'll need to puree them. Use a blender or food processor to puree, adding the cumin and chili. Don't overblend; you should try to retain some texture.) Set the refried beans aside while you prepare the remaining ingredients.

Peel, seed, and mash the avocado; peel one of the tomatoes and mash it with the avocado. Season with lemon juice, salt, and chili powder to taste; set the guacamole aside. Chop the remaining tomatoes and place in a separate bowl.

Whip the ricotta in a blender, with a mixer, or with a whisk, and stir in the yogurt. (Don't use the blender or mixer for thi. or the mixture will become too runny.) Set aside.

Toss the sprouts with the salad dressing.

Have all the ingredients, in their separate bowls, within easy reach.

Heat some safflower oil in a large skillet and add salt. Sauté the tortillas, a few at a time, on both sides until crisp, and drain on paper towels. (Be careful not to burn them, which will happen very quickly once they are crisp.)

Now assemble your *chalupas*. Spread a spoonful of black beans over the tortilla crisp. Top this with a layer of the yogurt-ricotta mixture, then a layer of the guacamole. Over this sprinkle some grated cheddar cheese, and top with the sprouts tossed with the salad dressing, the black olives, the chopped tomatoes, and a sprinkling of sunflower seeds and the remaining chopped coriander. If any salad dressing remains, sprinkle it over the chalupas.

Serve with hot sauce, if desired, on the side.

6 servings

Menu Suggestions

Hors d'oeuvres: Stuffed Mushrooms (page 65)
Soups: Sopa de Ajo (page 103), Stracciatella (page 95), Escarole (page 120)
Salads: Mixed Green (page 238), Spinach (page 238), Green Bean, Almond, and Mushroom (page 245)
Desserts: Fresh fruit (see page 276), Oranges Grand Marnier (page 279), Strawberry and Cassis Sherbet (page 301)

WHOLE-WHEAT PIE CRUST

You'll find the crust here is a vast improvement over the usual bland pie pastry—it has a buttery, nutty taste that is truly scrumptious. It can be made up to three days in advance and refrigerated, or it can be frozen (a frozen crust takes only half an hour to thaw out). This recipe will make two 9-inch crusts, so you can use one now and freeze the other for a later date. It will also make one large crust, for use in such recipes as Tomato Quiche on page 152.

1 cup whole-wheat pastry flour
½ cup unbleached white flour
½ cup wheat germ
½ teaspoon salt, preferably sea salt
1 stick plus 2 tablespoons cold butter, or use half butter and half wheat-germ oil
   margarine (or any health margarine made by Hain)
3 to 4 tablespoons ice-cold water

Making the crust by hand: In a large bowl, combine the flours, wheat germ, and salt. Quickly cut in the butter and roll briskly between the palms of your hands to make sure that the butter is evenly distributed. Add the water, a tablespoon at a time, and blend with a fork. When you've mixed it into a dough, divide evenly into two balls.

Place a ball of dough on top of a piece of lightly floured waxed paper. Press it down with your hand and place another piece of lightly floured paper on top. Roll it out with a rolling pin; peel off the top paper, turn the crust into a buttered pie plate, and then peel off the other paper. Press the dough into the pie pan and pinch a pretty scalloped edge around the rim. Repeat with the other ball of dough; then refrigerate both crusts for 2 hours, covered with plastic wrap, or freeze (to freeze, cover with plastic and place in plastic bags or wrap in foil).

Making the crust with a food processor: The action of the food processor makes the dough very moist, and it's easier to press it into the pie pan than roll out, as it tends to stick to the waxed paper. Place the flours, wheat germ, and salt in the container of your food processor, fitted with the steel blade. Flick on four times to combine the ingredients. Cut the *cold* butter into tablespoon-sized pats and place in the bowl. Flick on and off ten times. Pour in 3 tablespoons ice-cold water and turn on the machine. The mixture should take on a pie-dough consistency in about 20 seconds and roll up onto the blade. If it doesn't, dribble in a little more water. As soon as the dough balls up onto the blade turn off the machine. Remove and divide into two balls. Butter a piepan and press one ball flat between the palms of your hands. Place in the center of the pie pan, and then, working from the center out, press out the dough. Push from the heel of your palm out toward your fingertips, and keep spreading out the dough, turning the pan with your other hand, so that it spreads up the sides of the pan evenly all the way around. Pinch a pretty scalloped edge around the rim. Repeat with the other ball of dough; refrigerate or freeze as described above.

Completing both methods: Preheat the oven to 350 degrees. Pierce the bottom of each crust with a fork or weigh it down with dried beans on a piece of foil (to keep it from buckling). Prebake in the preheated oven for 5 minutes; cool before filling.

Enough for two 9-inch pie shells

SPINACH AND ONION QUICHE

Quiche is essentially a custard flavored with cheese. But traditional quiche is very rich, calling for cream, butter, and eggs. So instead of cream I use a combination of milk and spray-dried milk. The "enriched milk" makes a considerable difference in the calorie count, at virtually no expense to flavor or texture.

Because the crust can be made far in advance and the filling only takes about 5 minutes to put together, quiche is an excellent dish to make when you are short on time. You needn't use spinach and onions—any blanched vegetable will do. Sautéed mushrooms work well, too. Combining sautéed onions with any vegetable you use will add a distinctive flavor and appealing texture. The important ingredient here is the cheese, which is always Swiss or French Gruyère, or a combination of Gruyère and Emmenthaler; I sharpen it with a little Parmesan.

Since the use of enriched milk makes this a relatively light dish, a hearty soup such as Pistou (page 95) or a rich Ratatouille (page 92) would be a suitable accompaniment, along with a green salad or marinated vegetables. For dessert, I would choose fruit, either fresh or poached in wine; certainly avoid anything made with eggs.

½ recipe Whole-Wheat Pie Crust (page 149)
½ pound fresh spinach, stemmed and washed carefully
½ cup minced onion
1 tablespoon butter or oil
3 large eggs, at room temperature

1 cup milk, enriched with 2 tablespoons spray-dried milk, or 1 cup water plus ⅓
    cup spray-dried milk (do this in a blender)
¼ teaspoon salt, preferably sea salt
1 grind of pepper
    Dash of Worcestershire sauce
    Pinch of freshly grated nutmeg
1 cup grated Gruyère cheese or half Gruyère and half Emmenthaler
¼ cup freshly grated Parmesan cheese

Prepare a 9-inch pie shell as directed in the pie crust recipe; after you prebake it for 5 minutes, set it aside and let it cool.

Blanch the spinach by plunging it into boiling water for 10 to 15 seconds, then drain it and run it under cold water. Squeeze out the liquid by twisting the spinach in a towel; chop fine.

Sauté the onion in the butter or oil until crisp-tender; set aside.

Beat the eggs and blend with the milk, then beat in the salt, pepper, Worcestershire, and nutmeg.

In a large bowl, toss together the onion, spinach, and the cheeses. Spread half the mixture over the bottom of the prepared pie shell. Pour the egg-milk mixture over, and top with the remaining cheese mixture.

Bake at 350 degrees for 30 to 40 minutes, or until firm to the touch. Let cool for 10 minutes before serving.

6 to 8 servings

Menu Suggestions

See the suggestions at the beginning of the recipe; other good soups for
    accompaniment would be A Different Onion Soup (page 112), Blender
    Gazpacho (page 135), or A Rich Tomato Soup (page 104).

ASPARAGUS QUICHE

For the spinach, substitute 1 cup pieces of asparagus or other green vegetable, steamed briefly.

6 to 8 servings

MUSHROOM QUICHE

Substitute 1 cup sliced mushrooms for the spinach. Sauté the mushrooms, and a clove of minced garlic if you wish, with the minced onion in the butter or olive oil until tender. Toss together with the cheeses and proceed with the recipe.

6 to 8 servings

For the spinach, substitute 1 cup minced fresh herbs, such as parsley, fennel, chives, thyme.

6 to 8 serving

TOMATO QUICHE

This satisfying dish is also good cold. The crust and the tomato part of the filling can be done in advance. You *must* cook the tomato mixture until it is dry and thick, or your quiche will be runny. Be sure to let this sit for 20 to 30 minutes before you serve it to allow it to become firm.

    4 to 5 large ripe tomatoes, peeled
    1 onion, finely chopped
    2 tablespoons butter
      Pinch of thyme
      Salt, preferably sea salt, and freshly ground pepper
    4 eggs, beaten
 1½ cups milk, enriched with 3 tablespoons spray-dried milk
    ½ cup freshly grated Parmesan cheese
    8 ounces Swiss cheese, grated
    1 full recipe Whole-Wheat Pie Crust (page 149), prebaked for 5 minutes in an
      oblong baking dish or deep, round pie pan

Chop two of the peeled tomatoes; you should have 2 cups. (Add one more tomato if you fall short.) Slice the remaining tomatoes and set aside.

In a skillet or frying pan, sauté the onion in the butter until tender. Add the chopped tomatoes, thyme, and a little salt and pepper; cover and simmer for 10 minutes. Uncover the pan, mash the tomatoes with the back of a spoon, and cook, uncovered, over low heat until the mixture is dry and thick, about 30 minutes. Set aside to cool.

Preheat the oven to 350 degrees.

Beat together the eggs, milk, and ½ teaspoon salt. Stir in the grated cheeses and the cooled tomato mixture.

Line the bottom of the prepared pie crust with the sliced tomatoes, then pour in the cheese, milk, and egg mixture.

Bake for 30 to 45 minutes, until a knife inserted in the center comes out clean. Remove from the oven and allow to sit for 20 to 30 minutes before serving.

6 to 8 serving

Menu Suggestions

Soups: Vichyssoise (page 121), Puree of Asparagus (page 110), Miso-Vegetable (page 127), A Different Onion (page 112)

Salads: Mixed Green (page 238), Spinach (page 238), World of Sprouts (page 239), Salade Niçoise (page 241), Green Bean, Almond, and Mushroom (page 245)

Desserts: Fresh fruit (see page 276), Bananas Poached in White Wine (page 277), Oranges Grand Marnier (page 279), Peaches Marsala (page 282)

ADZUKI BEAN COBBLER

Don't be put off by the seemingly strange combination of ingredients in this recipe; it's always a hit. Apple concentrate gives it a special zip, and the lattice crust sets off the deep red beans to make this a lovely dish.

You can cook the beans and make the pie crust in advance, and assemble and bake at the last minute.

1 cup dried adzuki beans, washed
3 cups water
1 recipe Whole-Wheat Pie Crust (page 149)
1 onion, chopped
2 cloves garlic, minced or put through a press
1 tablespoon safflower oil
2 teaspoons salt, preferably sea salt, or to taste
1 tablespoon butter
1 apple, peeled, if desired, and sliced
½ teaspoon ground cinnamon, or to taste
¼ teaspoon freshly grated nutmeg
½ cup currants
½ cup sunflower seeds
1 green pepper, seeded and sliced
½ sweet red pepper (if available), seeded and sliced
3 tablespoons apple concentrate (available in natural foods stores)
1 peach, peeled and sliced (optional)

Soak the washed adzuki beans for several hours in the 3 cups water.

Make the pie crust as directed, saving half for a lattice top crust. Roll it out and line your pie pan, then refrigerate for 2 hours. Ten minutes before the refrigeration time is up, preheat the oven to 350 degrees.

Prebake the crust for 5 minutes.

Sauté the onion and garlic in the oil in a medium-sized saucepan until the onion is tender. Add the adzukis and water and bring to a boil. Add the salt, then cover and reduce the heat. Simmer for 1 to 2 hours, until the adzukis are tender. Drain over a bowl and retain 1 cup liquid from the beans.

Melt the butter in a skillet and sauté the apple with the cinnamon, nutmeg, and currants for 5 minutes. Stir in the sunflower seeds and remove from the heat. Combine with the adzukis and their liquid and the remaining ingredients; stir the mixture together well. Correct the salt and cinnamon, then turn the mixture into the pie shell and top with a lattice crust. Bake at 350 degrees for 40 minutes.

6 to 8 servings

Menu Suggestions

Soups: Corn Chowder (page 267), Cream of Wheat Berry (page 109), Almond (page 131)

Salads: Coleslaw (page 256), Mixed Green (page 238), Brown Rice (page 245), World of Sprouts (page 239)

Side Dish: Yorkshire Puddings with Cornmeal (page 229)

Desserts: Indian Pudding (page 293), Baklava (page 296), Grapefruit with Port (page 282)

DEEP-DISH VEGETABLE PIE

A perennially popular dish. Soybeans add complementary protein; another idea would be tofu, sautéed with onion. You can use whatever vegetables you have on hand, and you may decide on a different sauce.

As always, the crust can be made well in advance, and the sauce can be made a day or two in advance and refrigerated. Remember to soak and cook the soybeans ahead of time.

For the crust:
1 recipe Whole-Wheat Pie Crust (page 149)
1 egg, beaten

For the sauce:
3 tablespoons butter
½ onion, minced
3 tablespoons flour (whole-wheat pastry flour or unbleached white, or a combination)
2 cups hot Vegetable Stock (page 91) or Tamari-Bouillon Broth (page 91)
1 clove garlic, minced or put through a press
Salt, preferably sea salt, and freshly ground pepper to taste
1 bay leaf

¼ teaspoon dried marjoram
¼ teaspoon oregano
  Pinch of dried thyme
2 to 3 tablespoons tomato paste (optional)
2 tablespoons red wine (optional)

For the vegetable filling:
1 onion, chopped
½ cup sliced fresh mushrooms
1 tablespoon butter or safflower oil
½ cup diagonally sliced or matchstick-cut carrots
1 cup broccoli florets
½ cup cauliflower florets
½ cup fresh or frozen peas
½ cup shredded cabbage
¾ cup cooked soybeans or soy flakes (¼ cup dried; see page 25)
½ cup raw peanuts
¼ cup chopped fresh parsley

Prepare and roll out two-thirds of the pie crust and use it to line a deep baking dish; reserve the remainder for the lattice topping. Refrigerate for 2 hours.

Ten minutes or so before the refrigeration time is up, preheat the oven to 350 degrees. Brush the chilled crust with beaten egg and prebake for 5 minutes, then set aside to cool.

Prepare the sauce. Melt the butter and sauté the minced onion for a few minutes, then add the flour and cook, stirring, for a few minutes longer. When the roux is just beginning to brown, slowly stir in the hot stock, beating all the while with a whisk. Stir until the sauce is smooth and thick.

Add the garlic, salt, pepper, and herbs and let simmer on very low heat for about 15 minutes. (If you want a tomato-y *sauce aurore*, stir in the optional tomato paste and red wine.) Remove the bay leaf and set aside while you prepare the vegetable filling.

Sauté the onion and mushrooms in the butter or safflower oil until tender. Steam the carrots, broccoli, cauliflower, and peas for 5 minutes (if using frozen peas, simply thaw them out).

Toss all the vegetables together with the raw peanuts, soybeans, and parsley and turn into the prebaked pie shell. Cover with the sauce, moving the vegetables around so the sauce can reach those on the bottom.

Make a lattice topping with the remaining dough and bake at 350 degrees for 45 minutes.

6 to 8 servings

ASPARAGUS OR BROCCOLI DEEP-DISH PIE

Instead of the mixed vegetables, use 4 cups chopped, steamed asparagus or broccoli. Make the above sauce but omit the bay leaf, marjoram, oregano, red wine, and tomato sauce and stir in ¾ cup Gruyère cheese and 3 tablespoons dry white wine as a last step before pouring the sauce over the vegetables.

6 to 8 servings

Menu Suggestions:

Soups: Vichyssoise (page 121), Potato-Cheese (page 114), Curry of Eggplant (page 132)
Salads: Mixed Green (page 238), Salade Niçoise (page 241), Marinated Vegetables Vinaigrette (page 74), Avocado and Citrus (page 239)
Desserts: Fresh fruit (see page 276), Bavarian Crème au Café (page 286), Apricot Soufflé (page 289), Millet-Raisin Pudding (page 292)

KASHA PIE

Kasha pie has a nutty, soothing flavor and aroma and a fluffy texture. But you'll need something green to serve along with it—broccoli or peas. If you like, you can blanch the vegetables and stir them into the filling just before you bake the pie.

The kasha and sauce may be made up to a day in advance; in fact, this is the best way to use up leftover kasha. And of course you can make your crust well in advance.

1 recipe Whole-Wheat Pie Crust (page 149)
2 eggs, beaten separately
2½ cups Vegetable Stock (page 91)
½ teaspoon salt, preferably sea salt
1 carrot, sliced
1 onion, chopped
1 rib celery, chopped
1 cup raw buckwheat groats
½ cup chopped almonds or pecans
⅔ cup cooked soybeans or soy flakes (¼ cup dried; see page 25) (optional)
1 recipe White Wine Sauce (page 258)

Make the pie crust, then line a deep pie pan with half the crust and save the other half for a top crust. Refrigerate for 2 hours.

Ten minutes before the refrigeration time is up, preheat the oven to 350 degrees. Brush the crust with egg and prebake the pie crust for 5 minutes.

Using the stock, salt, carrot, onion, celery, and 1 beaten egg, cook the buckwheat groats as described in the recipe for Kasha Filling for Stuffed Mushrooms on page 67. Combine the cooked groats with the almonds or pecans and, if you wish, ⅔ cup cooked soybeans.

Have the white wine sauce ready.

Fill the prebaked pie crust with the kasha mixture and pour the sauce over. Roll out the top crust and cover the pie; pinch the top and bottom crusts together. Slash or pierce the top crust to allow steam to escape. Brush with the remaining beaten egg.

Bake at 350 degrees for 30 to 40 minutes, until the top crust is golden, and serve, with a bright vegetable side dish such as Gingered Broccoli (page 231) or steamed asparagus.

6 to 8 servings

Menu Suggestions

Soups: Egg Drop with Bean Sprouts (page 94), Turkish Cucumber (page 139), Apple-Spice (page 136), Blender Gazpacho (page 135)

Serve the salad and dessert of your choice; eggs in the dessert would be complementary.

CHEESE SOUFFLÉ

The prospect of making a soufflé always intimidated me—until I gathered my courage and found out how simple it is. You start off with a classic sauce base enriched with egg yolks. Then all you do is beat the egg whites and fold them into the sauce with the cheese, or cheese and vegetables, or fruit (in the case of a dessert soufflé).

This cheese soufflé is a delightful main course. Serve it with a hearty soup such as Pistou (page 96) or Ratatouille (page 92) and a crisp salad. It makes a perfect luncheon or brunch dish, too. Fruit, fresh or poached in wine, or a fruit pie or tart (see pages 294–95) is a good complement for dessert. Avoid (obviously) soups and desserts that call for eggs.

(continued)

158

A soufflé looks spectacular when it comes out of the oven. You must have a clear idea of when you are going to eat it, so you can start baking it 35 to 40 minutes beforehand. However, you can do the sauce base one or two days ahead, and if you like you can even have the complete soufflé mixture made up to 2 hours before baking. Try to remember to take the eggs out of the refrigerator a few hours before you make the soufflé, because they need to be at room temperature for the whites to set right; if you forget, place them in a bowl of warm water for a few minutes.

If the soufflé is done and your guests are not yet ready for it, turn off the oven and leave the door shut. This will delay the falling; your soufflé should still be dramatically puffed up when you serve it.

 3 tablespoons butter
 ¼ cup flour (whole-wheat pastry flour or unbleached white, or a combination)
 1½ cups hot milk
    Salt, preferably sea salt
 ⅛ teaspoon freshly ground pepper
    Pinch of freshly grated nutmeg
 6 eggs, at room temperature, plus 2 egg whites
 ¼ teaspoon cream of tartar
 1½ cups grated Gruyère cheese or sharp white Cheddar, loosely packed
 ¼ cup freshly grated Parmesan cheese

You will need a medium-sized, heavy-bottomed saucepan, a whisk, and a wooden spoon for the sauce, and another saucepan to heat the milk in. Have a 3-quart bowl and a clean dry whisk or egg beater for the egg whites; and a buttered soufflé dish with a collar (see directions below).

In a medium saucepan, heat the butter and stir in the flour to make a roux. Cook for a few minutes over low heat, stirring with a wooden spoon; allow the roux to bubble but not to brown.

Meanwhile, heat the milk, and when it is hot slowly stir it into the roux, using a whisk. Stir quickly and thoroughly to mix well, then continue to stir over moderate heat until the very thick sauce comes to a boil; cook for 1 minute, stirring and bringing the sauce up from the bottom and sides of the pan. (Don't be alarmed by the thickness of the sauce; you're about to thin it out with egg yolks.) Remove the saucepan from the heat and stir in 1 teaspoon salt, the pepper, and the nutmeg.

Now separate the eggs, one by one, stirring each egg yolk into the sauce and adding each white to a mixing bowl containing the two extra whites; set the sauce aside. (At this point the sauce may be refrigerated for one or two days, tightly covered. If you do refrigerate the sauce base beforehand, reheat it gently in a double boiler before folding in the egg whites.)

Beat the egg whites, which should be at room temperature, until they begin to foam. Add the cream of tartar and a pinch of salt and continue beating until the egg whites are satiny and form peaks when lifted with the spatula or beater. Do not overbeat; the whites should remain smooth.

Now stir one-quarter of the egg whites into the sauce base with a spatula; this will lighten up the sauce so the folding procedure will be easier. Pour the sauce base into the middle of the bowl of egg whites. Fold the egg whites into the sauce with your spatula by gently scooping the sauce from the middle of the bowl, under the egg whites to the side of the bowl, up over the egg whites back to the middle of the bowl. With each fold, sprinkle in a handful of the Gruyère and Parmesan cheeses and give the bowl a quarter turn, making sure you reserve 2 tablespoons of the Parmesan; continue this folding process until the mixture is homogenous. You should work rapidly yet lightly, and the process should take no more than a minute.

Prepare your soufflé dish. Butter it and dust it with the 2 tablespoons Parmesan. Using waxed paper or aluminum foil, make a collar by wrapping a cylinder of the paper around the dish and taping or tying it; the cylinder should extend 2 to 3 inches above the edge of the soufflé dish. Now gently spoon in the soufflé mixture. At this point you may set the mixture aside for up to 2 hours, inverting a large bowl over it (or placing a piece of waxed paper or foil over the top of the collar), or bake it.

Preheat the oven to 375 degrees.

Bake the soufflé for 35 to 40 minutes. If you wish—or dare—stick a thin skewer in to see if it's done. If the skewer comes out nearly clear, and the top of the soufflé is golden, the soufflé is done. If it comes out very wet, bake for another 5 to 7 minutes. Remove from the oven, detach the collar, and serve immediately.

6 to 8 servings

CHEESE SOUFFLÉ WITH VEGETABLES

Fold in one or two cups of blanched chopped vegetables—asparagus, spinach, broccoli, green beans—along with the cheese.

6 to 8 servings

Menu Suggestions

See the suggestions at the beginning of the recipe (page 157).

OEUFS POCHÉS EN SOUFFLÉ À LA FLORENTINE

This is a dramatic dish for a brunch, luncheon, or dinner. Like a surprise ball, it reveals one delight after another on the inside. Most of the steps can be done a day or two ahead of time. The eggs can be poached in advance—in fact, they must be—and kept refrigerated in a bowl of cold water; the sauce base for the soufflé and the creamed spinach can be made a day or two in advance and refrigerated, covered (warm the sauce through before folding in the beaten egg whites). If you do all these things in advance, all you will have to do before the final assembly is whip the egg whites and fold them into the sauce base with the cheese. These conveniences are especially helpful if you are serving this for brunch; they will allow you a few more hours of sleep.

Once assembled, like other soufflés, this can sit up to 2 hours before being baked. Like other soufflés, this will fall if not served right away.

The first time I made this dish, for a large brunch, the biggest challenge was poaching the eggs. I went through several dozen before I got the twenty or so that I needed. The biggest problem was that the eggs would stick to the pan and tear when I tried to remove them, a problem I solved by buttering the surface of my pan generously. I've tried to use an egg poacher in the preparation of this dish, but find it unsatisfactory because the top surface of the poached egg is so thin that it breaks easily and the yolk runs out. Below is what I've found to be the easiest method for poaching eggs:

Butter a large frying pan and fill it with water 2 to 3 inches deep. Bring to a boil and add 2 tablespoons vinegar (this helps to set the eggs), then reduce the heat so the water simmers very gently.

Break an egg into a tea cup. Lower the cup into the water and let it sit there for 15 seconds, then carefully tilt the cup, holding it right above the water, and let the egg slide into the simmering water.

For regular poached eggs you would cook the eggs for 4 minutes before removing from the water with a slotted spoon. Place immediately in cold water to stop the cooking and wash off the vinegar. For the poached eggs in this dish, though, cook only 3 to 3½ minutes, as they will heat through again when baked.

Make note of the order in which you put each egg in the water so you can take them out in order.

Don't worry if the cooked whites of your eggs are irregular and look messy. Trim them down with a sharp knife after they have cooled; remember that they will be hidden in a puffed, golden soufflé.

For the eggs and creamed spinach:
  1 pound fresh or frozen spinach
  1 tablespoon minced green onions, both white part and green, or shallots
  2 teaspoons butter
  1 tablespoon whole-wheat pastry flour or unbleached white flour
    Salt, preferably sea salt, and freshly ground pepper to taste
    Freshly grated nutmeg to taste
  ¾ cup cream or half-and-half, more if necessary
  6 three-inch rounds or halved slices toasted whole-wheat bread (Mixed Grains Bread on page 38 is great)
  6 eggs, poached as described above and chilled in cold water

For the soufflé:
  3 tablespoons butter
  3 tablespoons unbleached white flour (or a mixture of whole-wheat pastry flour and unbleached white)
  1 cup hot milk
  4 eggs, at room temperature, plus 1 egg white
    Salt, preferably sea salt, and freshly ground pepper
    Pinch of freshly grated nutmeg
  ¼ teaspoon cream of tartar
  ¾ cup grated Gruyère cheese

For the garnish:
    Chopped fresh parsley

If you are using fresh spinach, wash and remove the stems and blanch in boiling salted water. Drain, squeeze out excess water, and chop. If you are using frozen spinach, allow to thaw, squeeze out excess water, and then chop.

In a heavy saucepan or skillet, sauté the green onions or shallots in the butter until tender. Stir in the spinach and toss to mix; sprinkle in the flour and toss again. Cook for about 2 minutes, then add salt and pepper to taste and a little freshly grated nutmeg. Stir in the cream or half-and-half and cook, stirring, for about 5 minutes over low heat. The spinach should be creamy but should hold its shape in a spoon. If it begins to dry out, thin it out with a little more cream or half-and-half. Correct the seasonings and remove from the heat.

Make a soufflé mixture, using the same procedure as for Cheese Soufflé (page 157), beginning with the making of the roux and continuing through the folding of the cheese into the soufflé mixture—but this time set aside 3 tablespoons of the cheese.

(continued)

162

Preheat the oven to 375 degrees; butter a flat 2-quart oblong baking dish.

Carefully remove the poached eggs from the cold water with a slotted spoon or your hands and drain on a kitchen towel. Arrange the croutons in rows in the baking dish. Place a mound of creamed spinach—2 to 3 tablespoons—on each crouton. Make a depression with the back of a spoon in each mound of spinach and carefully place a poached egg on top. Spoon the soufflé mixture over all, filling up the entire baking dish and mounding it over the poached eggs. Top each mound with a pinch of the remaining cheese.

Bake for 25 to 30 minutes, until the soufflé is puffed and beginning to brown. Remove from the oven, garnish with chopped fresh parsley, and serve immediately, cutting square portions with a mound in the middle of each.

Note: For a really rich and extravagant (and high-calorie) dish, serve with White Wine Sauce (page 257). Then you will have something truly extraordinary.

6 servings

Menu Suggestions

Soups: A Different Onion (page 112), A Rich Tomato (page 104), Madrilène (page 142), Puree of Asparagus (page 110)

Salads: Mixed Green (page 238), Tomatoes and Fresh Herbs (page 247), Salade Niçoise (page 241)

Desserts: Fresh fruit (see page 276), Grapefruit with Port (page 282), Pears Poached in Red Wine with a Touch of Cassis (page 277)

SOUFFLÉ ROLL WITH MUSHROOM AND BROCCOLI FILLING

This is an impressive variation on a soufflé, and it will look especially dramatic if you line your serving platter with lettuce leaves and garnish it with herbs and tomato wedges or radishes. As for the soufflé, the sauce base can be done in advance; the mushroom filling may also be done in advance and kept tightly covered for a day or two in the refrigerator. Before filling the "roulade," reheat the filling gently and warm the sauce base in a double boiler before folding in the egg whites.

The mushroom and broccoli filling makes this a richer dish than the traditional soufflé, so I would serve it with a lighter soup and a nice green salad.

For the soufflé roll:
   Ingredients for Cheese Soufflé (page 158), omitting the two extra egg whites

For the filling:
   2 tablespoons butter
   1 tablespoon olive oil
   ½ cup minced onion
   1 clove garlic, minced or put through a press
   1½ cups sliced fresh mushrooms
   ¼ teaspoon dried thyme
   3 tablespoons unbleached white flour (or a mixture of whole-wheat pastry flour
      and unbleached white)
   1½ cups hot Vegetable Stock (page 91) or Tamari-Bouillon Broth (page 91)
   ¼ cup dry white wine
      Salt, preferably sea salt, and freshly ground pepper to taste
   2 tablespoons chopped fresh parsley
   1 cup broccoli florets, steamed briefly (until bright green) and chopped

For the garnish:
      Freshly grated Parmesan cheese (optional)
      Chopped fresh parsley and chopped fresh mushrooms (optional)
   1 cup White Wine Sauce (page 257; optional)
      Parsley sprigs and tomato wedges or radish roses

Follow the procedure for the cheese soufflé through the folding in of the egg whites and cheese; fold in all the Parmesan.

Preheat the oven to 375 degrees. Butter a jelly-roll pan; make sure the sides and corners are especially well buttered. Line it with buttered waxed paper, which should extend lengthwise an inch over the ends.

Spoon the soufflé mixture into the pan and bake for 30 to 40 minutes, or until just beginning to brown.

Meanwhile, prepare the filling. Heat the butter and oil in a medium-sized saucepan and sauté the onion and garlic until the onion is tender. Add the mushrooms and thyme and sauté for 3 minutes, then add the flour and stir well with a wooden spoon. Continue to sauté the mixture, stirring all the while, until the mushrooms are tender and aromatic; be careful not to let it brown.

Now carefully whisk in the stock or broth. Keep stirring until you have a smooth sauce, then add the wine and boil for 1 minute, stirring. Reduce the heat and season to taste with salt and freshly ground pepper, then add the chopped parsley and simmer for about 10 minutes. Stir in the broccoli florets and simmer for 5 minutes more, then remove from the heat. At this point you may hold the sauce, covered, in the refrigerator for one to two days (reheat to use); or simply set aside until you are ready to fill the soufflé roll.

When the soufflé is firm, remove it from the oven and gently spread the mushroom sauce in an even layer over it. Carefully roll the soufflé up lengthwise, lifting the ends of the waxed paper gently and rolling it up like a jelly roll (the paper should come away easily if it has been generously buttered). Roll the "roulade" off the baking sheet and onto a platter and sprinkle with Parmesan cheese, fresh chopped parsley, and fresh chopped mushrooms; or top with white wine sauce. Surround with parsley sprigs and tomato wedges or radish roses.

Slice crosswise to serve.

6 to 8 servings

Menu Suggestions:

Soups: A Different Onion (page 112), Blender Gazpacho (page 135), Miso-Vegetable (page 127), Fruit (page 99)

Salads: Mixed Green (page 238), Tomatoes and Fresh Herbs (page 247), Crudité (page 73)

Desserts: Pears Poached in Red Wine with a Touch of Cassis (page 277), Pineapple Boats (page 281), Baked Apples (page 283)

SQUASH SOUFFLÉ

Squash soufflé has a delicate flavor and is wonderfully light and nutritious. It has the puffed-up quality of a traditional soufflé—but you won't have to bother with making a cream sauce or separating the eggs.

You can assemble this dish a few hours before you bake it.

1½ pounds yellow squash or a mixture of yellow squash and zucchini
 1 tablespoon salt, preferably sea salt, more as necessary
 ½ onion, minced
 1 tablespoon butter or safflower oil
 4 eggs, beaten
 ¾ cup grated Cheddar or Gruyère cheese
 ½ cup cottage cheese
 ½ cup whole-wheat bread crumbs
 2 tablespoons chopped parsley
   Freshly ground pepper to taste
 2 tablespoons melted butter

Preheat the oven to 350 degrees.

Grate the squash and toss with the salt. Let sit for 20 minutes.

Meanwhile, sauté the onion in the butter or oil until tender. Combine with the beaten eggs, grated cheese, cottage cheese, bread crumbs, parsley, and salt and pepper to taste.

Squeeze out the excess water from the squash and rinse well. Squeeze in a towel to dry, then stir into the egg-cheese mixture. Turn into an oiled casserole or soufflé dish and pour the melted butter over the top.

Bake for 45 minutes and serve immediately.

6 to 8 servings

Menu Suggestions

Hors d'oeuvres: Vegetable Platter with Assorted Dips (page 77), Stuffed Mushrooms (page 65)

(continued)

166

Page 166

Soups: Fresh Pea (page 107), Tomato-Rice (page 122), A Rich Tomato (page 104)

Salads: Mixed Green (page 238), Garbanzo Bean (page 254), Marinated Vegetables Vinaigrette (page 74)

Desserts: Pears Poached in Red Wine with a Touch of Cassis (page 277), Bananas Poached in White Wine (page 277), any fruit tart (see page 294), Peaches Marsala (page 282)

SPANOKOPITA
Greek Spinach Pie

This is a spectacular dish for company—a golden, puffy spinach pie with a savory filling and a rich, crisp crust—and it makes a wonderful hors d'oeuvre (see page 71). It's most impressive when baked just before serving, but you can assemble it a day in advance. It takes about an hour to put together. After it's baked and cooled, it can be frozen. The reheated *spanokopita* won't be puffed out and golden like the "original," but it will still have a magnificent flavor.

Sometimes the sheets of packaged filo dough stick together and tear as you try to pull them apart. Don't be too discouraged if this happens. If some of the filo in your *spanokopita* is in shreds, nobody will really see it. It just slows you down (and tries your patience) when you're putting the dish together.

- 2 pounds fresh spinach or 2 packages (10 or 12 ounces each) frozen spinach
  Salt, preferably sea salt
- 1 onion, chopped
- ½ pound fresh mushrooms, sliced
  Olive oil and butter
- 1 clove garlic, minced or put through a press
  Freshly ground pepper to taste
- 6 eggs
- ½ pound feta cheese
- ½ cup freshly grated Parmesan cheese
- ¼ cup chopped fresh parsley
- 1 teaspoon oregano
- ¼ teaspoon dried rosemary (optional)
- ¼ pound (1 stick) butter
- 1 pound filo dough

If you are using fresh spinach, wash the spinach and remove the tough stems. Place in a large bowl and sprinkle heavily with salt. Rub the salt into the leaves by taking them up, a bunch at a time, and rubbing them between your hands; the volume of the spinach will decrease before your very eyes. Tear the spinach up as you do this. Rinse the salt off thoroughly and dry the spinach, squeezing it in bunches in a towel. (If you are using frozen spinach, just let it thaw and squeeze out excess moisture).

Sauté the onion and mushrooms in a little olive oil and butter with the garlic and salt and pepper to taste. When both the onions and mushrooms are tender, remove from the heat.

Beat the eggs in a large bowl and crumble in the feta cheese; add the Parmesan, then the spinach, onions, and mushrooms. Stir in the parsley, oregano, rosemary, some freshly ground pepper, and a little salt (remembering that the feta is very salty).

Preheat the oven to 375 degrees.

Melt the butter and brush a 2-quart or 3-quart oblong baking pan with it. Spread your filo dough out flat next to the pan. Take a sheet and lay it in the pan, letting the edges come out over the pan. Take another sheet and lay it on top of the first, not directly but in such a way that its edges extend over different parts of the pan. Brush with butter. Continue to layer the sheets of filo, brushing every other one with butter and turning each one slightly so that the edges fan out over the sides of the pan, until you have about eight sheets left.

Now spread the spinach mixture evenly over the filo dough in the pan, pushing it into the corners. Take the edges of the filo and fold them in over the spinach mixture.

Take the remaining sheets of filo and layer them one by one over the spinach mixture, again brushing every other sheet with butter, but this time pushing the edges down into the sides of the pan. It is difficult to do this neatly; just rumple the edges down into the sides of the pan (they will form a nice crisp edge after baking). Brush the top of the *spanokopita* with butter and make ½-inch-deep diagonal slashes across it with a sharp knife.

Bake for 50 minutes, until the crust is puffed up and golden; it will shrink from the sides of the pan. Cut into squares or diamond shapes and serve immediately.

6 to 8 servings

Menu Suggestions

Hors d'oeuvres: Vegetable Platter with Assorted Dips (page 77), Marinated Vegetables à la Grecque (page 76)

Soups: Egg-Lemon (page 111), Curry of Eggplant (chilled) (page 132), A Rich Tomato (page 104), Leek (page 113)

(continued)

Salads: Cucumber (page 243), Mixed Green (page 238), Tomatoes and Fresh Herbs (page 247), Tabouli (page 240)

Desserts: Fresh fruit (see page 276), Bananas Poached in White Wine (page 277), Oranges Grand Marnier (page 279)

PIPÉRADE

This dish comes from the Basque region of Spain and southern France. It's hardly more complicated than scrambled eggs, yet it's as memorable as a soufflé. The green peppers give it a rich, full-bodied flavor.

It's a nice Sunday evening dinner.

2 tablespoons olive oil or butter
1 pound onions, sliced
1 clove garlic, minced or put through a press
4 green peppers, seeded and sliced in thin strips
2 red peppers, seeded and sliced in thin strips (if unavailable use green peppers)
1 pound tomatoes, peeled and chopped
  Salt, preferably sea salt, and freshly ground pepper
½ teaspoon oregano
½ teaspoon dried marjoram
6 to 8 eggs, beaten

In a heavy frying pan, heat the olive oil or butter and sauté the sliced onion with the garlic until tender. Add the peppers and cook a few more minutes, then add the tomatoes, salt, pepper, oregano, and marjoram. Stir this all together, then cook the mixture, covered, for about 15 minutes, until it is saucy and fragrant.

Pour in the beaten eggs and stir as for scrambled eggs. Remove from the heat as soon as the eggs have set and serve.

6 to 8 servings

Menu Suggestions

Hors d'oeuvres: Tiropites (page 69), Nachos with Black Bean Topping (page 72)

Soups: Black Bean (page 128), Pistou (page 96), Minestrone (page 118)

Salads: World of Sprouts (page 239), Mixed Green (page 238), Water Cress and Mushroom (page 247)

Desserts: Light Cheesecake (page 291), Pecan Pie (page 295), Raspberries in Red Wine (page 282)

OMELETS

Omelets are an essential part of a vegetarian cook's repertoire. They're fast, versatile, and nutritious, and they can be filled with almost anything. In fact, the best omelets are often made from the leftovers in your refrigerator. Savory tomato-based leftovers from such dishes as Eggplant Parmesan (page 178) or Ratatouille (page 92) make excellent fillings.

There are two kinds of omelets. One is the folded omelet, which is wrapped around its filling. The other—from Spain, Italy, and the south of France—is flat, like a pancake. Eggs and filling are beaten together and cooked at the same time. The flat omelet has an advantage: you can cook it in advance and reheat it, or even eat it cold.

Use about ¼ cup filling per person. If you try to put too much inside a folded omelet, it may break apart as you turn it onto the plate.

For a two-egg omelet, either folded or flat, you will need the following:

1½ teaspoons butter, more as necessary
  2 eggs
    Salt, preferably sea salt, and freshly ground pepper
    Milk or cream
  ¼ cup of the filling of your choice (see pages 170–72), prepared and heated if necessary

Method 1: The folded omelet. Be sure you have everything you need ready beforehand, including the serving plate. The folded omelet happens fast.

Heat your omelet pan slowly. Start to melt the butter in the pan. Break the eggs into a bowl, add a little salt and pepper and a drop or two of milk or cream, and beat thirty times with a fork or whisk.

Meanwhile, the butter will have melted and begun to sizzle. Tip the pan from side to side to coat the bottom evenly, then turn up the heat to medium. As soon as the sizzling stops—and not a moment later—pour in the egg mixture. Tilt the pan with a rotating wrist motion so the bottom is coated with egg. As soon as you see that a thin layer of egg is cooked, shake the pan vigorously by pushing it away from you and then jerking it toward you. (It is this motion of the pan that assures a fluffy omelet and prevents it from browning.) If the jerking motion is not moving the egg mixture enough for the runny egg on top to flow underneath the cooked layer, lift the edge of the cooked layer with a spatula as you shake the pan so the egg can run underneath.

After a few shakes of the pan, place your filling in the center of the omelet, making a "line" of filling going across the diameter of the omelet.

Continue to jerk the pan so the omelet folds over on itself. If you are afraid
of spilling the eggs out over the side of the pan, shake the pan with one
hand while lifting the sides of the omelet with a spatula, allowing the un
cooked egg to run underneath. Then, still shaking the pan, fold the omele
over with the spatula. Tilt the pan and roll the omelet out onto the serving
plate, helping it along if necessary with the spatula. This entire operation
should take about 1 minute.

Keep in mind that the center of the omelet should be undercooked
because once it's closed up it continues to cook in its own heat for a minute
or so.

Method 2: The flat omelet. The procedure for the flat omelet is not a
fast. Heat the butter and olive oil in an omelet or frying pan. Mix togethe
your eggs, salt and pepper, milk or cream and beat thirty times with a for
or whisk. Stir in your filling and mix well. Pour the mixture into the pa
and lower the flame. When a thin layer of egg has set, begin to gentl
shake the pan and continue cooking for 4 to 5 minutes. When the omele
has just about set, place the pan under the broiler for 2 to 4 minutes t
finish it off. It should puff up. Serve immediately, cut in wedges like a pie
or cool and chill.

Note: Be careful not to let the butter burn.

LEFTOVER RATATOUILLE, EGGPLANT PARMESAN, OR SPAGHETTI SAUCE FILLING

For this recipe, use leftovers from Ratatouille (page 92), Eggplant Par
mesan (page 178), or Soybean Spaghetti Sauce (page 215).

Have your filling heating in a separate pan; spoon on (or in) ¼ cup pe
person. For a folded omelet (see page 169), sprinkle 1 teaspoon of grated
Parmesan and 1 teaspoon of sunflower seeds over the filling before you fol
the omelet, and top the omelet with grated Parmesan and chopped fresl
parsley. For a flat omelet (see above), add the extra Parmesan and parsle
to the egg-filling mixture and top with Parmesan and chopped fresh parsley

FINES HERBES FILLING

Use whatever herbs you happen to have on hand for this. My favorite
are parsley, tarragon, chives, basil, fennel and dill. Though they are stron
herbs, I like fresh rosemary and thyme as well. Chop up a cupful and add
little minced garlic and, if you wish, some grated Parmesan. Use 1 table
spoon for each two-egg omelet. Top with a sprinkling of herbs and more
Parmesan.

CHEESE FILLING

Use 3 to 4 tablespoons grated cheese per two-egg omelet. I suggest Cheddar, Gruyère, Jarlsberg, or Emmenthaler, and the addition of a little Parmesan will give it a little zip. Garnish with parsley, which you may also combine with the cheese. Toasted buttered croutons are also a nice touch.

VEGETABLE FILLING

Anything you have on hand will do. Asparagus and broccoli are my favorites, and mushrooms. Blanch green vegetables and chop in small pieces. If you are using mushrooms, sauté first in butter or olive oil with a little onion and garlic, salt, and pepper. Use ¼ cup per person, and combine if you wish with a tablespoon of grated Parmesan or Gruyère.

AVOCADO FILLING

2 ripe avocados
½ cup very finely chopped chives or green onion
2 tablespoons lemon juice
  Salt, preferably sea salt, and freshly ground pepper to taste

Mash the avocados to a very smooth puree. Add the remaining ingredients and mix well. Use about ¼ cup of this mixture per omelet.

Enough for 6 two-egg omelets

SPINACH AND MUSHROOM FILLING

1½ cups blanched, chopped spinach
¼ pound fresh mushrooms, sliced and sautéed until tender
3 tablespoons cream or half-and-half
  Salt, preferably sea salt, and freshly ground pepper to taste

Combine the spinach and mushrooms, then stir in the cream and salt and pepper to taste. Use ¼ cup per omelet.

Enough for 6 two-egg omelets

SPICED APPLE FILLING

2 apples, peeled, if desired, then cored and sliced thin
¼ cup raisins
½ to 1 teaspoon ground cinnamon
½ teaspoon freshly grated nutmeg
½ teaspoon ground allspice
1 to 2 tablespoons butter
  Mild honey to taste (optional)

Sauté the apples with the raisins and spices in butter until they begin to soften; remove from the heat before they get mushy. Add a little honey, if you wish, then divide the mixture evenly among your omelets, folded (see page 169) or flat (see page 170).

Enough for 6 two-egg omelets

BEAN SPROUT FILLING

 4 green onions, both white part and green, chopped
 1 tablespoon safflower or vegetable oil
   Dash of tamari
1½ cups mung bean or alfalfa sprouts

Sauté the green onions in the oil for a few minutes. Add the tamari and sprouts, then stir together and remove from the heat. Divide equally among your omelets, folded (see page 169) or flat (see page 170).

Enough for 6 two-egg omelets

CURRIED ORANGE FILLING

 1 tablespoon butter
1½ teaspoons curry powder
 2 to 3 oranges, peeled and sectioned
 ½ cup plain yogurt, homemade (see page 259) or commercial, or buttermilk
 1 teaspoon chopped fresh mint

Heat the butter and sauté the curry powder for 1 minute. Add the orange sections and sauté, stirring, for 3 minutes. Remove from the heat, place in a bowl, and stir in the yogurt and mint. Divide among your omelets, folded (see page 169) or flat (see page 170), and serve the omelets with Chutney (page 235).

Enough for 6 to 8 two-egg omelets

Menu Suggestions

Omelets make a simple main course with just about any eggless hors d'oeuvre, soup, salad, or dessert.

CRÊPES

I love the concept of the crêpe, a paper-thin pancake wrapped around the filling of your choice. It's a pity that the mystique of crêpes, their French name, and their high restaurant price have kept many people from attempting them, because they're easy to make and to store. They may be stored in the refrigerator for a few days, or frozen (stack them between pieces of waxed paper to avoid sticking and seal well in plastic, or wrap in a clean, dry cloth). They thaw quickly, so if you have a supply in the freezer you can make wonderful meals in no time.

The three crêpe recipes that follow are just a few suggestions to start you off. Leftovers make good fillings, and a popular crêpe in France is one filled with a fried egg and cheese—so, you see, one needn't get very fancy.

I use a traditional crêpe pan. If you have an inverted crêpe pan (see Method 2 below), omit the oil or melted butter.

3 large eggs
⅔ cup milk
⅔ cup water
3 tablespoons sesame oil or melted butter (for Method 1 only)
½ teaspoon salt, preferably sea salt
1 cup whole-wheat pastry flour (or half whole-wheat pastry flour and half unbleached white)

Put the eggs, milk, water, oil or butter, and salt in a blender. Turn it on and slowly pour in the flour. Whirl it all at high speed for 1 minute.

Alternatively, sift together the flour and salt and beat in the eggs. Gradually add the liquids and the oil or butter, beating vigorously with a whisk, and strain through a sieve.

Refrigerate the batter for 1 to 2 hours. (This will allow the flour particles to swell and soften so the crêpes will be light.)

Method 1: Using a standard crêpe pan: For this method, use a 6- or 7-inch crêpe pan or a cast-iron or no-stick skillet. Have the batter ready in a bowl, with a whisk on hand for stirring, as the flour tends to settle and the batter will need to be stirred before making each crêpe. Also have on hand a ¼-cup measure (preferably a ¼-cup ladle, available in restaurant supply stores) and a plate to stack the finished crêpes on.

Place the pan over moderately high heat and brush the bottom with butter. When the pan *just* begins to smoke, remove from the heat and pour in slightly less than ¼ cup batter, then tilt the pan to distribute the batter evenly. (Don't get nervous and think you should look like a crêperie chef; just slowly and methodically tilt the pan from side to side and watch the batter distribute itself evenly. Eventually you will be able to do it faster.) Return the pan to the heat and cook for about 1 minute. Loosen the edges gently with a spatula, and if the crêpe comes up from the pan easily, turn and cook for about 30 seconds on the other side. (If the crêpe sticks, wait for another 30 seconds, then turn.) Turn the crêpe from the pan onto a plate, with the first (or "good") side down; this will make filling the crêpes easier, since you want this golden side to show.

(continued)

Brush the pan again with butter and continue with the remainder of the batter, a scant ¼ cup at a time. After the first three or four crêpes, you will not have to brush the pan with butter every time.

You might have a problem with the crêpes sticking to the pan. There are a few things to be careful about. First, make sure that your pan is well seasoned and your batter is well blended so the flour doesn't settle. Do not panic if the first four or five crêpes stick. It might take about that many to get the pan sufficiently saturated with butter. Also, don't try to turn the crêpes until they come away from the pan easily, or they will tear.

Proceed as directed in each of the three crêpe recipes that follow.

Method 2: Using an inverted crêpe pan: These pans make a nice, even, thin crêpe, but there is always some crêpe batter that you can't use up because it is too far down in the pie pan. Place your batter in a pie pan and heat the crêpe pan, inverted, over a moderate flame. If a drop of batter sizzles when you drop it on the pan, the pan is ready. Dip it evenly into the pie pan. A surface of batter will adhere immediately and begin to cook. (If the crêpe pan is too hot, the batter will immediately fall off, back into the pie pan. If this happens, allow the pan to cool for a minute, then dip it into the pie pan again.) Place the pan, inverted again, over the flame and cook for about 30 seconds. Loosen gently around the edges with a spatula and let the crêpe fall off onto a plate. The "good" side, the side you want to show when you roll the crêpe up, will be up when the crêpe falls onto the plate; you will have to turn it over to fill it.

Proceed as directed in each of the three crêpe recipes that follow.

20 to 30 pancakes

ALMOND-CHEESE STUFFED CRÊPES

The almond-cheese filling for these crêpes is exceptionally delicious. The ricotta-egg mixture is fluffy, and the ground almonds provide a wonderful crunch. Nutmeg makes it really special.

 1 recipe Crêpes (page 172)
12 ounces ricotta
 2 eggs
 1 cup almonds, chopped very fine or ground in a blender
 ½ cup freshly grated Parmesan cheese
 1 cup plain yogurt, homemade (see page 259) or commercial
 ¼ to ½ teaspoon salt, preferably sea salt, or to taste
   Freshly grated nutmeg to taste
   White Wine Sauce (page 258)

Have your crêpes stacked and ready to fill.

Preheat the oven to 325 degrees; butter a 2-quart baking dish. Blend the ricotta and eggs together in a blender or in a large bowl with a whisk. Stir in the almonds, Parmesan, and yogurt. Season with salt and nutmeg to taste.

Place 2 to 3 tablespoons filling on the less-cooked side of each crêpe, then roll up in either of two ways: like an enchilada (see illustration 1) or like a blintz (see illustration 2), with the sides folded over the filling first. (For these crêpes I prefer the latter method, because the filling is runny and the crêpes folded at the sides will contain it better.) Place the crêpes side by side in the buttered baking dish.

Cover the baking dish with foil to keep the moisture in and bake for 30 minutes. Serve hot, with the white wine sauce.

6 to 8 servings

Menu Suggestions

Hors d'oeuvres: French Bread (page 45) and Baba Ganouch (page 60), Marinated Vegetables Vinaigrette (page 74)

Soups: A Different Onion (page 112), Blender Gazpacho (page 135), Puree of Asparagus (page 110), A Rich Tomato (page 104)

Salads: Mixed Green (page 238), Spinach (page 238), Water Cress and Mushroom (page 247), Tender Lettuce and Orange (page 242)

Desserts: Fresh fruit (see page 276), Pears Poached in Red Wine with a Touch of Cassis (page 277), Strawberry and Cassis Sherbet (page 301), Peaches Marsala (page 282), Raspberries with Red Wine (page 282)

RATATOUILLE-CHEESE CRÊPES

A perfect way to use up leftover *ratatouille,* and a quick, easy, and satisfying main course. The sauce is remarkably simple: it's just a puree.

As for any crêpe dish, the crêpes may be made in advance and frozen or refrigerated. You can also make the *ratatouille* in advance, if you're making it especially for this recipe; it gets better as it matures.

1 recipe Crêpes (page 172)
1 recipe Ratatouille (page 92)
½ cup freshly grated Parmesan cheese
½ cup half-and-half or cream
  Tomato paste (optional)
  Chopped fresh basil or parsley for garnish

Have your crêpes stacked and ready to fill.

Preheat the oven to 300 degrees; butter a 2-quart baking dish.

Set aside 2 cups of the *ratatouille* and about 2 tablespoons of the Parmesan. Place 2 to 3 tablespoons of the remaining *ratatouille* on each crêpe, sprinkle with some of the remaining Parmesan, and roll up. Place side by side in the buttered baking dish, cover the dish with foil, and heat the crêpes through in the oven for 20 minutes.

Meanwhile, make a sauce by pureeing the 2 cups *ratatouille* in a blender or food processor. Place this puree in a saucepan and heat through, thinning it out with the half-and-half or cream (If you want a more tomato-y taste, add some tomato paste.)

Remove the baking dish from the oven, pour the puree over the crêpes, and sprinkle them with the reserved Parmesan. Garnish with fresh basil or parsley and serve.

6 to 8 servings

Menu Suggestions

Hors d'oeuvres: Fresh Fruit and Nuts (page 80), Cheese Fondue (page 84), Soya Pâté (page 58)

Soups: Leek (page 113), Fresh Pea (page 107), Cheese and Black Bread (page 106)

Salads: Salade Niçoise (page 241), Green Bean, Almond, and Mushroom (page 245), Crudité (page 73)

Desserts: Indian Pudding (page 293), Millet-Raisin Pudding (page 292), Light Cheesecake (page 291)

CRÊPES FLORENTINE

These have a rich spinach filling that can be made a day ahead of time and kept refrigerated, tightly covered. The spinach is creamed with a luxurious mushroom-cheese sauce and further enriched with cottage cheese and egg.

    1 recipe Crêpes (page 172)
    3 tablespoons butter
    2 tablespoons minced green onion, shallot, or white onion
    1 clove garlic, minced or put through a press
    1 cup diced fresh mushrooms
    3 tablespoons flour (whole-wheat pastry flour or unbleached white, or a combination)
    3 cups hot milk
    1½ pounds fresh spinach, stemmed and washed, or 1½ packages (10 ounces each) frozen spinach
    2 tablespoons dry white wine
    1 cup grated Gruyère cheese
        Salt, preferably sea salt, and freshly ground pepper to taste
        Freshly grated nutmeg to taste
    1 cup cottage cheese
    2 eggs, beaten

Have your crêpes stacked and ready to fill. Heat the butter in a heavy-bottomed, 2-quart saucepan. Add the onion, garlic, and the diced mushrooms and sauté until the onion is tender and the mushrooms cooked through, 3 to 5 minutes. Add the flour and stir together to make a roux. Cook, stirring, for a few minutes, then slowly whisk in the hot milk and bring to a simmer, stirring. Once the sauce is smooth and has begun to thicken, allow to simmer over very low heat for about 10 minutes, stirring occasionally.

Meanwhile, prepare the spinach. Blanch fresh, stemmed spinach in salted boiling water; drain and squeeze out excess liquid, then chop. (Or thaw frozen spinach, squeeze out excess liquid, and chop.) Place in a 2- or 3-quart bowl.

Stir the white wine into the sauce and add ¾ cup of the Gruyère. Season to taste with salt, freshly ground pepper, and a little nutmeg, then stir until all the cheese is melted.

Combine the cottage cheese and beaten eggs and add to the spinach. Stir in 1 cup of the sauce; mix together. Correct the seasoning, and if you would like a creamier filling add a little more sauce, making sure that you reserve enough to top the crêpes.

Preheat the oven to 350 degrees; butter a 2- or 3-quart baking dish.

(continued)

Place 2 heaping tablespoons of filling on each crêpe, roll up, and place side by side in the buttered baking dish. Sprinkle the remaining cheese over the top and bake for 20 to 30 minutes, until bubbly.

Heat the remaining sauce through, pour over the crêpes, and serve.

6 to 8 servings

GÂTEAU DE CRÊPES À LA FLORENTINE

Make the crêpes, filling, and sauce as directed above. Butter a baking dish and lay a crêpe in it, golden side up. Spread a spoonful of mushroom sauce over this, and layer another crêpe over the sauce. Spread this crêpe with the spinach filling. Continue alternating crêpes spread with Florentine filling and sauce, setting aside a small amount of sauce for the top, until you have used up all your crêpes. Sprinkle the remaining cheese over the top crêpe.

Bake at 350 degrees for 20 to 30 minutes, until bubbling hot and slightly browned on top. Pour on the remaining sauce, cut into pie-shaped wedges, and serve.

6 to 8 servings

Menu Suggestions

Soups: Leek (page 113), Egg-Lemon (page 111), A Different Onion (page 112)

Salads: Mixed Green (page 238), Tomatoes and Fresh Herbs (page 247)

Desserts: Fresh fruit (see page 276), Raspberries in Red Wine (page 282), Pears Poached in Red Wine with a Touch of Cassis (page 277)

EGGPLANT PARMESAN

Eggplant Parmesan is a rich, filling dish. To complete the menu, you'll want just a light soup and green salad, and a light dessert. Like Black Bean Enchiladas (page 144), it's a dependable choice for my catered dinners, and most of it can be prepared ahead.

The tomato sauce can be made a few days in advance, and the casserole can be assembled a day in advance and refrigerated *before* you bake it. But do *not* use aluminum foil to cover it. The aluminum reacts with the tomato sauce and sheds itself onto the casserole; you will be alarmed to find holes in the foil and bits of gray all over the top of your beautiful eggplant Parmesan. So use plastic wrap when you store it.

As with every casserole, every part of the whole should taste good.

Grate your own Parmesan if you have the time, for it makes all the difference in the world. And use good olive oil and bread crumbs.

Avoid running out of sauce by being sparing with the ingredients when you start to assemble the casserole, and becoming more extravagant as you near the top.

½ cup olive oil, approximately
1 onion, chopped
3 cloves or more garlic, minced or put through a press
1 green pepper, chopped (optional)
4 cups chopped tomatoes
1 can (12 ounces) tomato paste
1 teaspoon salt, preferably sea salt, or to taste
  Freshly ground pepper to taste
1 tablespoon fresh basil or 1 teaspoon dried, or to taste
1 teaspoon oregano, or to taste
  Pinch of ground cinnamon
1 large or 2 small eggplants
½ cup whole-wheat flour
1 pound mozzarella cheese, sliced or grated
½ to 1 cup whole-wheat bread crumbs
1 cup freshly grated Parmesan cheese

In a Dutch oven or large saucepan heat about 2 tablespoons of the olive oil and sauté the onion with half the garlic and the optional green pepper until tender. Add the tomatoes, remaining garlic, tomato paste, ½ teaspoon salt, and pepper to taste and let simmer for 1 hour, while you prepare the eggplant. Add the basil and oregano after the first half hour. Toward the end of the cooking time, add the cinnamon to the sauce and correct the seasoning; you may wish to add more garlic, salt, oregano, or basil.

"Steam" the eggplant according to the directions on page 23, but keeping it in the oven for only 10 minutes and piercing it several times with a skewer instead of scoring with a knife.

When the eggplant is cool enough for you to handle, slice it in lengthwise pieces about ¼ inch thick. Meanwhile, in a bowl, combine the flour and ½ teaspoon salt. Dip the eggplant slices in this mixture, a few at a time, and sauté on both sides in the remaining olive oil until crisp. Drain well on paper towels. When the slices are cool enough, cut them in half crosswise.

Preheat the oven to 350 degrees.

Oil a 2½ or 3-quart casserole or baking dish. Place ¼ inch of tomato sauce on the bottom, then add a layer of eggplant slices. Cover with some of the mozzarella, a thicker layer of sauce, a sprinkling of bread crumbs, and then of Parmesan. Continue in this order—eggplant, mozzarella, sauce, bread crumbs and Parmesan—finishing up with a lavish helping of sauce, bread crumbs, and Parmesan.

Bake for 30 to 40 minutes and serve immediately.

6 to 8 servings

Menu Suggestions

Hors d'oeuvres: Spinach Gnocchi (page 192), homemade bread (see pages 38–48) with Herb Butter (page 61), Vegetable Platter with Assorted Dips (page 77)

Soups: Stracciatella (page 95), Escarole (page 120)

Salads: Mixed Green (page 238), Spinach (page 238)

Desserts: Italian Fruit Compote (page 278), Bavarian Crème au Café (page 286)

STUFFED EGGPLANT

Many of the ingredients in this fresh, colorful dish will be familiar to you from other stuffed eggplant recipes. But you'll never forget this version. The difference is in the nuts, which give this a sensational texture.

This dish is easier to prepare if you have a grapefruit knife for scooping the eggplant out of the skin.

1 to 2 large or 3 to 4 small eggplants, prepared as directed on page 23, but "steamed" for 15 to 20 minutes
3 tablespoons olive or safflower oil
1 medium or large onion, sliced
2 cloves garlic, minced or put through a press
1½ green peppers, seeded and diced
¼ cup almonds, cut in half lengthwise
¼ cup chopped brazil nuts
¼ cup sunflower seeds or pignolia (pine nuts)
⅓ cup whole-wheat bread crumbs
2 tomatoes, peeled and sliced
Salt, preferably sea salt, and freshly ground pepper to taste
1 tablespoon lime juice, or to taste
½ cup freshly grated Parmesan cheese

When you remove the eggplant from the hot oven to cool, reduce the oven heat to 325 degrees; oil a large rectangular baking dish.

When the "steamed" eggplant halves are cool, carefully scoop out the pulp, leaving just enough pulp in the skins to give them some structure and enable them to hold the filling. Dice the eggplant pulp and set aside for a moment.

Heat the olive or safflower oil in a wok or large skillet and sauté the onion, garlic, and green pepper for 5 minutes. Add the eggplant and continue to sauté for 10 minutes longer.

Add all the remaining ingredients except 2 tablespoons of the Parmesan, then cover and cook over a low flame for 10 to 15 minutes, or until the eggplant is tender, stirring occasionally to prevent sticking. Adjust the seasoning and remove from the heat.

Fill the eggplant shells with the mixture, sprinkle with the remaining Parmesan, and place in the oiled baking pan. Heat through in the oven for 20 minutes.

Slice larger eggplants crosswise to serve.

6 to 8 servings

Menu Suggestions

Hors d'oeuvres: Sliced cantaloupe, Marinated Vegetables Vinaigrette (page 74)

Soups: Puree of Asparagus (page 110), A Rich Tomato (page 104), A Different Onion (page 112); or serve Fettucine con Pesto Genovese (page 188) as a first course

Salads: Mixed Green (page 238), Spinach (page 238), Water Cress and Mushroom (page 247)

Side dishes: See the grains side dishes on pages 226–28; or serve steamed vegetables

Desserts: Fresh fruit (see page 276), Peach Pie (page 294), Soufflé Grand Marnier (page 290)

ITALIAN SOYBEAN-GRAINS CASSEROLE

This is the model meatless protein dish. The grains and soybeans complement each other, and the cheese and wheat germ give the dish another protein push. It is the best way I can think of to introduce whole soybeans into your diet. (I once served this to four hundred people at a conference on world hunger.) The grains and soybeans soak up the tasty tomato sauce, the zucchini adds a fresh vegetable crunch and flavor, and it's all very satisfying.

You can assemble this a day in advance and refrigerate it before baking. As for Eggplant Parmesan (page 178), do *not* cover with aluminum foil; the aluminum will react with the tomato sauce. Use plastic wrap. You will have to remember to soak and cook the whole beans and to cook the grains in advance. The tomato sauce can be made up to a few days in advance.

1 onion, chopped
2 or more cloves garlic, minced or put through a press
¼ cup olive oil
8 tomatoes, chopped
1 can (6 ounces) tomato paste
1 teaspoon oregano
1 tablespoon chopped fresh basil or 1 teaspoon dried
   Salt, preferably sea salt, and freshly ground pepper to taste
2 zucchini, sliced
   Vegetable salt
2 cups cooked soybeans or soy flakes (⅔ cup raw; see page 25)
2 cups cooked brown rice or bulgur (1 cup raw; see page 25) or 1 cup each, mixed
4 ounces Cheddar cheese, sliced or grated
½ cup wheat germ

Sauté the onion and garlic in 2 tablespoons of the olive oil until the onion is tender. Add the tomatoes, tomato paste, and seasonings, then cover and simmer for 30 minutes.

Sauté the zucchini in the remaining oil until just beginning to be tender and translucent. Sprinkle with a little vegetable salt and drain on paper towels.

Preheat the oven to 350 degrees; oil a 2-quart casserole.

Combine the soybeans and grains with 1 cup of the sauce and spread them over the bottom of the prepared casserole. Layer the zucchini over the grains and beans. Pour on the remaining sauce, sprinkle on the cheese, and top with wheat germ.

Bake for 30 minutes.

6 to 8 servings

Menu Suggestions

Soups: Cream of Raw and Cooked Mushroom (page 101), Leek (page 113), Stracciatella (page 95)

Salads: Mixed Green (page 238), Spinach (page 238), Water Cress and Mushroom (page 247)

Desserts: Bavarian Crème au Café (page 286), Italian Fruit Compote (page 278), Bananas Poached in White Wine (page 277)

PICANTE ZUCCHINI

This looks like a squash Parmesan, but the flavors are *picante,* and the rosemary and coriander add an unusual touch to the sauce.

3 medium zucchini (about 1½ pounds), sliced ¼ inch thick
  Peanut or safflower oil as needed
1 sprig fresh rosemary or ¼ teaspoon dried
3 sprigs fresh coriander (*cilantro*)
1 mild chili (or a hot one, according to your taste and the tastes of your guests)
3 cloves garlic
½ to 1 teaspoon salt, preferably sea salt
1 can (6 ounces) tomato paste
1½ pounds tomatoes, peeled and chopped
8 ounces cheddar cheese, grated or sliced

Sauté the sliced zucchini in oil until it begins to be tender and transparent on both sides. Drain on paper towels.

Grind the rosemary, coriander, chili, garlic, and salt together in a mortar. Add this herb mixture to the tomato paste and the tomatoes in a saucepan. Cook, stirring, for 30 minutes.

Preheat the oven to 350 degrees; oil a 2-quart casserole or baking dish.

Spread the cooked zucchini on the bottom of the prepared pan. Pour the sauce over and top with the grated or sliced cheese.

Bake for 45 minutes.

Note: If you desire a more substantial dish, line the bottom of the casserole with cooked brown rice or bulgur.

6 to 8 servings

Menu Suggestions

Hors d'oeuvres: Tiropites (page 68), French Bread (page 45) with Soya Pâté (page 58) or Potted Roquefort (page 63), Garbanzo Bean Salad (page 254), which should be used in place of a soup

Soups: Cream of Raw and Cooked Mushroom (page 101), Miso-Vegetable (page 127), Dill (page 117)

Salads: Mixed Green (page 238) with Cucumber Cream Dressing (page 261), Avocado and Citrus (page 239), Garbanzo Bean (page 254)

Desserts: Spiced Fruit- and Nut-Filled Crêpes (page 284), Strawberry and Cassis Sherbet (page 301)

THE BEST PIZZA IN TOWN

You'll never go back to your local pizza parlor after this one. You can make the crusts in advance and freeze them before prebaking. If you have room in your freezer, I recommend that you go ahead and roll the dough out, and then place it on the pizza pans; that way it will only take an hour to thaw out. If you don't have room, punch down the dough and roll it into a ball, wrap it in plastic, and freeze. It should take about 4 hours to thaw completely.

The sauce, too, like any good tomato sauce, can be made in advance. These pizzas then take minutes to assemble and bake. They're great for a party.

For the dough:
- 2 tablespoons (2 envelopes) active dry yeast
- 1¼ cups warm water
- 2 tablespoons honey
- ¼ cup olive or safflower oil
- 1 teaspoon salt, preferably sea salt
- 1 cup soy flour
- 2½ cups whole-wheat flour, plus additional flour for kneading
  Cornmeal
- 1 egg, beaten

For the sauce:
- 3 tablespoons olive oil
- 1 cup chopped onions
- 4 cloves garlic, minced or put through a press
- 4 cups chopped tomatoes
- 1 can (12 ounces) tomato paste
- 1 tablespoon oregano
- 1 tablespoon chopped fresh basil or 1 teaspoon dried
- 1 bay leaf
  Pinch of ground cinnamon
  Salt, preferably sea salt, and freshly ground pepper to taste

For the topping:
- 1 pound mozzarella cheese, sliced or grated
- ½ cup freshly grated Parmesan cheese
  Garnish or garnishes of your choice (see below)

Dissolve the yeast in the water with the honey, then combine with the oil and salt in a large bowl. Mix in the soy flour, then the 2½ cups whole-wheat flour, a cup at a time. Turn out onto a floured board and knead until smooth and elastic. Put into a large oiled bowl; cover with a damp towel and place in a warm spot. Let rise until doubled in volume, about 1½ hours.

Meanwhile, make the sauce.

In a 3- or 4-quart saucepan, heat the oil and sauté the onion until tender. Add the garlic and cook for 2 minutes, then add the remaining sauce ingredients. Bring to a simmer and simmer for 1 hour, stirring occasionally. (If a thicker sauce is desired, cook longer.) Remove the bay leaf before pouring over the pizza.

Preheat the oven to 400 degrees.

Punch the dough down and knead again for a few minutes to make it easy to handle, then divide it into three pieces (or four if you're using 10-inch pans). Roll each piece out to a thickness of about ¼ inch (or thinner) and place on cookie sheets or pizza pans oiled with olive oil and dusted with cornmeal. Pinch a lip around the edge to contain the sauce, then brush with beaten egg.

Prebake for 7 minutes, then set aside to cool slightly. Meanwhile, turn up the oven heat to 450 degrees.

Sprinkle about one-third of the mozzarella over the prebaked pizza crusts. Pour the tomato sauce over each and sprinkle with equal amounts of the remaining cheese. Top with the garnish or garnishes of your choice and bake for 10 to 15 minutes.

Note: You can top your pizzas with any of the suggestions below, singly or in combination:

Sliced fresh mushrooms, sautéed in butter and olive oil with salt and freshly ground pepper

Sliced green pepper

Pitted, sliced black olives

Sliced artichoke hearts

Sliced eggplant, sautéed in olive oil with garlic, salt, and freshly ground pepper

Sliced onion, sautéed in olive oil until crisp-tender

Sliced zucchini, sautéed in olive oil with garlic, salt, and freshly ground pepper

Sliced pimientos

3 to 4 pizzas

(*continued*)

186

Menu Suggestions

Hors d'oeuvres: Spinach Gnocchi (page 192), Marinated Vegetables Vinai-
    grette (page 74), Marinated Vegetables à la Grecque (page 76), Gar-
    banzo Bean Salad (page 254), Marinated White Beans (page 195)
Soups: Minestrone (page 118), Pistou (page 96), Sopa de Ajo (page 103)
Salads: Niçoise (page 241), Mixed Green (page 238)
Desserts: Italian Fruit Compote (page 278), Bavarian Crème au Café (page
    286), Apricot Soufflé (page 289)

DELICATE HOMEMADE PASTA

To me, pasta is the most sensuous of foods. Its texture is light and
smooth, its flavor elusive. A few years ago I took a class in ravioli making
from Ann Clark, a marvelous cook who teaches French cooking in Austin.
This recipe is my whole-wheat version of her excellent pasta. It has a
slightly nutty flavor, and is not as starchy as commercial pasta.

Unless you're using a food processor, you'll find that as you make the
dough little bits of flour will crumble off. Resist the temptation to incorporate these tiny pieces; the dough must be uniform in order to roll out well,
and any little bits you try to attach will flake off when you roll it out or
when you cook it.

You can make up the dough a day in advance, wrap it in plastic and a
damp towel, and keep it refrigerated until you're ready to roll it out.

This recipe makes enough for 24 lasagne noodles, or 24 to 30 ravioli 3 x
3 inches, or enough fettucini to feed 6 to 8 big eaters.

1 cup whole-wheat pastry flour
1 cup unbleached white flour
1 teaspoon salt, preferably sea salt
2 large eggs, at room temperature
2 teaspoons olive oil
2 tablespoons water, more as necessary

Sift together the flours and salt and pour out on a clean, dry board.
Shape into a mound, then make a well in the center with the "walls" of
flour even all around (see illustration). Crack the eggs into the well and add
the oil. Using a fork, mix the flour together with the egg mixture, keeping
the "well" intact by cupping one hand around the wall of flour while you
brush flour from the top of the wall into the well, incorporating it into the
egg mixture. The mixture of eggs and flour will get very sticky; keep incorporating flour with the fork while you continue to confine the flour with
your other hand so it doesn't scatter itself all over your working surface.
(You won't be able to get all the flour incorporated, and some flakes of the

mixture won't be absorbed, but don't be concerned with this small amount—you'll have plenty of pasta.)

When you have incorporated all the flour you can into the egg mixture, sprinkle with the water. This may make the mixture sticky. Sprinkle with a little more flour—just a little—so you can handle the dough, and mix the dough vigorously with your hands. This is fun; you just squeeze the dough in your hands, from one end to another, back and forth and from hand to hand. When the dough is smooth and elastic, knead it for 5 minutes. (You can do this on the board or by continuing to squeeze it.) Shape the dough into a ball, wrap it in a damp towel, and let rest for 30 minutes to 1 hour.

Divide the dough into two parts. Roll out as thin as possible (here a heavy rolling pin comes in very handy, as does an aggressive frame of mind). Slam the pin down onto the dough and roll in one direction. Lift the pin, slam it down again, and roll in another direction. The dough will shrink back a little, so roll it thinner than you want to. Cut it into desired shapes—ravioli, fettucini, lasagne, manicotti—and place on waxed paper until ready to cook. If storing, allow to dry and wrap in plastic. Keep in a cool, dry place.

To cook the pasta, bring a large pot of water to a boil. Add 1 teaspoon salt per quart of water and 1 tablespoon olive oil. Drop in the pasta—it should float to the surface very quickly—then turn down the water to a gentler boil and count 2 minutes. Drain and serve immediately.

6 to 8 generous servings

LASAGNE

This is always a popular dish for big dinners. Like the Eggplant Parmesan on page 178, it can be assembled in advance—and don't use aluminum foil for storage for this dish either.

12 lasagne noodles (whole-wheat or semolina), homemade (page 186) or commercial

1 recipe Soybean Spaghetti Sauce (page 215) or the tomato sauce used in Eggplant Parmesan (page 178)

1 pound ricotta or cottage cheese

1½ cups freshly grated Parmesan or Romano cheese

1½ cups whole-wheat bread crumbs

1¼ pounds mozzarella cheese, sliced

Butter

Preheat the oven to 350 degrees; oil a 3-quart lasagne pan or baking dish.

(continued)

Cook the lasagne noodles according to the directions at the end of the preceding recipe, if homemade, or on the package; drain.

Mix about 1 cup of the sauce in with the ricotta or cottage cheese to moisten; in a separate bowl, combine the Parmesan or Romano and the bread crumbs.

Cover the bottom of the prepared lasagne pan with a thin layer of sauce. Sprinkle a layer of the bread crumb-Parmesan mixture over this, then make a layer of the lasagne noodles. Cover the noodles with a layer of mozzarella, then a layer of ricotta.

Now start again: sauce, bread crumbs and Parmesan, noodles, mozzarella, ricotta. Finish up with a lavish layer of sauce and sprinkling of bread crumbs and Parmesan; dot with butter and bake for 40 minutes.

6 to 8 servings

Menu Suggestions

See the menu suggestions for Soybean Spaghetti Sauce (page 215).

FETTUCINE CON PESTO GENOVESE

Pesto is one of my favorite foods. Fresh basil is essential; after all, *pesto* is the definitive statement about this fragrant herb.

Usually *pesto* includes ground pignolia or sunflower seeds, but I find they result in a gummy sauce, so I've omitted them from my recipe. The important elements are the basil, garlic, olive oil, and parsley. If you wish, you can sauté pignolia or sunflower seeds and sprinkle them over the top of the dish when you serve it. The rich green sauce, by the way, keeps for several days in the refrigerator.

For those who wish to avoid the carbohydrates in pasta, the variation that follows will be welcome, not only for this dish but also as a base for other sauces; it also makes an excellent first course.

For the pesto:
   2 to 3 cups loosely packed fresh basil leaves, to taste
   ½ teaspoon salt, preferably sea salt
   2 medium or large cloves garlic
   ½ cup freshly grated Parmesan cheese
   2 teaspoons lemon juice (optional)
   ⅔ cup olive oil
   ⅓ cup pignolia (pine nuts) or sunflower seeds, sautéed in a little oil (optional)

For the pasta:
  6 quarts water
  1 tablespoon salt, preferably sea salt
  Olive oil
  1 pound fettucini noodles (whole-wheat or semolina), homemade (see page 186)
    or commercial
  3 to 4 tablespoons butter

Combine the basil, salt, and garlic and blend together in a blender or food processor. If you are not using a blender or food processor, place those ingredients in a large mortar and chop and blend using a pestle. Add the cheese. Blend these ingredients until you have a homogenous paste. Add the lemon juice. (The sauce tends to turn a dull green at the surface, and the lemon juice will prevent this somewhat.)

Now, by tablespoons or in a slow stream, add the olive oil, blending or mixing until the mixture cannot absorb any more. (If you wish to thin the sauce out, use tablespoonfuls of water from the boiled pasta.)

Bring the water to a rolling boil and add the salt and a little olive oil, to keep the pasta from sticking together. Dump in the fettucini, a handful at a time, stirring with a wooden spoon, again to keep the noodles from sticking together.

Cook the noodles in the rapidly boiling water until *al dente*, which means just tender to the bite—*not* mushy, but not raw. Test commercial fettucini after 5 to 7 minutes (homemade after 2) by tasting, and continue to test every minute; the cooking process should not take longer than 10 minutes for commercial pasta (and homemade pasta will float to the surface very quickly).

Place a large colander in the sink and drain the pasta carefully. Toss immediately in a warm serving bowl with the butter and *pesto*. Sprinkle with sautéed pignolia or sunflower seeds, if you wish, and serve. Pass a bowl of freshly grated Parmesan.

6 to 8 servings

SQUASH WITH PESTO

This variation comes from my friend Marguerite Mullen, a great cook and caterer.

Instead of using pasta, use 2 pounds zucchini or yellow squash. Grate the squash and salt it, using about ½ teaspoon salt. Let sit for 10 to 15 minutes, then squeeze out the moisture and rinse under cold water. Squeeze dry and sauté gently in 2 tablespoons olive oil until the squash is fragrant

and tender but not mushy. Toss with butter and *pesto*.
Serve immediately, with additional grated Parmesan on the side.

6 to 8 servings

Menu Suggestions

Soups: Leek (page 113), Stracciatella (page 95), Cream of Raw and Cooked
Mushroom (page 101), A Rich Tomato (page 104)
Salads: Mixed Green (page 238), Spinach (page 238), Tomatoes and Fresh
Herbs (page 247)
Desserts: Italian Fruit Compote (page 278), any fruit pie (pages 294–95),
Soufflé Grand Marnier (page 290)

FETTUCINE CON FUNGHI

Pasta with Mushrooms

Fettucine con funghi will fill your kitchen with the savory smell of simmering mushrooms seasoned with thyme, garlic, parsley, and wine. It's a
light and elegant main course with a luxurious abundance of mushrooms.
The sauce can be made up to three hours in advance and held, covered, on
top of the stove. But don't cook the pasta until minutes before you wish to
serve.

For the sauce:
   3 dried Chinese mushrooms plus 1 cube vegetable bouillon in 2½ cups water, or
      2 cups Vegetable Stock (page 91) or Garlic Broth (page 92)
   2 tablespoons olive oil
   2 tablespoons butter
   1 to 2 cloves garlic, minced or put through a press
   4 to 5 green onions, both white part and green, sliced
1½ to 2 pounds mushrooms (depending on how thick with mushrooms you want
      your sauce to be), sliced
   3 tablespoons flour (whole-wheat pastry flour or unbleached white, or a combi-
      nation)
  ¼ cup chopped fresh parsley
  ½ teaspoon dried thyme
  ¼ cup dry white wine
  ½ teaspoon salt, preferably sea salt
      Freshly ground pepper to taste
      Pinch of freshly grated nutmeg

For the pasta:
6 quarts water
3 tablespoons olive oil
1 tablespoon salt
1 pound fettucini noodles (whole-wheat, semolina, or spinach), homemade (see page 186) or commercial

For the dish:
1 cup freshly grated Parmesan cheese
2 tablespoons chopped fresh parsley

Simmer the dried mushrooms and bouillon cube in the water for 30 minutes; measure out 2 cups of this stock. Or heat the vegetable stock or garlic broth in a small saucepan.

Heat the olive oil in a large frying pan, wok, or saucepan and add the butter; the flame should be medium-low. Sauté the garlic and green onions for 1 minute, then add the mushrooms and sauté, stirring, for about 3 minutes, until they begin to cook through. Add the flour and stir well with a wooden spoon. Continue to cook, stirring constantly, for another 3 minutes. Add the parsley and thyme.

Slowly pour in the 2 cups hot stock (mushroom or vegetable) and stir until the liquid is slightly thickened. Add the white wine, salt, and pepper. Stir together well and simmer, uncovered, over low heat for 20 minutes, stirring occasionally. Add the nutmeg.

Meanwhile, heat the 6 quarts water in a large pot. When it begins to boil, add the olive oil and salt.

If the sauce is ready (and if you're just about ready for this course), drop in the fettucini. Cook until tender, about 5 to 10 minutes (unless the noodles are homemade, in which case they will be ready 2 minute after they float to the top of the water), then drain carefully in a colander. Place in a warm, buttered serving dish and pour the mushroom sauce over the pasta, reserving ¾ cup sauce for the top.

Sprinkle in ¾ cup of Parmesan cheese and toss the noodles well. Ladle the remaining sauce over the top, and sprinkle with the remaining Parmesan. Garnish with the chopped fresh parsley and serve immediately, as a first or main course.

6 to 8 servings

Menu Suggestions

Soups: Leek (page 113), Fresh Pea (page 107), Puree of Asparagus (page 110), A Rich Tomato (page 104)

(continued)

Salads: Salade Niçoise (page 241), Mixed Green (page 238), Salade Mimosa
(page 248), Beet and Endive (page 248)
Desserts: Bavarian Crème au Café (page 286), Apricot Soufflé (page 289),
Raspberries in Red Wine (page 282)

SPINACH GNOCCHI

Gnocchi are Italian dumplings. Roman *gnocchi* are made with potatoes;
the delicious Florentine *gnocchi* here are spinach, with ricotta and Parmesan, and lightened up with egg. The mixture can be made a day in advance and refrigerated, and you can also roll the dumplings, as long as you
seal them well. They are excellent with homemade pasta, and can also
serve as an hors d'oeuvre.

1½ pounds fresh spinach or 2 packages (10 ounces each) frozen spinach
  2 tablespoons butter
  8 ounces ricotta
    Salt, preferably sea salt, and freshly ground pepper to taste
    Freshly grated nutmeg to taste
  2 eggs, beaten
  3 tablespoons flour (whole-wheat pastry flour or unbleached white, or a combi-
    nation), plus ¼ to ½ cup additional for dusting
  ½ cup freshly grated Parmesan cheese
  5 quarts water

If you are using fresh spinach, wash and stem, then blanch very
quickly; squeeze out excess water and chop fine. Allow frozen spinach to
thaw and squeeze out excess water; chop fine.

Heat the butter in a saucepan over very low heat and add the spinach,
ricotta, salt and pepper to taste, and nutmeg. Using a wooden spoon, stir
and mix together well, and cook for 5 minutes. Remove from the heat and
stir in the beaten eggs, 3 tablespoons flour, and 5 tablespoons of the Parmesan. Refrigerate for at least 2 hours.

Place the additional flour on a plate. Take up the spinach-ricotta mixture by heaping half-teaspoons or teaspoons (depending on how large you
want them), and roll in the flour, forming little balls coated with flour.

Bring the 5 quarts of water to a boil in a large pot. Add 5 teaspoons salt
then drop in the *gnocchi*, one by one. After they float to the top, wait 3 or
4 minutes and remove with a slotted spoon. Place in a serving dish and top
with the remaining Parmesan.

Note: You may also toss with unsalted butter and additional Parmesan
or serve with White Wine Sauce (page 257) or tomato sauce.

If you're serving the *gnocchi* as hors d'oeuvres (for which a sample menu follows), place on a warm platter with toothpicks.

6 to 8 servings

Suggested Menu

Spinach Gnocchi (see above)
Eggplant Parmesan (page 178)
Mixed Green Salad (page 238)
Pears Poached in Red Wine with a Touch of Cassis (page 277)

Menu Suggestions

Soups: Leek (page 113), Tomato-Rice (page 122), Ratatouille (page 92)
Side Dish: Whole-Grain Pasta with Butter and Herbs (page 228)
Desserts: Oranges Grand Marnier (page 279), Orange Dessert Crêpes (page 285)

BLACK BEAN FEIJOADA WITH SPICED RICE

My Brazilian dinner guests were apprehensive when I announced that I would be serving a vegetarian version of this Brazilian stew—but they loved it. I use all black beans instead of meat, adding oranges to give the dish a special tang. It's especially warming in cold weather. The spiced rice should be served with this to make a tasty, protein-complementary meal.

2 cups dried black beans, washed
1 large onion, chopped
3 cloves garlic, minced or put through a press
1 tablespoon safflower oil
6 cups Vegetable Stock (page 91) or water
1 bay leaf
¼ teaspoon freshly ground pepper
2 oranges, whole or halved
1 teaspoon salt, preferably sea salt, or to taste
2 ribs celery, chopped
1 tomato, chopped
   Spiced Rice (see below)

Soak the beans in the stock or water overnight, or at least for several hours.

In a large flameproof bean pot or Dutch oven, sauté the onion and garlic in the oil until the onions are tender. Add the beans, stock or water, bay leaf, and pepper.

Bring the beans to a boil, add the remaining ingredients (except for the rice), and simmer, covered, for 2 to 3 hours. After the first hour remove the lid and simmer, uncovered.

When the beans are tender, remove about one-third of them and mash. Return the beans to the pot and continue cooking until the mashed beans thicken the mixture.

Serve accompanied by the rice.

6 to 8 servings

SPICED RICE

For the rice:

  1 onion, chopped
  3 cloves garlic, minced or put through a press
  2 tablespoons olive oil
  1 tablespoon butter
  2 tomatoes, peeled and coarsely chopped
2½ cups cooked brown rice (1 cup raw; see page 25)

For the sauce:

  Juice of 1 lemon
  2 tomatoes, peeled
  1 small onion, quartered
  2 cloves garlic
  1 teaspoon chili sauce
  1 fresh hot green chili (optional)
  ¼ cup wine or cider vinegar
  ½ teaspoon salt, preferably sea salt
  Liquid from the finished *feijoada* (see above)

Sauté the onion and garlic in the olive oil and butter until the onion is tender and golden. Add the tomatoes and simmer a few minutes, then stir in the cooked rice and mix well.

Keep warm over low heat until ready to serve (unless you make it far in advance—then just heat over a medium flame shortly before serving).

When ready to serve, put all the sauce ingredients (except the *feijoada* liquid) in a blender container and liquefy. Stir in liquid from the *feijoada* to taste and serve over the rice.

6 to 8 servings

Menu Suggestions

Hors d'oeuvres: Fresh fruit (see page 276), Quichettes (page 64), Tiropites (page 69), Spinach Gnocchi (page 192)

Salads: Spinach (page 238), Spinach and Citrus (page 249), Water Cress and Mushroom (page 247)

Desserts: Orange Dessert Crêpes (page 285), Pineapple with Kirsch (page 282), Grapefruit with Port (page 282)

MARINATED WHITE BEANS

This is one of my favorite dishes; it's always a big success at dinner parties, with pasta and a vegetable dish on the side, or on a bed of leaf lettuce. It makes an elegant starter, main course, or salad.

For the beans:
2 cups small dried white beans, washed
1½ quarts water
2 tablespoons olive oil
1 onion, chopped
3 cloves garlic, minced or put through a press
1 bay leaf
1 teaspoon salt, preferably sea salt, or to taste

For the salad:
¼ to ½ cup chopped fresh parsley
4 green onions, both white part and green, sliced
2 tablespoons fresh herbs (basil, marjoram, thyme, fennel)
1 green pepper, seeded and chopped
1 red pepper (if available), seeded and chopped
¼ cup freshly grated Parmesan cheese
Cherry tomatoes (optional)

For the marinade:
Juice of 1 lemon
¼ cup vinegar
1 clove garlic, minced or put through a press
1 teaspoon prepared Dijon-style mustard
½ teaspoon oregano
1 teaspoon chopped fresh basil or ½ teaspoon dried
¼ teaspoon dried tarragon
Salt, preferably sea salt, and freshly ground pepper to taste
¾ cup olive oil

Wash the beans and soak in the water overnight or at least for several hours.

(continued)

In a heavy-bottomed flameproof bean pot or Dutch oven, heat the olive oil and sauté the onion and garlic until the onion is tender. Add the beans, water, bay leaf, and salt. Bring to a boil, then cover, reduce the heat, and cook for 1 to 2 hours, until the beans are tender but still firm. Remove from the heat, drain, and remove the bay leaf.

In a 2- or 3-quart bowl, toss the cooked beans together with the parsley, green onions, herbs, green and red peppers, and the freshly grated Parmesan.

Combine the lemon juice, vinegar, garlic, mustard, and the seasonings, in a small bowl. Stir in the olive oil, then toss with the bean mixture and refrigerate for several hours. Before serving, garnish with fresh cherry tomatoes, if desired.

6 to 8 servings

Menu Suggestions

Soups: Tortilla (page 100), Almond (page 131), Tomato-Rice (page 122)

Salads: Avocado and Citrus (page 239), Spinach and Citrus (with oranges) (page 249), Beet and Endive (page 248), Tomatoes and Fresh Herbs (page 247)

Vegetable side dishes: Shredded Zucchini Sauté (page 233), Broccoli Moutarde (page 233), steamed green beans or asparagus, Sprout-Stuffed Artichokes (page 231)

Desserts: Strawberry and Cassis Sherbet (page 301), Oranges Grand Marnier (page 279), any dessert soufflé (see pages 288–91)

VEGETABLE PAELLA

There are few entrées that can match the dramatic impact of paella, a Spanish creation traditionally made with seafood, chicken, and sausages. This version is a bountiful array of vegetables, exquisitely seasoned. The rice is colored a rich yellow and subtly flavored by that aristocrat of spices, saffron. For an absolutely beautiful company dinner, cook and serve it in a wok or paella pan.

2 cups raw brown rice
6 cups Vegetable Stock (page 91) or water
2 onions, sliced thin

4 cloves garlic, minced or put through a press
3 green peppers, seeded and sliced thin
2 tomatoes, sliced
¼ cup olive oil
½ to 1 teaspoon salt, preferably sea salt, or to taste
1 teaspoon saffron threads
1 bay leaf
2 cups cooked garbanzo beans (¾ cup dried; see page 25)
1 package (10 ounces) frozen peas, thawed, or 2 cups fresh peas, briefly steamed until bright green
1 cup sliced black olives
8 pimientos, sliced
½ cup almonds, whole or cut in half
1 jar (6 ounces) artichoke hearts (optional)

Cook the rice in 3 cups of the stock or water until the stock is absorbed.

In a large, heavy-bottomed skillet, wok, or flameproof casserole, sauté the onions, garlic, peppers, and tomatoes in the olive oil until the onions are tender.

Stir in the rice, remaining stock or water, salt, saffron, bay leaf, and garbanzos. Cover and cook over low heat until the water is nearly absorbed, about 30 minutes. Add the peas, olives, and pimientos; do not stir. Continue cooking, uncovered, until all the water is absorbed.

Garnish with the almonds and/or artichoke hearts and serve.

6 to 8 servings

Menu Suggestions

Soups: Lentil (page 129), Blender Gazpacho (page 135), Fresh Pea (page 107)

Salads: Mixed Green (page 238), World of Sprouts (page 239), Spinach (page 238)

Desserts: Bavarian Crème au Café (page 286), Light Cheesecake (page 291), Oranges Grand Marnier (page 279)

FALLAFELS

Fallafels are the Middle Eastern equivalent of tacos or hamburgers. The actual *fallafels* are deep-fried or browned croquettes made from a seasoned *hommos*. These are stuffed into pita breads, the Middle Eastern round, flat breads with pouches in the middle. Along with the croquettes you can stuff the pitas with tomatoes, sprouts, green peppers—anything you wish. Both whole-wheat and white-flour pita breads are available in major supermarkets or natural foods stores.

The *hommos* and the sesame spread can be made up to two days in advance. But the stuffed pitas should not sit too long before you serve them, or they will get soggy. *Fallafels* are excellent fare for a buffet. Place the ingredients in pretty bowls and let people fill their own.

For the sesame spread:
   1 cup sesame tahini
   ¼ cup lemon juice
   2 cloves garlic, put through a press
      Salt, preferably sea salt, to taste
      Hot water, if necessary

For the fallafels:
   6 to 8 pita breads, preferably whole-wheat
   1 recipe Garbanzo Bean Croquettes (page 86)
   2 to 3 tomatoes, chopped
   1 cup alfalfa sprouts or chopped lettuce doused with ¼ cup Vinaigrette (page 261)
   1 cup diced cucumber
   ½ cup pitted, sliced ripe olives
   ¼ cup chopped fresh parsley or mint, or both (mint is great)
      Leaf lettuce

Prepare the spread first. Blend together the sesame tahini, lemon juice, garlic, and salt. (The mixture should be as spreadable as mayonnaise; if it's too stiff, thin out with hot water.)

Make a slit at one end of a pita bread and open it up. Spread the inside generously with the sesame spread, then fill halfway with the croquettes. Fill the rest of the pita with the tomato, sprouts or lettuce, cucumber, olives, and parsley or mint. Continue until you have filled all the pitas, then place on a platter lined with leaf lettuce and serve.

Or serve the ingredients separately, as a buffet (like Extraordinary Chalupas on page 147).

6 to 8 servings

Menu Suggestions

Soups: Curry of Eggplant (page 132) Egg-Lemon (page 111), Turkish Cucumber (page 139), Dill (page 117)
Salads: Tabouli (page 240), Cucumber (page 243), Spinach (page 238)
Desserts: Fresh fruit (see page 276) and cheese, Soufflé Grand Marnier (page 290), Pineapple Boats (page 281), Strawberry and Cassis Sherbet (page 301)

VEGETABLE SHISH KEBAB

Vegetable shish kebab is a gastronomic delight—and an utterly beautiful dish besides. Serve it over Saffron Brown Rice (page 227), or Indonesian Rice (page 227). Egg Rolls (page 80) make a good accompaniment, too.

For the marinade:
    2 cups tamari, more if necessary
    2 cups water, more if necessary
    3 tablespoons curry powder
    2 tablespoons freshly grated gingerroot or 1 tablespoon ground ginger
    3 bay leaves
    1 onion, sliced very thin
    4 cloves garlic, sliced or put through a press
      Salt, preferably sea salt, and freshly ground pepper

For the vegetables:
    1 pint cherry tomatoes
    4 green peppers, seeded and quartered or cut in eighths (if very large)
    4 onions, cut in eighths or quartered
    ½ to ¾ pound mushrooms, stems removed
    1 zucchini, sliced
    3 potatoes, unpeeled, cut in pieces and steamed until crisp-tender
    ½ fresh pineapple, peeled, cored, and chunked

For the sauce:
    1 cup marinade (see above)
    1 teaspoon freshly grated gingerroot or ½ teaspoon ground ginger
    1 teaspoon mild honey
    1 tablespoon dry sherry
    1 tablespoon arrowroot or cornstarch dissolved in a little marinade

Combine the ingredients for the marinade in a large bowl. Prepare the vegetables and marinate for several hours at room temperature. (If the marinade does not completely cover the vegetables, add tamari and water in equal proportions.)

Either prepare a fire in your grill or barbecue pit, preheat the oven to 400 degrees, or light the broiler.

Place the marinated vegetables on skewers, alternating them to make a colorful arrangement. Roast the kebabs over the open fire, under the broiler, or in the hot oven, basting with the leftover marinade (making sure you set aside 1 cup for the sauce); this should take about 30 minutes.

Meanwhile, prepare the sauce. Heat the marinade with the ginger, honey, and sherry. Stir in the dissolved arrowroot or cornstarch and bring to a boil to thicken.

Serve the kebabs over either of the rices suggested above, or over couscous, accompanied by the sauce

Note: Any leftover marinade may be frozen and reused.

6 to 8 servings

Menu Suggestions

Hors d'oeuvres: Egg Rolls (page 80), Won Tons with Spinach and Tofu Filling (page 204), Tempura'd Tofu with Dipping Sauces (page 84)

Soups: Fruit (page 99), Apple-Spice (page 136), Cabbage-Cheese (page 116)

Salads: Cucumber (page 243), Shredded Fruit and Vegetable (page 253), World of Sprouts (page 239)

Desserts: Bavarian Crème au Café (page 286), Soufflé Grand Marnier (page 290), Light Cheesecake (page 291)

STIR-FRY CHINESE TOFU AND VEGETABLES NO. 1

This is most definitely *not* the notorious ascetic rice and vegetables associated with the old vegetarianism ("R & V," we used to call them). The sauce is rich and satiny, and the flavors and aromas are subtle. You can use other vegetables, though for this particular version I like to use green and white ones.

After experimenting with techniques for this recipe, I'm most satisfied with steaming some vegetables and stir-frying others, and then mixing them together with the sauce at the last minute. I will give you a choice of methods here. It *is* easier to stir-fry everything in a wok, but then you have to keep adding oil, thereby sacrificing the delicacy of the vegetables. If you are using the second steam-and-fry technique, a tiered Chinese steamer will help to eliminate space and utensil problems.

This dish is cooked quickly just before serving, so organization is essential. Have all your vegetables cut and in separate bowls, and mix your sauce well in advance.

Serve over the grain of your choice; my favorites are millet, brown rice, and couscous.

For the sauce:
   5 tablespoons Vegetable Stock (page 91) or water
   4 tablespoons tamari
   2 tablespoons dry sherry
   1 to 2 teaspoons Pernod (anise-flavored liqueur) or anisette, or ½ teaspoon crushed aniseed plus 1 teaspoon mild honey
   2 teaspoons cider vinegar or wine vinegar
   ½ teaspoon freshly grated gingerroot or ¼ teaspoon ground ginger
   1 tablespoon arrowroot, more as necessary

For the vegetables:
   2 tablespoons safflower or peanut oil, more as necessary
   1 onion, sliced
   1 clove garlic, minced or put through a press
   ½ to 1 teaspoon freshly grated gingerroot or ¼ to ½ teaspoon ground ginger
   2 squares tofu, diced
   1 tablespoon sesame seeds
   3 tablespoons water, approximately (for Method 2 only)
   1 tablespoon tamari (for Method 2 only)
   ½ cup raw peanuts
   1 small can (4 ounces) water chestnuts, drained, then quartered or sliced
   ½ pound snow peas, strings removed
   ½ pound asparagus, sliced on the diagonal in 2-inch pieces, or 1 cup broccoli florets, or 1 zucchini, sliced on the diagonal in ¼-inch pieces
   ½ cup sliced fresh mushrooms
   1 cup diced *tender* turnips
   1 cup sliced yellow squash or cauliflower florets
     Handful of soybean or mung sprouts
   ½ cup raw cashews

For the dish:
   3 to 4 cups hot, cooked millet, brown rice, coriscons, or other grain of your choice (1½ cups raw; see page 25)
   1 tablespoon chopped fresh coriander (*cilantro*) (optional)

Before you start to cook the vegetables, by either method, have the sauce ready. Blend together the ingredients and stir well.

(*continued*)

202

Method 1: Stir-frying: Heat the oil in a wok or large frying pan and add the onions, garlic, and ginger. Stir-fry—that is, fry quickly, keeping the vegetables moving at all times with a paddle or wooden spoon—until the onion starts to become translucent. Add the tofu and sesame seeds and stir-fry for 5 minutes. Add the peanuts and each remaining vegetable one at a time, stir-frying each about 3 minutes, or until there is a definite color change (green vegetables should become bright green and white vegetables should start to become translucent). Add the cashews last.

Stir the sauce one more time and pour over the vegetable mixture; toss until the sauce thickens and glazes the vegetables. (If this doesn't happen within 3 minutes, dissolve another 2 teaspoons arrowroot in a little water and stir it into the mixture.)

Serve immediately over the hot, cooked grain, sprinkled with the chopped fresh coriander.

Method 2: Steaming and stir-frying: Heat the oil in the wok and stir-fry the onion and garlic with the ginger until the onion starts to become translucent. Add the tofu and the sesame seeds and stir-fry for a few minutes; then add about 3 tablespoons water and 1 tablespoon tamari. Cover and let simmer while you steam the remaining vegetables (except for the bean sprouts).

In a tiered bamboo or stainless-steel steamer, steam each vegetable just until crisp-tender and fragrant. The green vegetables should be bright green and beautiful, which should only take 5 minutes; the squash, turnips, and cauliflower should steam for about 10 minutes. When the vegetables are done, remove them from the heat and set aside.

Add the raw peanuts and cashews to the wok and cook, stirring, about 3 minutes. Now add the steamed vegetables and the raw bean sprouts; toss together. Give the sauce one last stir and add to the wok; stir until the sauce thickens and the vegetables are glazed, adding more arrowroot as in Method I, if necessary.

Serve immediately, sprinkled with fresh coriander over the hot, cooked grain.

6 to 8 servings

Menu Suggestions

Hors d'oeuvres: Egg Rolls (page 80), Won Tons with Spinach and Tofu Filling (page 204), Soya Pâté (page 58)

Soups: Cream of Raw and Cooked Mushroom (page 101), Egg Drop with

Bean Sprouts (page 94), Noodle-Bean (page 125), Thick Cabbage
(page 126), Cheese and Black Bread (page 106)
Salads: Cucumber (page 243), with Cucumber-Cream Dressing (page 261),
Marinated Lentil (page 252), Water Cress and Mushroom (page 247),
Mixed Bean (page 252)
Desserts: Any dessert soufflé (see pages 288–91), Bavarian Crème au Café
(page 286), Pumpkin Pie (page 273), any fruit pie (see pages 294–95)

STIR-FRY CHINESE TOFU AND VEGETABLES NO. 2

Here's a stir-fry with a much different character from the previous one.
The colors of the first stir-fry are shades of green and brown; this one, besides the brilliant green of the broccoli, has the oranges, reds, and yellows
of carrots, tomatoes, and yellow squash. The tomatoes and basil give it a
hint of sweetness.

 2 tablespoons peanut or safflower oil, more as necessary
 ½ teaspoon freshly grated gingerroot or ¼ teaspoon ground ginger
 1 clove garlic, minced or put through a press
 1 onion, sliced
 2 squares tofu, diced
 2 carrots, sliced diagonally
   Handful of sesame seeds
 1 rib celery, sliced diagonally
 ½ cup raw peanuts
 1 yellow squash or zucchini, sliced diagonally
 2 cups broccoli florets or 1 cup broccoli florets plus 1 cup cauliflower florets
   Salt, preferably sea salt, or vegetable salt to taste
 2 tomatoes, sliced
 ¼ teaspoon dried basil
 2 tablespoons tamari, more if necessary
 1 tablespoon arrowroot or 2 teaspoons cornstarch, more if necessary
 ¼ cup water
 2 tablespoons dry sherry (optional)
 3 to 4 cups hot, cooked millet, brown rice, couscous, or other grain of your
   choice (1½ cups raw; see page 25)

Heat a wok or heavy skillet; add 2 tablespoons oil, the ginger, and the
garlic. Starting with the onion and tofu, sauté one vegetable at a time, stirring constantly and cooking only until you notice a color change (about 2
minutes). Either push the vegetable to the side or remove completely
before adding the next. Add oil as needed.

(*continued*)

Cook the vegetables in this order: onions and tofu, (with the ginger and garlic); carrots and sesame seeds; celery and raw peanuts; squash; brocco (or broccoli and cauliflower). With the addition of each vegetable, sprinkl with a little salt or vegetable salt. The onions will become translucent; th carrots will become a more distinctive yellow in the center and the orang will darken. The squash will begin to look translucent and bright aroun the edges; the broccoli will also become bright green, and the cauliflowe if you use it, will begin to look translucent.

After all the vegetables except the tomatoes have been sautéed, retur them all to the pan with the tomatoes, basil, and the tamari. Cover an simmer together over very low heat for 10 to 15 minutes, allowing th flavors to mingle. Taste and add salt or tamari, if necessary.

Mix the arrowroot or cornstarch with the water and sherry and stir wel to dissolve. Pour over the vegetables and toss, over a low flame, until th sauce thickens and glazes the vegetables.

Serve immediately, over the hot, cooked grain.

6 to 8 serving

Menu Suggestions

Hors d'oeuvres: Egg Rolls (page 80), Won Tons with Spinach and Tofu Fil ing (page 204), Soya Pâté (page 58)

Soups: Noodle-Bean (page 125), Egg Drop with Bean Sprouts (page 94) Tamari-Noodle with Green Beans (page 124), Thick Cabbage (pag 126)

Salads: Spicy Tofu (page 243), Green Bean, Almond, and Mushroom (pag 245), Mixed Bean (page 252), Cole Slaw (page 256)

Desserts: Apricot Soufflé (page 289), Light Cheesecake (page 291), Caro Brownies (page 301), Indian Pudding (page 293)

WON TONS WITH SPINACH AND TOFU FILLING

These make a nice hors d'oeuvre for a crowd, as well as a delightfu main dish. The spinach can be washed and stemmed well in advance; onc that task is done, making the spinach filling is a quick process. You ca make the filling up to a day in advance and refrigerate it, covered, althougl it's best to make the won tons right after you finish the filling. If you wisl to put the won tons together and hold them for an hour, place them o waxed paper, or they will stick to the dish.

This filling is so delicious that you may want to eat it *without* the wo tons.

Oil (safflower, peanut, or vegetable), both for stir-frying and deep-frying
½ cup chopped green onion, both white part and green
1 large clove garlic, minced or put through a press
½ to 1 teaspoon freshly grated gingerroot
2 squares tofu, diced small
¼ cup sesame seeds
10 ounces fresh spinach, washed and stemmed, or 1 package (10 ounces) frozen
   spinach, thawed and excess moisture squeezed out
2 to 3 tablespoons tamari, or to taste
1 tablespoon water
2 teaspoons dry sherry
1 package won ton wrappers
1 egg, beaten

Heat 2 tablespoons safflower oil in a wok or large skillet with a lid and sauté the green onion with the garlic and fresh ginger for 3 minutes.

Add the diced tofu and the sesame seeds and stir-fry for 3 to 5 minutes over a medium-high flame, adding more oil if necessary. Add the spinach and continue to stir until it is completely coated with oil. Add the tamari, water, and sherry, then cover and cook over a medium flame for 5 minutes.

Remove the lid, turn up the flame, and cook over high heat until the liquid in the wok has evaporated; this should take only a minute or two. (If a large amount of liquid remains, remove the wok from the heat and pour some of it off.) Remove from the heat and correct the seasonings.

Now remove the entire mixture from the wok and chop fine, either by hand or with a food processor (with the processor, just a second or two of chopping will be sufficient). Place a level teaspoonful of the chopped mixture in the middle of each won ton skin. Fold the skin diagonally, to make a triangle (see illustration), then take the two ends of the triangle and join them together at the tips. Seal with a little beaten egg.

(continued)

Heat 1 quart of oil in a wok or deep-fryer to a temperature of 370 degrees. Carefully drop in the won tons; they should float up to the surface right away. Turn them or spoon the hot oil over the top to ensure even browning. As soon as they are golden brown, remove from the oil with a slotted spoon and drain on paper towels.

40 won tons

Menu Suggestions

Soups: Cream of Wheat Berry (page 109), Curry of Eggplant (page 132), Apple-Spice (page 136)
Salads: Avocado and Citrus (page 239), Potato-Egg with Chilled Broccoli (page 251), Garbanzo Bean (page 254)
Desserts: Indian Pudding (page 293), Light Cheesecake (page 291), Gingerbread Soufflé (page 289), Millet-Raisin Pudding (page 292)

VEGETABLE TEMPURA WITH TAHINI-TAMARI SAUCE, SERVED WITH BUCKWHEAT NOODLES

For this dish you will have to have your vegetables and batter prepared in advance, and you can prepare the tahini-tamari sauce up to one or two days beforehand. Keep the sauce well covered in the refrigerator, and reheat it gently before serving. The deep-frying is done just before serving, as are the noodles. If you have a good chafing dish, you can put a small dish of sauce at each place setting and let each guest tempura his own vegetables.

Buckwheat noodles have a delicious, nutty flavor, like kasha.

Use the recipe for Tempura'd Vegetables on page 81 and the recipe for Tahini-Tamari Sauce on page 83.

Combine the sauce ingredients and thin out with spoonfuls of hot water. Dip the tempura into this sauce and serve with ½ pound buckwheat noodles (*soba*), cooked *al dente* (about 4 minutes) in a pot of salted boiling water, along with a tablespoon of oil, and drained.

6 to 8 servings

Menu Suggestions

Soups: Lentil (page 129), Curry-Flavored Lentil (page 130), Cabbage-
Cheese (page 116), Puree of White Bean (page 97), Puree of Straw-
berry (page 140)
Salads: Mixed Green (page 238), Tomatoes and Fresh Herbs (page 247),
World of Sprouts (page 239), Mixed Bean (page 252)
Desserts: Fresh fruit (see page 276), Gingerbread Soufflé (page 289),
Light Cheesecake (page 291)

SWEET AND SOUR CABBAGE

This is one of the quickest, cheapest, and easiest dishes in this section.
It's simple, comforting, and utterly satisfying.

2 tablespoons safflower or peanut oil, more as needed
1 onion, sliced
2 carrots, sliced diagonally
½ cup raw peanuts
½ head cabbage, shredded or chopped
2 tomatoes, sliced
⅓ cup mild honey
⅓ cup wine vinegar or cider vinegar
½ teaspoon salt, preferably sea salt
1 tablespoon arrowroot or 2 teaspoons cornstarch

Heat the oil in a wok or large skillet. Add the onion and stir-fry for
3 minutes, until beginning to wilt. Push to one side or remove from the
pan and add the carrots and peanuts; stir-fry for 3 minutes.

Push the carrots to one side and add the cabbage. Stir-fry for 3 minutes,
then add the tomatoes and toss everything together. Cover, reduce the
heat, and simmer for 10 minutes, as you prepare the sweet and sour sauce.

Combine the honey, vinegar, and salt and blend well, then stir in the
arrowroot or cornstarch. Stir the sweet and sour sauce into the vegetables
and toss the mixture until the sauce thickens and glazes the vegetables.

Serve over hot, cooked brown rice or another grain of your choice (see
page 25).

6 to 8 servings

Menu Suggestions

Soups: Egg Drop with Bean Sprouts (page 94), Apple-Spice (page 136),
Meatless Mulligatawny (page 133)

(*continued*)

Salads: Spicy Tofu (page 243), Mixed Bean (page 252), World of Sprouts (page 239)

Desserts: Any dessert soufflé (see pages 288–91), or crêpes (see pages 283–86), Apple Pie (page 294)

CURRIED TOFU AND VEGETABLES OVER MILLET OR BULGUR

For several years I had been trying to develop a really fine curry. Finally I tasted a marvelous one at a friend's restaurant. The secret, she revealed, is to sauté the seasonings with the onions for a long time. This brings out their aromas without overcooking any of the vegetables.

I use creamy buttermilk to thicken the curry, so it's quite delicious but low in calories.

3 tablespoons butter
1 tablespoon peanut oil
1 teaspoon mustard seed
1 teaspoon cuminseed, crushed in a mortar
½ teaspoon ground coriander
½ teaspoon ground cloves
½ teaspoon chili powder
1 teaspoon turmeric
2 to 3 teaspoons curry powder
½ teaspoon salt, preferably sea salt, or to taste
1 onion, sliced
1 clove garlic, minced or put through a press
1 teaspoon freshly grated gingerroot or ½ teaspoon powdered ginger
1 cup diced tofu
½ cup raw peanuts
½ cup raw cashews or sliced almonds
½ cup raisins
1 green pepper, seeded and sliced
½ cup diagonally sliced or matchstick-cut carrots
1 cup cauliflower florets
1 cup broccoli florets
1 yellow squash, sliced
2 cups shredded red cabbage
½ cup green peas, steamed until bright green
½ cup Vegetable Stock (page 91)
1 cup buttermilk
1 tablespoon chopped fresh coriander (*cilantro*)
3 to 4 cups hot, cooked millet or bulgur (1½ cups raw; see page 25)

Heat the butter and oil over low heat in a heavy-bottomed Dutch oven, wok or large skillet with a lid. Sauté all the spices, from the mustard seed through the salt and starting with 2 teaspoons of curry powder, with the onion, garlic, and ginger for 15 minutes, stirring often. Add the tofu, peanuts, cashews, raisins, and green pepper and cook, stirring, for 5 minutes.

One at a time, and in the order listed, add the remaining vegetables except the peas and toss for 3 minutes, adding more butter or oil if they begin to stick. Keep the heat low.

After you add the cabbage, pour in the ½ cup stock. Cover and simmer for 10 minutes, until the vegetables are cooked through but still have some body. Add the peas and stir together.

Remove from the heat and let cool for a minute, then stir in the buttermilk and coriander. Adjust the seasoning—you may want to add a little curry powder or salt—and serve immediately, over the hot, cooked millet or bulgur and accompanied by the side dishes listed below.

6 to 8 servings

Menu Suggestions

Soups: Vichyssoise (page 120), Puree of White Bean (page 97), Apple-Spice (page 136)

Salads: Shredded Fruit and Vegetable (page 255), Grated Carrot (page 253)

Side dishes: Chutney (page 235), Banana Raita (page 235), Cucumber Raita (page 235), Lentil Dahl (page 229)

Desserts: Bavarian Crème au Café (page 286), Gingerbread Soufflé (page 289), Strawberry and Cassis Sherbet (page 301), Indian Pudding (page 293)

CURRY SALAD

I love it when we make this in my cooking class, or I make it for a catering job, because I get to eat leftovers for as long as they last (usually not too long). It's one of my favorites, and is included in this section because it's such a good main dish in itself, especially on a warm evening. At first the combination of ingredients might sound strange to you, but you'll see that they make a remarkable dish with a fresh, health-giving quality. The combination of the grains, soy grits, and garbanzo beans, with the Parmesan and yogurt in the dressing, makes this a good example of a "complementary" protein dish.

(continued)

Remember to cook the beans and grains in advance, and give the sala·
a little time to marinate.

1 recipe Curry Dressing (page 262)
1 recipe Mary's Basic Salad Dressing (page 260) or Vinaigrette (page 261)
1½ to 2 cups broccoli florets, steamed briefly until bright green
¼ cup whole almonds
1½ to 2¼ cups cooked brown rice (¾ to 1 cup raw; see page 25)
1 to 1½ cups cooked wheat berries (½ cup raw; see page 25)
⅓ cup soy grits, cooked with the wheat berries or with the brown rice (add ·
  cup more water)
1¼ cups cooked garbanzo beans (½ cup dried; see page 25)
1 teaspoon salt, preferably sea salt
½ cup freshly grated Parmesan or Romano cheese
2 ribs celery, chopped
1 cucumber, peeled (if bitter or waxed) and sliced
4 green onions, both white part and green, chopped
¼ cup raisins
¼ cup sunflower seeds
¼ cup peanuts, lightly roasted
¼ cup cut green beans, steamed briefly until bright green
1 green pepper, seeded and chopped
1 head leaf lettuce, separated into leaves and washed
  Halved cherry tomatoes for garnish

Prepare the curry dressing by combining the mayonnaise and yogurt and
stirring in the seasonings; have the other salad dressing prepared and
ready.

Set aside some of the broccoli and almonds for garnish. Toss the re·
mainder together with all the other salad ingredients (except for the lettuce
and cherry tomatoes) and the dressings, first with Mary's or the vinaigrette
and then with the curry.

Line a salad bowl with the lettuce leaves and mound the salad on top.
Decorate with the reserved broccoli florets and almonds and cherry toma·
toes.

Serve immediately or else chilled.

6 to 8 servings

Menu Suggestions

Hors d'oeuvres: Sesame Eggplant Rounds with Hommos (page 86), Vege·
  table Platter with Assorted Dips (page 77)
Soups: Bulgarian Cucumber (page 138), Turkish Cucumber (page 139),
  Puree of Strawberry (page 140)

Salads: Watermelon-Fruit Extravaganza (page 280), Shredded Fruit and Vegetable (page 255)

Desserts: Strawberry and Cassis Sherbet (page 301), Peaches Marsala (page 282)

FRUIT CURRY

Since fruit is such an excellent companion to curries, why not make it the main item? This scrumptious dish is sweet and crunchy. The fruit caramelizes while the curry matures, and it smells divine as it cooks.

3 tablespoons peanut oil or butter
1 tablespoon curry powder
1 teaspoon freshly grated gingerroot or ½ teaspoon ground ginger
2 bananas, sliced
2 apples, sliced
2 peaches, peeled and sliced
2 pears, sliced
¼ pound seedless grapes
¼ cup raw cashews, halved lengthwise
¼ cup brazil nuts, coarsely chopped
¼ cup almonds, halved lengthwise
½ cup raisins or currants
1 tablespoon mild honey
½ to 1 cup orange juice

Heat the oil or butter over a medium flame in a wok or large skillet and sauté the curry powder and ginger for about 2 minutes. Add the fruit, one kind at a time, tossing gently each time to coat with oil; add the nuts and raisins. Continue tossing until the fruit begins to bubble, then add the honey and pour in the orange juice. Reduce the heat, cover, and simmer for 20 to 30 minutes, stirring occasionally to prevent sticking.

Serve with Saffron Brown Rice (page 227) or couscous and Chutney (page 235).

6 to 8 servings

Menu Suggestions
Soups: Lentil (page 129), or Curry-Flavored Lentil (page 130)
Salads: Cucumber (page 243), Shredded Fruit and Vegetable (page 255)
Desserts: Bavarian Crème au Café (page 286), Baklava (page 296), Light Cheesecake (page 291)

THE ALL-TIME SOYBEAN GROUND BEEF SUBSTITUTE

This is a great-tasting, protein-rich filler that I use for Soyburgers (page 213), Soybean Spaghetti Sauce (page 215), Chili (page 214), and Lasagne (page 187)—and other dishes that usually call for ground beef. I really dislike the idea of vegetarian "substitutes" for meat, but in practical terms that's what this recipe is. However, it bears *no* resemblance to the "texturized soy protein" now marketed in natural foods stores.

Be forewarned on two counts:

1. The first step in this recipe, the cooked ground soybeans, is not at all appetizing; you soak soybeans overnight, then grind them and cook them to get a very bland product, which you then cook again with seasonings. It's a necessary prerequisite for the second step, the savory ground soybeans, which taste marvelous and will make your kitchen smell terrific.

2. This recipe takes a few hours to make. Since it freezes well, I suggest that you set aside a block of time and make a big batch. Freeze it in small containers and thaw it out as you need it.

STEP 1: COOKED GROUND SOYBEANS

1½ cups dried soybeans
4½ cups water
 1 teaspoon salt, preferably sea salt
 1 small onion

Soak the soybeans overnight in the water, salted. In the morning grind the beans, a cup at a time, in a blender with the onion, adding enough water to cover; you can use the soaking water. (You can also use a food mill, with less satisfactory results.) The ground soybeans will resemble creamed corn.

Place the ground soybeans in a saucepan or Dutch oven that is at least twice their volume. (This is important: the soybeans are full of air and will bubble up dramatically, and if your pot isn't big enough, they will boil over.) If you have not used up all the soaking water in the grinding, add up to 2 cups to the pot. Over medium heat, bring the mixture to a boil *slowly* (so the soybeans don't burn and stick to the pan); add a little salt, reduce the heat, and cover. Simmer until the liquid is absorbed, about 1½ hours. (The soybeans may stick to the pan despite your precautions, but they'll come off easily with some soaking.)

At this point you can store the soybeans, covered, in the refrigerator, or seal them in glass or plastic containers and freeze.

Or you can go on to the next step.

6 cups

STEP 2: SAVORY GROUND SOYBEANS

1 onion, minced
3 tablespoons safflower or vegetable oil
1 clove garlic, minced or put through a press
2 tablespoons powdered vegetable broth or 3 vegetable bouillon cubes
1 cup tomato juice or pureed tomato (2 tomatoes)
1 tablespoon Worcestershire sauce
1 to 2 tablespoons soy sauce
½ teaspoon vegetable salt (optional)
3 cups Cooked Ground Soybeans (see page 212)

In a wok or large heavy-bottomed skillet, sauté the onion in the oil with the garlic until tender. Add broth or bouillon cubes (mashing the bouillon cubes with the back of a spoon to dissolve), tomato juice, and seasonings and cook for a few minutes. Add the cooked ground soybeans and stir until well blended, then cook, uncovered, over a medium flame until almost dry, about 40 minutes. Stir from time to time to prevent sticking.

This will keep for three to five days in the refrigerator and freezes very successfully.

3 cups

SOYBURGERS

3 eggs
3 cups Savory Ground Soybeans (see above)
½ cup minced green pepper
½ cup grated carrot
½ cup sprouts (mung, lentil, or sunflower), chopped
1½ cups fresh whole-wheat bread crumbs or toasted wheat germ, or a combination
½ cup sesame seeds
Safflower oil for frying

Beat the eggs in a large bowl and stir in the soybeans, green pepper, grated carrot, sprouts, and 1 cup of the bread crumbs or wheat germ. (This mixture can be made several hours ahead of time and stored in the refrigerator in a covered container. Don't freeze it, though; the vegetables will lose their crunch if you do.) Shape into patties and set aside.

Mix the remaining bread crumbs or wheat germ with the sesame seeds on a plate. Dip the soyburgers in this mixture and fry in oil in a skillet until browned, about 5 minutes on each side. (You may have trouble keeping the soyburgers together; just be patient and use your spatula to press them down and to lift them—carefully—into and out of the frying pan. Don't try to do this over a grill.)

These can also be broiled in a baking dish. Turn when browned on one side, about 10 to 15 minutes.

Serve on whole-wheat bread or buns

8 to 10 burgers, depending on size

Suggested Menus

Almost any soup, salad, and dessert make good accompaniments; see the following sample menus:

Cheese Fondue (page 84), with raw vegetables as dippers
Soyburgers (see above)
Gingered Broccoli (page 231)
Mixed Green Salad (page 238)
Pineapple Boats (page 281)

Tempura'd Vegetables with Assorted Dips (page 81)
Potato-Tomato Soup (page 115)
Soyburgers (see above)
Tomatoes and Fresh Herbs (page 247)
Spiced Fruit- and Nut-Filled Crêpes (page 284)

CHILI

I vow to enter the Texas Chili Cook-off with this recipe someday. Some of the staunchest chili lovers I know have encouraged me.

8 tomatoes
2 tablespoons safflower or vegetable oil
2 onions, chopped
3 cloves garlic, minced or put through a press
1 green pepper, seeded and chopped
3 cups Savory Ground Soybeans (page 213)
1 to 2 jalapeño peppers, chopped fine
1 can (15 ounces) tomato sauce
1 tablespoon chili powder, or to taste
1 tablespoon ground cumin
2 tablespoons chopped fresh coriander (*cilantro*) (optional)
   Salt, preferably sea salt, to taste
1 cup cooked pinto or kidney beans (optional)

Chop half the tomatoes and puree the rest; combine and set aside.
In a large saucepan, heat the oil and sauté the onion, garlic, and green

pepper. When the onion is tender, add the soybeans, tomatoes, jalapeños, tomato sauce, and spices. Cover and simmer for 1 hour, stirring occasionally. Correct the seasoning and add the cooked beans, if desired, shortly before serving.

Serve with Corn Bread (page 53) or corn tortillas.

6 to 8 servings

Menu Suggestions

Salads: Mixed Green (page 238), Spinach and Citrus (page 249), Guacamole (page 242), Crudité (page 73)

Side dishes: Steamed green vegetables, Beets Moutarde (page 233), Yorkshire Puddings with Cornmeal (page 229)

Desserts: Pineapple with Kirsch (page 282), Peaches Marsala (page 282), Light Cheesecake (page 291)

SOYBEAN SPAGHETTI SAUCE

This sauce can be made a day or two in advance. It freezes well.

8 tomatoes
1 carrot
2 tablespoons safflower or vegetable oil
2 onions, chopped
4 cloves garlic, minced or put through a press
1 green pepper, seeded and chopped (optional)
2 cups Savory Ground Soybeans (page 213)
1 can (12 ounces) tomato paste
   Salt, preferably sea salt, and freshly ground pepper to taste
1 teaspoon oregano
1 tablespoon chopped fresh basil or 1 teaspoon dried
1 zucchini, sliced (optional)
   Dash of ground cinnamon
   Canned or bottled tomato sauce (optional)
2 to 4 teaspoons mild honey (optional)

Chop half the tomatoes and puree the rest; either puree the carrot with the tomatoes or slice it thin.

In a large saucepan or Dutch oven, heat the oil and sauté the onion, garlic, and green pepper until the onion is tender. Add the soybeans, the tomatoes (both pureed and chopped), the carrot, and the tomato paste. Bring to a simmer, then cover and cook gently for 1 hour. Add salt, pepper, the oregano, and basil and simmer, uncovered, for another 30 minutes to an hour, stirring occasionally.

(continued)

216

Add the zucchini about 30 minutes before the end of the cooking tim and the cinnamon about 10 minutes before. (The cinnamon brings out th sweet garlic and tomato flavors.) Correct the seasoning.

If the sauce is not tomato-y enough, add some canned or bottled toma sauce and cook, uncovered, until it reaches the desired thickness. (Som times Italian tomato sauce can taste bitter. If yours does, add 2 to 4 te spoons honey.)

Serve over whole-grain or semolina spaghetti, cooked as directed c page 26.

8 cu

Menu Suggestions

Hors d'oeuvres: Sliced oranges, Mushroom Pâté (page 59), French Brea (page 45) and Herb Butter (page 61)
Soups: Stracciatella (page 95), Thick Cabbage (page 126), Leek (page 11
Salads: Mixed Green (page 238), Spinach (page 238), Water Cress an Mushroom (page 247)
Desserts: Italian Fruit Compote (page 278), Pears Poached in Red Wir with a Touch of Cassis (page 277), Light Cheesecake (page 291), Bava ian Crème au Café (page 286)

FRUITED BAKED BEANS WITH CHUTNEY

Here's another sweet and pungent dish, this time with the warming, fa miliar taste of Boston baked beans and the exotic touch of chutney. You ca use soybeans instead, but the traditional navy beans are my favorite.

2 cups dried navy beans, washed
1 quart water
1½ teaspoons salt, preferably sea salt, or to taste
1½ teaspoons dry mustard
1 onion, chopped fine
½ cup Chutney (page 235), minced
Freshly ground pepper
2 apples, sliced
3 peaches (in season), peeled and sliced
½ cup dried apricots
¼ to ½ cup mild honey, or to taste
¼ cup molasses
½ cup plain yogurt, homemade (see page 259) or commercial

Soak the beans in the water overnight, or for at least several hours. Cook in the soaking liquid with 1 teaspoon salt for about 1 hour, until tender but not mushy. Drain, reserving 1 cup of the liquid.

In a small bowl, dissolve the mustard in the bean liquid and combine with the finely chopped onion, the chutney, and salt and pepper to taste. Stir this into the beans.

Preheat the oven to 325 degrees; oil a 2-quart casserole or baking dish.

Pour half of the bean mixture into the prepared casserole. Top with a layer of sliced apples, peaches, and apricots, then pour in the rest of the bean mixture and top with the rest of the fruit. Combine the honey and molasses and pour evenly over the top.

Cover and bake for 1 hour, then remove the cover and bake for another 30 minutes. About 5 minutes before removing from the oven, pour on the yogurt.

Serve steaming hot, with Corn Bread (page 53) or brown rice.

6 to 8 servings

Menu Suggestions

Soups: Corn Chowder (page 267), Fruit (page 99), Cream of Wheat Berry (page 109)

Salads: Mixed Green (page 238), Avocado and Citrus (page 239), Salade Mimosa (page 248), Brown Rice (page 245)

Desserts: Fresh fruit (see page 276) and cheese, Light Cheesecake (page 291), Peaches Marsala (page 282), Pecan Pie (page 295)

POTATOES GRUYÈRE

This is a rich, satisfying dish that goes well with a tomato-y soup and a crisp, green salad.

    1 cup plain yogurt, homemade (see page 259) or commercial
    6 ounces Gruyère or other Swiss cheese, grated
    1 onion, chopped
    2 tablespoons chopped fresh chives or green onion tops
    5 large potatoes, unpeeled and sliced thin
    ½ teaspoon salt, preferably sea salt, or to taste
      Freshly ground pepper
    ½ cup whole-wheat bread crumbs or toasted wheat germ
    2 tablespoons butter

Preheat the oven to 350 degrees; butter a 2-quart baking dish or casserole.

(continued)

Combine the yogurt, cheese, onion, and chives.

Place a layer of half the potatoes on the bottom of the prepared baking dish. Salt and pepper them generously, then cover with half the yogurt mixture.

Repeat with another potato layer and the remaining yogurt mixture.

Top with the bread crumbs or wheat germ, dot with the butter, and cover with a buttered lid. Bake at 350° for 1½ hours.

6 to 8 servings

Menu Suggestions

Hors d'oeuvres: Tempura'd Vegetables with Assorted Dips (page 81), Little Spanokopitas (page 71), Crudité Salad (page 73)
Soups: Blender Gazpacho (page 135), A Rich Tomato (page 104), Egg Drop with Bean Sprouts (page 94), Miso-Vegetable (page 127)
Salads: Mixed Green (page 238), Beet and Endive (page 248), Fig and Mint (page 248), Shredded Fruit and Vegetable (page 255)
Desserts: Carob Marble Cake (page 300), Peaches Marsala (page 282), Raspberries in Red Wine (page 282)

POTATO PANCAKES

These crisp, tasty potato pancakes consist mainly of grated potatoes held together with egg and a small amount of bread crumbs. They're not doughy like batter pancakes, but more like thin sheets of hashed brown potatoes. They're wonderful with yogurt and applesauce and a full-bodied salad.

  5 large potatoes, peeled
 ⅓ cup finely chopped onion
  1 teaspoon salt, preferably sea salt
  3 large eggs, beaten
 ¼ cup whole-wheat bread crumbs or matzo meal
    Freshly ground pepper to taste
    Safflower oil and butter for frying

Grate the potatoes and press out excess water. Measure 3½ cups grated potatoes into a mixing bowl. Stir in the onion, salt, eggs, and bread crumbs; add freshly ground pepper to taste.

In a large, heavy-bottomed skillet, heat equal amounts of safflower or vegetable oil and butter; there should be about ¼ inch melted butter and oil. Drop the pancake batter by heaping spoonfuls into the pan and flatten with the back of the spoon. Fry for a few minutes on each side, until crisp and golden. Drain on paper towels and serve immediately, or keep the pancakes warm in the oven.

6 to 8 servings

Serve topped with plain yogurt, homemade (see page 259) or commercial, and Homemade Applesauce (page 258).

Menu Suggestions

Soups: Cream of Raw and Cooked Mushroom (page 101), A Rich Tomato (page 104), Fresh Pea (page 107), Rose Hips (page 141)

Salads: World of Sprouts (page 239), Mixed Green (page 238), Green Bean, Almond, and Mushroom (page 245), Cole Slaw (page 256)

Desserts: Pears Poached in Red Wine with a Touch of Cassis (page 277), Dried Fruit Compote (page 279), Pineapple with Kirsch (page 282)

COUSCOUS WITH VEGETABLES

Of all the grains, I find couscous the most delicate and tasty. They're precooked hard-cracked granules of semolina wheat, which you can cook quickly by a soak-and-steam method. You can also use a *couscousière*, which is a steamer made specifically for couscous. I've been quite satisfied with the first method, in which the only special equipment one needs is a colander.

Sometimes the little grains of couscous tend to stick together (which is why it is steamed instead of boiled). If after cooking they become sticky or gummy, just separate the grains with forks or with your hands.

One can go through an elaborate series of steps to make couscous. The best and most complete treatment of couscous cookery is to be found in Paula Wolfert's *Couscous and Other Good Food from Morocco.* [1] The simple method I am giving you here comes right off the back of the package, and it works well for me.

(continued)

[1] New York: Harper & Row, 1973.

⅔ cup dried garbanzo beans
5 cups water
Salt, preferably sea salt
½ onion, chopped
1½ carrots, sliced
2 cloves garlic, minced or put through a press
1 teaspoon dried thyme
1 bay leaf
½ teaspoon dried rosemary
1½ cups raw couscous
1 onion, sliced
2 tablespoons safflower oil
½ teaspoon ground cinnamon
¼ teaspoon freshly grated nutmeg
½ cup pignolia (pine nuts), raw cashews, almonds, or sunflower seeds
1 zucchini, sliced
1 yellow squash, sliced
1 cup fresh or frozen green peas
Freshly ground pepper to taste

Wash the garbanzos and soak in 2 cups of the water for several hours.

Place the garbanzos and their soaking water in a saucepan and bring to a boil. Add 1 teaspoon salt, the chopped onion, one-third of the sliced carrots, one clove of the garlic, the thyme, bay leaf, and rosemary. Cover, reduce the heat, and cook for 1 hour, or until the garbanzos are tender.

Place a colander or strainer over a bowl and drain the beans; reserve the liquid. Set both aside.

Place the couscous in a bowl and pour the remaining 3 cups water, salted, over it. Let sit for 10 to 15 minutes, until the water is absorbed. The couscous will now be soft; fluff it with a fork or with your hands.

In a saucepan that will fit beneath a colander (or in the bottom of a *couscousière*), sautè the sliced onion and the other clove of garlic in the oil with the cinnamon and nutmeg until the onion is tender. Add the nuts, the remaining vegetables, including the remaining sliced carrots, and the garbanzos and toss together. Now pour in enough of the liquid from the beans to cover by ½ to 1 inch.

Place the couscous in a colander, sieve, or the top part of a *couscousière* and set it over the vegetable mixture, making sure that the bottom of the colander does not touch the liquid (remove some of the liquid if it does). Wrap a towel or cheesecloth around the space between the sides of the colander and the pot so that the steam will come up only through the colander. Now cover the couscous with a towel or with the lid of the pot, and bring the liquid to a simmer.

When you see the steam coming through, count 10 minutes. Remove the couscous from the pot and place in a large bowl. Pour the vegetable-stock mixture over the couscous and toss with forks. Adjust the seasoning and serve at once.

Note: Other vegetables, such as eggplant, green beans, broccoli, and cauliflower, may be used.

6 to 8 servings

Menu Suggestions

Hors d'oeuvres: Sesame Eggplant Rounds with Hommos (page 58), Soya Pâté (page 58), Mushroom Pâté (page 59)
Soups: Curry of Eggplant (page 132), Dill (page 117), Fruit (page 99), Thick Cabbage (page 126)
Salads: Mixed Green (page 238), Shredded Fruit and Vegetable (page 255), Beet and Endive (page 248), Spinach (page 238)
Desserts: Any of the fruit pies on pages 294–95, Oranges Grand Marnier (page 279), Pumpkin Pie (page 273)

COUSCOUS WITH FRUIT

Couscous is superb with fruit; it makes an excellent breakfast as well. Leftovers can be heated through in a double boiler and served with yogurt.

1½ cups raw couscous
4 cups water
   Salt, preferably sea salt
2 tablespoons butter
1 teaspoon ground cinnamon
¾ teaspoon freshly grated nutmeg
¾ teaspoon ground allspice
2 apples, peeled (if waxed), cored, and chopped
¾ cup slivered almonds or pignolia (pine nuts)
½ cup chopped dried apricots
½ cup currants
1 pear, cored and chopped
1 cup apple juice

Pour 3 cups of the water, salted, over the couscous in a bowl and let sit for 10 minutes, until the water is absorbed and the couscous is fluffy.

Melt the butter in a saucepan that will fit under a colander (or use the bottom of a *couscousière*), and sprinkle in the cinnamon, ½ teaspoon nutmeg, and ½ teaspoon allspice. Add the apples, nuts, dried apricots, and currants and sauté for 5 minutes. Stir in the pear, the remaining 1 cup water, and the apple juice. (If the fruit is not covered with liquid, add a little more water or apple juice.)

Place the couscous in a colander or in the top part of a *couscousière* above the fruits in their liquid. Seal off the space between the colander and the pot with a towel or with cheesecloth. Cover and bring the liquid to a boil. Let steam for 10 minutes, then remove the couscous from the pot and place in a large bowl. Toss with the fruit and nuts in their liquid and adjust the seasoning. Sprinkle the top with the remaining allspice and nutmeg and serve at once.

6 to 8 servings

Menu Suggestions

Hors d'oeuvres: Hommos (page 57) and Mixed Grains Bread (page 38), Garbanzo Bean Croquettes (page 86), Tempura'd Tofu with Assorted Dips (page 81)
Soups: Curry of Eggplant (page 132), Cheese and Black Bread (page 106), Puree of Strawberry (page 140)
Salads: World of Sprouts (page 239), Cucumber (page 243), Avocado and Citrus (page 239)
Desserts: Any dessert soufflé (see pages 288–91), Baklava (page 296)

CURRY STUFFED PEPPERS

Here is an unusual curry filling for peppers. It's a nice break from the traditional cheese or brown rice stuffing. I prefer nice light millet for this dish, but any grains (including leftover ones) will do.

You can make the filling and stuff the peppers a day in advance.

6 to 8 green peppers
3 tablespoons peanut or safflower oil
1 onion, chopped
1 clove garlic, minced or put through a press
2 teaspoons curry powder, more to taste
½ cup sliced fresh mushrooms
1 carrot, cut in matchsticks 1½ inches long
1 cup mixed sliced almonds and raw cashews
1½ cups raw millet, cooked (see page 25) with ¼ teaspoon saffron

½ cup raisins (optional)
1 to 1½ cups cooked lentils (½ cup dried; see page 25)
1 cup fresh or frozen green peas, steamed until bright green
½ teaspoon salt, preferably sea salt, or to taste
1 cup Curry Dressing (page 262), plain yogurt, or buttermilk

Preheat the oven to 350 degrees.

Blanch the peppers for 5 minutes in boiling water. Rinse in cold water, then cut off the tops and remove the seeds and white membranes. Drain upside down while you prepare the filling.

Heat the oil in a wok or large skillet and sauté the onion with the garlic and curry powder for 10 minutes. Add the mushrooms and cook for another 5 minutes; add the carrots and nuts and cook for 5 minutes longer, stirring. Add more oil, if necessary, then add the millet, raisins, lentils, peas, and salt. Toss everything together for a few minutes and correct the seasoning.

Fill each pepper with this mixture. Set them in a baking dish, place in the preheated oven, and bake for 30 minutes.

Pour over the curry dressing, yogurt, or buttermilk and serve.

6 to 8 servings

Menu Suggestions

Hors d'oeuvres: Fresh fruit (see page 276), French Bread (page 45) and Soya Pâté (page 58), Potted Roquefort Spread (page 63)

Soups: Curry of Eggplant (page 132), Dill (page 117), Turkish Cucumber (page 139), Apple-Spice (page 136)

Salads: Mixed Green (page 238), Cucumber (page 243), World of Sprouts (page 239)

Desserts: Bananas Poached in White Wine (page 277), Baked Apples (page 283), Watermelon-Fruit Extravaganza (page 280)

STUFFED ZUCCHINI

This is a crunchy dish with a creamy sauce—especially good for those huge zucchinis that grow in your garden and appear in produce markets in summer and fall. Though the soybeans are not essential, I recommend that you include them; they provide complementary protein and blend well with the other ingredients besides.

You'll have to remember to cook the grains and soybeans beforehand, and you can make the tahini-tamari sauce in advance and store it, covered, in the refrigerator.

(continued)

1 huge or 2 medium zucchini, cut in half lengthwise
1 onion, chopped
1 clove garlic, minced or put through a press
2 tablespoons safflower oil, more as necessary
1 cup diced tofu
2 carrots, sliced diagonally or cut in matchsticks
¾ cup raw peanuts
    Vegetable salt to taste
2 ribs celery, sliced diagonally
⅔ to ¾ cup cooked soybeans or ¾ cup cooked soy flakes (⅓ cup raw; see page 25) (optional)
3 cups cooked bulgur or millet (1 cup raw; see page 25)
1 tablespoon tamari, or to taste
1 cup warm Tahini-Tamari Sauce (page 83)

Preheat the oven to 325 degrees.

Steam the zucchini for 5 minutes, then scoop out the seeds and stringy part of the pulp.

Sauté the onion and garlic in the oil, with the tofu, until the onion is tender. Add the carrots and peanuts, sprinkle with a little vegetable salt, and stir-fry for 3 minutes. Add the celery and stir-fry for 3 minutes more, then add the soybeans or soy flakes. Add a little more oil and stir in the cooked bulgur or millet and the tamari. Toss with the vegetables and heat through, adding more tamari if desired.

Stuff the zucchini with the mixture, then place in an oiled baking dish and bake in the preheated oven for 30 minutes.

Remove from the oven, pour on the warm tahini-tamari sauce, and serve.

6 to 8 servings

Menu Suggestions

Hors d'oeuvres: Fresh fruit (see page 276), Won Tons with Spinach and Tofu Filling (page 204), Egg Rolls (page 80)

Soups: A Rich Tomato (page 104), Miso-Vegetable (page 127), Puree of White Bean (page 97)

Salads: Mixed Green (page 238), World of Sprouts (page 239), Spinach (page 238), Water Cress and Mushroom (page 247)

Desserts: Fresh fruit (see page 276), Apricot Soufflé (page 289), Spiced Fruit- and Nut-Filled Crêpes (page 284)

SOME GRAIN, LEGUME, AND VEGETABLE SIDE DISHES

A curry is quite wonderful on its own, but with chutney and *raita* on the side it becomes truly outstanding. Grains will enhance a delicate Chinese vegetable dish and soak up its sublime, gingery sauce.

There are several criteria for choosing a side dish. Some give body to a main course and boost the protein. Grains, for example, complete the amino acid patterns of legumes, turning a curry or *feijoada* into a substantial meal. And grains and legumes can be dressed up: brown rice cooked with saffron takes on a beautiful yellow hue; add sherry-soaked currants, crunchy almonds and pungent chutney, and you have exciting Indonesian Rice (page 227). Lentils, refried and seasoned with cumin and curry, are transformed into mouthwatering Lentil Dahl (page 229), a perfect complement to Curried Tofu and Vegetables (page 208)

Very often the need for color will determine the choice of a side dish. Though beautiful in themselves, soufflés and dishes like Fruited Baked Beans with Chutney on page 216 and Kasha Pie on page 156 each display only one color, so your plate calls for another; perhaps the green of Broccoli Moutarde (page 233), or asparagus or artichokes. Or you might prefer the juicy red of Tomatoes and Fresh Herbs (page 247). Similarly, a main dish in which there is one predominating flavor or texture will go well with a "busy" side dish, like Chinese-Style Snow Peas and Water Chestnuts (page 230), Sprout-Stuffed Artichokes (page 231), or Indonesian Rice (page 227).

Sometimes the "main attraction" of your meal is in the spirit of a particular country. In this case, you'll most likely want to serve a side dish that conveys the same atmosphere. Whenever Black Bean Enchiladas (page 144) are requested for a catering job, so is Spanish Rice (page 226). Vegeta-

225

ble Shish Kebab (page 199) goes well with Saffron Brown Rice (page 227) or with couscous. Corn Bread (page 53)—or Yorkshire Puddings with Cornmeal (page 229)—accompanies my Chili (page 214).

When I go to a restaurant, I am as critical of the vegetables that are served on the side as I am of the entrée. If the vegetables are overcooked or drowned in butter, the restaurant gets a lower rating. I prefer my vegetables steamed just until they display their maximum bright color; this way they'll have a lively texture. If you boil them, they will lose not only their firmness but also many of their nutrients. Sometimes I like them braised in a little butter or enriched with a light sauce.

I hope these recipes will set your imagination going. You can try different vegetables with the same sauces and techniques, and experiment with new grains and legumes. There are enough recipes for side dishes to fill a book, but I've restrained myself here and limited this chapter to my favorites.

SPANISH RICE

This is a good accompaniment for any Mexican dish. You might have trouble with the rice sticking to the pan; watch it carefully and add water or stock as necessary. You can make this dish a day in advance and reheat it in the oven or over a low flame.

2 to 3 tablespoons olive or safflower oil, more as necessary
1 onion, sliced
3 cloves garlic, minced or put through a press
2 green peppers, seeded and sliced thin
1½ cups raw brown rice
2 cups peeled, chopped tomatoes
1 teaspoon salt, preferably sea salt
2 cups water or Vegetable Stock (page 91), more as necessary

In a wok, 10-inch frying pan, Dutch oven, or large saucepan, sauté the onion and one clove of the garlic in the safflower or olive oil until the onion begins to wilt. Add the green peppers and continue to sauté another 5 minutes. Add a little more oil and the rice and sauté, stirring, until the rice begins to smell toasty. Add the tomatoes, the remaining garlic, salt, and water and bring to a simmer. Cover and cook for 30 minutes, or until the water or stock is absorbed and the rice is tender, adding more water or stock as needed (if the rice sticks to the bottom of the pan it will burn).

Should some rice stick to the bottom of the pot, do *not* stir it up into the rest of the rice.

6 to 8 servings

SAFFRON BROWN RICE

Any time you want to dress up brown rice, saffron is the miracle seasoning. This rice goes well with curries and the Vegetable Shish Kebab on page 199.

1½ cups raw brown rice
 3 cups water
 1 teaspoon saffron threads
 ½ teaspoon salt, preferably sea salt
 2 tablespoons lemon juice
 ½ cup currants (optional)

Prepare the rice according to the directions on page 25, adding the saffron, salt, lemon juice, and currants when the water begins to boil.

6 to 8 servings

INDONESIAN RICE

A bright, colorful dish, excellent with curries, tempuras, shish kebabs, and stir-fries.

⅓ cup currants
   Dry sherry to cover
 1 small onion, diced
 2 cloves garlic, minced or put through a press
 ½ teaspoon freshly grated gingerroot or ¼ teaspoon ground ginger
 1 tablespoon safflower or peanut oil, more if necessary
 ⅓ cup slivered almonds
 ½ cup Chutney (page 235)
 1 recipe Saffron Brown Rice (see above), omitting the currants
 ½ teaspoon salt, preferably sea salt, or to taste

Soak the currants in the sherry for 30 minutes. In a wok or skillet, sauté the onion, garlic, and ginger in the oil until the onion is tender. Drain the currants and add, along with the almonds and chutney. Cook for a few minutes, then stir in the rice, adding more oil if necessary. Toss all the ingredients together over a medium flame for 5 minutes, then correct the seasoning and serve.

6 to 8 servings

WHOLE-GRAIN PASTA WITH BUTTER AND HERBS

Whole-grain pasta is now readily available in natural foods stores and food co-ops. There are several combinations—whole-wheat, soya, soy–whole-wheat, whole-wheat–sesame, on and on. Good egg noodles made with semolina flour are just as good and are available in Italian markets and import stores.

½ pound whole-grain pasta of your choice
1 tablespoon olive oil
4 tablespoons (½ stick) butter
¼ cup chopped fresh parsley
¼ cup freshly grated Parmesan cheese

Cook the pasta *al dente*, adding the tablespoon of olive oil to the water to prevent it from sticking together. Drain and turn into a warmed serving dish; immediately sliver the butter onto it and toss with the parsley and Parmesan.

6 to 8 servings

SOBA
Buckwheat Noodles

This has a wonderful nutty flavor.

½ pound buckwheat noodles
3 tablespoons sesame oil
1 tablespoon tamari (optional)

Cook the buckwheat noodles *al dente*, adding 1 tablespoon of the sesame oil to the cooking water. Drain and toss with the remaining sesame oil and the tamari.

6 to 8 servings

LENTIL DAHL

A *dahl* is an Indian mashed leguminous dish, an Indian "refried beans." You can make it with split peas or garbanzo beans, but lentils, with their distinctive flavor, have always been a favorite of mine. This is always successful at catered events; it's a good side dish for curries. The lentils will complement grains.

1 onion, chopped
1 clove garlic, minced or put through a press
½ teaspoon chili powder
½ teaspoon turmeric
½ teaspoon cuminseed
2 teaspoons curry powder
5 to 6 tablespoons safflower or peanut oil
1 cup dried lentils, washed
½ to 1 teaspoon salt, preferably sea salt, or more as desired
1 bay leaf
3 cups water, more if necessary
½ teaspoon ground cumin

Sauté the onion, garlic, ¼ teaspoon of the chili powder, the turmeric, cuminseed, and 1 teaspoon curry powder in 2 tablespoons of the oil. When the onion is tender, add the lentils, bay leaf, and water and bring to a boil. Add the salt, reduce the heat, and simmer until the lentils are tender and the water is absorbed, about 1 hour. (If the mixture becomes dry before the lentils are tender, add a little water.)

Heat the remaining 3 to 4 tablespoons oil in a skillet and add the ground cumin, remaining chili powder, and the remaining teaspoon curry powder. Fry the lentils in the same way that you refry beans (see page 148), mashing with a potato masher or the back of a spoon. (The mixture should be like a moist, textured puree and should hold its shape in a spoon; don't allow it to become too dry.) Turn into a warmed serving dish and serve with curries.

6 to 8 servings

YORKSHIRE PUDDINGS WITH CORNMEAL

A perfect, impressive complement for any bean dish, these puff up like soufflés and have the texture of a pudding. Serve them right away, as they fall quickly and are at their best pulled right from the oven.

(continued)

½ cup yellow cornmeal, preferably stone-ground
1 teaspoon salt, preferably sea salt
½ teaspoon dried marjoram
2 cups milk
4 eggs, beaten
Butter

In a bowl, stir together the cornmeal, salt, marjoram, and ½ cup of the milk.

Heat the remaining milk in the top of a double boiler or in a heavy-bottomed saucepan over low heat until just below the boiling point. Stir in the cornmeal mixture; stir until smooth.

Cover and cook the mixture over boiling water until all the liquid has been absorbed (this should not take very long; you will have a thick sputtering paste). Remove from the heat and cool to lukewarm; if pressed for time, you can cool it in the freezer.

When the mixture is lukewarm, beat in the eggs.

Preheat the oven to 350 degrees.

Place ¼ teaspoon butter in each well of your muffin tins or custard cups, or the equivalent amount in a 1½-quart baking pan, and place in the preheated oven until the butter is bubbly.

Turn the cornmeal mixture into the heated pans, filling the cups or the pan only half full. Bake for 10 minutes, then remove from the oven and dot again with butter, another ¼ teaspoon for each cup. Bake for 15 to 20 minutes longer, until puffed and beginning to brown.

Serve immediately; the puddings will fall very quickly, so make sure your guests see them when they are still puffed up and grand.

6 to 8 servings

CHINESE-STYLE SNOW PEAS AND WATER CHESTNUTS

5 tablespoons water
4 tablespoons tamari
1 tablespoon dry sherry
1 teaspoon Pernod (anise-flavored liqueur)
1 teaspoon freshly grated gingerroot or ½ teaspoon ground ginger
1 tablespoon arrowroot, more if necessary
1 pound snow peas, stringed
4 green onions, both white part and green, chopped

1 clove garlic, minced or put through a press
Safflower or peanut oil
1 small can (4 ounces) water chestnuts, drained, then sliced or quartered

In a small bowl, combine the water, tamari, sherry, Pernod, ginger, and arrowroot; set aside.

Steam the snow peas briefly, just until they are bright green. In a large skillet or wok, sauté the green onions with the garlic in a little oil until tender. Add the snow peas and water chestnuts and stir together. Add the sauce and stir until the vegetables are glazed, adding more arrowroot dissolved in a little water, if necessary.

Correct the seasoning and serve.

6 to 8 servings

GINGERED BROCCOLI

You can, of course, use other vegetables here. Whenever your menu calls for a crisp green side dish, this Oriental glazed broccoli will fit in beautifully.

1 teaspoon freshly grated gingerroot or ½ teaspoon ground ginger
2 tablespoons peanut or safflower oil
1 bunch broccoli, broken into florets (large ones cut in half lengthwise)
2 tablespoons mild honey
2 tablespoons soy sauce
¼ cup water
1 tablespoon arrowroot or 2 teaspoons cornstarch, dissolved in a little water

In a wok or skillet, sauté the ginger in the oil for 1 minute. Add the broccoli and cook, stirring, for 5 minutes.

Dilute the honey in the soy sauce and water. Pour over the broccoli, then cover and cook over a low flame for 10 minutes. Add the arrowroot or cornstarch dissolved in water and stir until the broccoli is glazed.

Serve immediately.

6 to 8 servings

SPROUT-STUFFED ARTICHOKES

I developed this dish in the spring, when my herbs were abundant and when I was discovering the magic of sprouts. Each kind of sprout has its

232

distinctive flavor—some mild, some peppery, some with a distinctive leguminous flavor like raw peas. They hold sauces and seasonings well, and can be the focal point of a meal. Artichokes also stand alone as an excellent hors d'oeuvre, first course, or side dish.

Sprout-stuffed artichokes are light and high in protein. They can be served as an hors d'oeuvre, as a main dish on a hot day or for a luncheon, or as a side dish. The artichoke leaves serve as scoopers for the sprout mixture, with the added treat of the flesh of the leaf. The dish can be assembled several hours before you wish to serve it.

 2 to 3 artichokes
    Juice of ½ lemon
 1 cup alfalfa sprouts
 1 cup mung bean sprouts
 1 cup lentil sprouts
 ½ cup sunflower seed sprouts
 4 green onions, both white part and green, chopped
 1 avocado, peeled, seeded, and diced
 ½ green pepper, seeded and diced
 ½ cup sunflower seeds
 ½ cup diced tofu
 ½ to 1 cup mixed, chopped fresh herbs (parsley, thyme, rosemary, tarragon, dill, basil)
 1 recipe creamy salad dressing of your choice (see pages 260–64)
    Lemon slices for garnish

Cut the stems off the artichokes and remove the tough bottom leaves; clip off the spiny tops of the other leaves. Plunge into water containing the juice of half a lemon (this helps prevent discoloration), then place in a large saucepan in 1 inch of freshly drawn tap water, or on a rack above it. Bring to a boil, then reduce the heat, cover, and steam for 45 minutes, or until the leaves pull away easily. Remove from the heat and run under cool water. Gently pull the middle leaves apart, exposing the choke. Take a spoon and carefully scoop out the choke and discard it.

Combine the sprouts, green onions, avocado, green pepper, sunflower seeds, tofu, and herbs and toss with the dressing of your choice. Now either fill the artichokes, placing a little sprout mixture between each leaf and filling the well above the heart; or, if the artichoke falls apart, arrange the leaves on a platter and place some sprout mixture on each leaf. Put the hearts in the center of the platter and mound the remaining sprout mixture on them.

Garnish with lemon slices and serve.

2 to 3 servings

BROCCOLI MOUTARDE

The mustardy flavor of this sauce will open up a new world of taste possibilities for you. Experiment with other vegetables; broccoli and the beets that follow are only suggestions.

1 bunch broccoli, trimmed and cut into florets
1½ teaspoons Dijon-style prepared mustard
½ cup light cream or half-and-half
    Salt, preferably sea salt, and freshly ground pepper to taste

Steam the broccoli until bright green. Mix the mustard and cream in a medium saucepan and simmer very gently for 1 minute. Add salt and pepper to taste, and the broccoli. Toss to coat evenly with the sauce, then cover and simmer gently for another 10 to 15 minutes.

Serve immediately.

6 to 8 servings

BEETS MOUTARDE

1 bunch (1 pound) beets
1½ teaspoons Dijon-style prepared mustard
½ cup light cream or half-and-half
    Salt, preferably sea salt, and freshly ground pepper to taste

Bake the beets at 350 degrees, skins on, for 45 minutes to an hour. Remove from the heat and peel off and discard the skins: cut the beets into matchsticks. Proceed as in Broccoli Moutarde (see above).

6 to 8 servings

MINTED FRESH PEAS

3 to 4 pounds unshelled tender, fresh green peas (3 to 4 cups shelled)
½ teaspoon salt, preferably sea salt
    Freshly ground pepper
1 to 2 tablespoons chopped fresh mint
1 to 2 tablespoons butter (optional)

Shell the peas and steam them until bright green and tender, about 15 minutes. Add salt and pepper, then toss with the mint. (Or, if you prefer, simmer in butter for 5 to 10 minutes and toss with the mint.)

Serve immediately.

6 to 8 servings

234

SHREDDED ZUCCHINI SAUTÉ

    2 pounds zucchini
      Salt, preferably sea salt
    ½ onion, minced
    1 clove garlic, minced or put through a press
    2 tablespoons safflower or olive oil
    1 green pepper, seeded and minced
    1 tablespoon tamari
    2 tablespoons freshly grated Parmesan cheese
      Freshly ground pepper to taste (optional)

Grate the zucchini and sprinkle generously with salt; let sit for 20 min utes. Squeeze out the moisture by twisting the grated zucchini in a towe Rinse and squeeze out the moisture again.

In a skillet or wok, sauté the onion and garlic in the oil until the onio is tender. Add the green pepper and sauté for 5 minutes, stirring or shak ing the pan. Add the zucchini and continue to stir-fry or shake the pa until it is tender and aromatic, about 5 to 10 minutes. Add the tamari an Parmesan and, if you wish, salt and pepper to taste.

6 to 8 servings

BAKED ACORN SQUASH

    3 acorn squash
    ¼ cup melted butter
    ⅓ cup mild honey
      Salt, preferably sea salt, to taste
      Ground cinnamon to taste

Preheat the oven to 375 degrees.

Cut the acorn squash in half with a sharp knife and remove the seeds Baste the cut side of each half with melted butter and honey and sprinkl on some salt and cinnamon.

Place in an oiled baking dish and bake for 1 to 1½ hours, basting ever 15 minutes with butter and a little honey. Remove from the oven when toothpick can pierce through to the skin easily.

Serve immediately.

6 servings

BANANA RAITA

A *raita* (from India) is a cooling, yogurt-based accompaniment to curries. Leftover banana *raita* is almost dessertlike, and a pleasure to have on hand.

  1 teaspoon butter
1½ teaspoons cuminseed
 ¼ teaspoon cardamom seeds
 ¼ teaspoon ground coriander
 ⅛ teaspoon cayenne pepper
  2 cups mashed ripe banana (about 3 medium bananas)
  2 cups plain yogurt, homemade (see page 259) or commercial

Melt the butter in a skillet. Pound the spices together in a mortar; they should not be completely crushed. Add them to the butter and stir for a few minutes, then quickly add the mashed banana.

Remove from the heat and stir in the yogurt. Transfer to a serving dish and chill well.

Serve with curry dishes.

6 to 8 servings

CUCUMBER RAITA

Leftover cucumber *raita* can be served as a salad.

  1 cucumber, peeled and minced
  1 cup plain yogurt, homemade (see page 259) or commercial
 ½ teaspoon salt
 ¼ teaspoon ground coriander
 ¼ teaspoon ground cumin

Combine all the ingredients; stir together and chill well.
Serve with curries.

6 to 8 servings

CHUTNEY

Make up a large batch of chutney once a year and you'll always have a welcome accompaniment to curries and other dishes. We usually see expensive jars of chutney on gourmet shelves; you'll be pleased when you see how easy it is to make your own. Your kitchen will be redolent with the fabulous smells as it simmers.

(continued)

2 cups cider vinegar
1½ cups mild honey
½ cup molasses
2 cloves garlic, minced or put through a press
1 tablespoon salt, preferably sea salt
1 tablespoon freshly grated gingerroot or 1½ teaspoons ground ginger
½ teaspoon freshly ground pepper
1 teaspoon ground cinnamon
2 tablespoons mustard seed
1 teaspoon ground cloves
1 teaspoon ground coriander
4 medium tomatoes, peeled and diced
1 onion, chopped fine
4 apples, peeled and diced
3 pears, peeled and diced
1 cup raisins
1 cup chopped dried figs

Combine the vinegar, honey, molasses, garlic, salt, ginger, and remaining spices and cook over a medium flame, stirring constantly, for 10 minutes.

Add the tomatoes and the remaining ingredients and bring to a boil. Cover and reduce the heat; simmer for 2 hours, until you have a chutney with a thick consistency. Adjust the seasoning.

If you are storing the chutney, seal it in hot, sterilized, airtight jars and store in a cool, dark place. Refrigerate the amount you wish to use in an airtight container.

Serve with curries.

4 quarts

SALADS

A salad alone can make a delightful meal, especially with all the imaginative variations in the recipes that follow. It can consist of both cooked ingredients and raw ones, fruits as well as vegetables, cheeses, eggs, nuts, grains, and legumes.

The variety of textures and flavors in your salad will depend on how exotic or varied the rest of your meal is. To accompany rich meals, choose simple salads, using the tenderest lettuce you can find. Reserve the more complicated salads to go along with soups and main dishes that are lighter in nature.

The salad is a good place to "sneak" protein into a meatless meal, in the form of roasted soybeans, perhaps, or tofu, sprouts, eggs, or cheese. Serve a rice salad ring around a lentil, garbanzo bean, or mixed-bean salad for a perfect complementary meal. This principle also applies to dressings: if you think the meal you are serving needs a protein boost, use a yogurt- or tofu-based dressing.

Make sure you wash your lettuce and other greens well. There is nothing worse than a gritty salad, especially when you've chosen beautiful, tender lettuce. You can wash lettuce well a day or two in advance if you drain it well, seal it in plastic bags, and refrigerate it. Make sure, too, that your lettuce is completely dry before you add it to the salad bowl.

If you like sprouts, try to keep some on hand at all times. They keep well and are always a welcome, nutritious addition to a salad. (See the instructions for sprouting on pages 26–27.)

These recipes feed six to eight people.

MIXED GREEN SALAD

A beautiful, lively contrast in textures and flavors.

¾ pound mixed lettuce (leaf lettuce, red tip, romaine, Boston), leaves separated
1 cucumber, scored with a fork or peeled (if very waxy or bitter), then sliced
1 green pepper, seeded and sliced in lengthwise strips
4 green onions, both white part and green, sliced
4 radishes, sliced
4 to 5 fresh mushrooms, sliced
3 ripe tomatoes, cut in wedges, or 8 to 10 cherry tomatoes
½ to 1 cup sprouts (alfalfa, mung bean, lentil), plus additional for garnish
2 tablespoons sunflower seeds or Roasted Soybeans (page 87), plus additional
   for garnish

Optional:
 ½ cup Marinated Broccoli Stems (page 76)
 2 hard-boiled eggs, sliced or diced
 ¼ cup grated or diced cheese
 ½ to 1 cup leftover grains or beans
   Chopped fresh herbs
   Pitted, sliced ripe olives

   Salad dressing of your choice (see pages 260–64)

Wash and dry the lettuce and prepare the other vegetables. Tear the lettuce in fairly large pieces and combine with the other ingredients, including any or all of the optional ones, in a large salad bowl. Toss just before serving with the dressing of your choice, scattering more sprouts, herbs, and roasted soybeans or sunflower seeds over the top for garnish.

6 to 8 servings

SPINACH SALAD

This salad traditionally includes crumbled bacon. Here the soybeans have the salty, crispy quality of bacon and work just as well.

½ to ¾ pound fresh spinach
6 large fresh mushrooms, sliced
3 to 4 green onions, sliced
¼ cup Roasted Soybeans (page 87)

Optional:
 ½ cup cooked garbanzo beans
 ½ cup cooked brown rice

3 tomatoes, cut in wedges
½ cup sprouts (alfalfa, mung bean, lentil)
  Sesame seeds
  Hard-boiled egg slices
  Salad dressing of your choice

Wash the spinach well and remove the stems; pat the leaves dry. Toss with the mushrooms, green onions, soybeans, and any other ingredients you wish to add, then with the dressing of your choice. I like Mary's Basic Salad Dressing (page 260) or Vinaigrette (page 261), or Tahini Dressing (page 264). Tofu Mayonnaise (page 260) and Green Dressing (page 262) are also very good.

6 to 8 servings

AVOCADO AND CITRUS SALAD

3 avocados
  Juice of 1 lemon
2 grapefruits or oranges (or one of each), peeled and white membranes removed, then sectioned
1 bunch water cress or leaf lettuce, leaves separated, then washed and drained
2 tablespoons minced green onion, both white part and green
1 recipe Poppy Seed Dressing (page 262)

Cut the avocados in half and remove the seeds; peel and slice according to the directions on page 19, then toss the slices with the lemon juice to avoid discoloration.

Arrange the avocado and citrus slices on a bed of water cress or leaf lettuce on a serving dish and sprinkle the minced green onion on top. Pour on the dressing and serve immediately.

6 to 8 servings

WORLD OF SPROUTS SALAD

This salad, one of my favorite meals, is a real treat. It's full of various textures and flavors and is very hearty.

Use the sprout mixture as described in the recipe for Sprout-Stuffed Artichokes (page 231) and toss with the dressing of your choice (see pages 260–64; I think creamy dressings are especially good). Line a salad bowl with lettuce leaves and fill with the already tossed sprouts mixture. Garnish with sliced tomatoes and serve.

6 to 8 servings

TABOULI

Tabouli is a splendid Middle Eastern salad combining bulgur and fresh herbs in a vinaigrette-like dressing. Fresh mint is essential here. This version uses garbanzo beans (or chick-peas), which boosts the protein.

3 cups boiling water, approximately
1½ cups raw bulgur
1 to 1½ cups cooked garbanzo beans (½ cup dried; see page 25)
½ to ¾ cup chopped fresh parsley
1 teaspoon chopped fresh dill
½ cup chopped fresh mint
1 cup minced green onion, both white part and green
½ cucumber, peeled (if bitter or waxy) and diced (optional)
4 tomatoes, diced
¼ cup lemon juice
¼ cup wine vinegar or cider vinegar
  Salt, preferably sea salt, and freshly ground pepper to taste
1 teaspoon Dijon-style prepared mustard
1 to 2 cloves garlic, crushed
1 cup olive oil
1 head romaine lettuce, leaves separated, then washed and drained
  Halved cherry tomatoes and cucumber slices for garnish

Pour enough boiling water over the bulgur to cover by 1 inch. Let stand for about 30 minutes, or until the bulgur is light and fluffy. When the bulgur is ready, drain off excess water by shaking it in a colander or sieve and then squeezing it with your hands.

Combine the bulgur with the garbanzos, parsley, dill, mint, green onion, diced cucumber, and tomatoes.

Combine the lemon juice, vinegar, salt, pepper, mustard, garlic, and olive oil. Pour over the salad; toss well and chill until ready to serve.

Line a bowl with the outer leaves of the romaine lettuce. Place the *tabouli* on top of the leaves, garnish with cherry tomatoes and sliced cucumbers, and serve, using the smaller inner lettuce leaves as dippers if you wish.

6 to 8 servings

SALAD NIÇOISE

There are many ways to present this dish. You can serve it as an hors d'oeuvre, with the vegetables arranged on a platter so that they can be handled easily with toothpicks or fingers. Or you can use a large bowl and toss everything together. If you want the salad to retain its composition in the bowl, toss each ingredient with the vinaigrette separately, then compose the salad bowl. Or put it all together in a beautiful salad bowl and toss it at the table.

The ingredients you use in the salad will depend on personal taste and what is in season. Most recipes call for anchovies, many for tuna. But the name *niçoise* does not dictate the use of these foods, and we will leave them out of our vegetarian version. I like to add a hard-boiled egg yolk to the vinaigrette; it makes a creamier dressing and adds protein to the overall content of the meal.

3 to 4 medium potatoes
¼ to ½ cup dry white wine
    Salt and freshly ground black pepper
1 tablespoon minced green onion, both white part and green
1 teaspoon chopped fresh parsley
1 recipe Vinaigrette (page 261), with a hard-boiled egg yolk mashed into it, if
    desired
1 head Boston or red tip lettuce, leaves separated, then washed and drained
½ pound fresh string beans, trimmed, steamed briefly, and then chilled
4 ripe tomatoes, sliced in wedges, or ½ pint cherry tomatoes, halved
1 cucumber, scored with a fork or peeled (if very waxy or bitter), then sliced
½ to ⅔ cup pitted black olives
½ cup alfalfa sprouts

Optional:
¼ cup whole almonds
1 green pepper, seeded and sliced crosswise
1 yellow squash, sliced
2 to 3 hard-boiled eggs, peeled and then halved or quartered
2 ribs celery, sliced

Wash the potatoes, leaving on the peel, and steam about 20 minutes, until tender to the fork. Remove from the heat and slice immediately into a bowl. Pour on the white wine and leave to cool for about 10 minutes, then toss gently with the salt and pepper, green onion, parsley, and ¼ cup of the vinaigrette. Cover and chill.

(continued)

For a platter: Toss all the components individually with the dressing. Line the platter with the lettuce leaves. In the center, place the string beans, garnished with almonds if you wish. Around the string beans make a circle of potatoes, interspersed with tomato wedges or cherry tomatoes. Circle the potatoes with cucumber and yellow squash, alternating colors and scattering olives here and there. Surround this with clumps of sprouts and the remaining olives and tomatoes. Rounds of green pepper can be placed on top of the arrangement, and the egg segments placed here and there.

In a bowl: You can design a similar arrangement in a large bowl. Either toss each ingredient separately before making the arrangement or toss the entire salad at the table (making sure everyone gets to see it beforehand).

6 to 8 servings

TENDER LETTUCE AND ORANGE SALAD

This delicate salad is perfect with a rich meal; the oranges are especially refreshing. It's also nice as a starting salad.

1 head Boston lettuce or tender red tip lettuce
2 oranges, peeled and white membranes removed, then cut in sections
1 to 2 tablespoons chopped fresh fennel or tarragon
2 tablespoons chopped fresh chives
1 recipe Mary's Basic Salad Dressing (page 260), Vinaigrette (page 261), or Orange Juice Dressing (page 263)

Wash and dry the lettuce and tear into large pieces, then toss together with the oranges, herbs, and chives. Toss with the dressing just before serving.

6 to 8 servings

GUACAMOLE

A popular Mexican salad of mashed avocados and tomatoes, this also serves as an hors d'oeuvre.

2 to 3 avocados, halved and peeled
1 clove garlic, minced or put through a press (optional)
1 large tomato, peeled and seeded
¼ cup finely minced onion
Juice of ½ lemon or lime, or to taste

Salt, preferably sea salt, to taste
Ground cumin and chili powder to taste
1 to 2 tablespoons mayonnaise (optional; see note below)
Chopped fresh chives or coriander (*cilantro*) for garnish

Place the avocado flesh in a bowl and mash with a fork or potato masher. If you are using the garlic, mash it along with the avocado. Mash until smooth, but allow the avocado to retain some of its texture. Chop the tomato and mash it in with the avocados, then add the onion, lemon juice, and salt, cumin, and chili powder to taste.

Note: If you are not serving the guacamole right away, place the seed in the middle and cover the guacamole with a thin film of mayonnaise; this will keep it from turning a brownish-olive color. When you wish to serve it, either scoop off the mayonnaise or stir it in, and remove the seed.

Garnish with chopped chives or coriander and serve.

6 to 8 servings

CUCUMBER SALAD

3 cucumbers, scored with a fork or peeled (if very waxy or bitter), then sliced very thin
4 green onions, both white part and green, sliced
2 to 4 tablespoons chopped fresh dill
2 tablespoons fresh mint (omit if you're using the mint dressing)
1 cup Mary's Basic Salad Dressing (page 260), Vinaigrette (page 261), Mint Dressing (page 264), or Cucumber Cream Dressing (page 261)

Toss together the cucumbers, green onions, dill, and optional mint with the dressing and refrigerate an hour or so before serving.

6 to 8 servings

SPICY TOFU SALAD

Tofu, walnuts, tomatoes, crunchy and succulent cucumbers, and green peppers combined with juicy oranges and bananas in a spicy sauce make this chilled salad one of the most refreshing I've ever eaten. An adaptation of an Indian chicken salad (with tofu replacing the chicken), it's seasoned with many of the raw ingredients of a curry. But if you don't like fresh coriander (*cilantro*) or hot chilies, this one isn't for you.

The composition is perfect—there's just enough fruit to temper the heat of the chili and spices, like a *raita* or chutney alongside a hot curry. This *picante* salad is good as a first course; serve a *raita* on the side, if you wish.

For the dressing:
    1 large tomato, peeled
    ¼ cup fresh coriander (*cilantro*) leaves
    ¼ cup fresh mint leaves
    1 small hot chili, fresh or canned
    1 clove garlic
    ½ teaspoon freshly grated ginger root or ¼ teaspoon ground ginger
    2 green onions, both white part and green, roughly sliced
    ¼ cup lemon juice
    ½ cup plain yogurt, homemade (see page 259) or commercial
    ½ teaspoon whole coriander seed
    Salt, preferably sea salt, and freshly ground pepper to taste

For the salad:
    3 cups diced tofu
    Safflower oil as needed
    1 clove garlic, minced or put through a press
    2 tablespoons tamari
    3 tablespoons water
    1 cucumber, peeled and diced
    1 large tomato, peeled and chopped
    1 small green pepper, seeded and diced
    ½ cup sliced fresh mushrooms (optional)
    3 green onions, both white part and green, chopped
    1 orange, peeled and white membrane removed, then sectioned
    1 banana, sliced and tossed with 1 tablespoon lemon juice
    ½ cup broken walnuts, plus 2 tablespoons for garnish

For the garnish:
    Leaf lettuce
    ½ cup alfalfa sprouts
    Fresh coriander (*cilantro*) leaves

Using a blender or food processor, puree the tomato with the fresh coriander, mint, chili, garlic, ginger, green onions, lemon juice, yogurt, coriander seeds, salt, and pepper. Adjust the seasoning to your taste and refrigerate the dressing while preparing the remaining ingredients.

In a skillet or frying pan, sauté the tofu in oil with the minced garlic for 5 minutes. Add the tamari and water and continue to cook, stirring occasionally, until the liquid evaporates. Remove from the heat, then toss the tofu gently with the cucumber, tomato, green pepper, mushrooms, green onions, orange sections, banana slices, and the ½ cup walnuts. Now pour on the salad dressing and toss again, gently. Refrigerate for 2 hours before serving.

To serve, place a piece of leaf lettuce on each plate and spoon the salad over; or line a salad bowl with lettuce leaves and fill with the tofu mixture. Garnish with sprouts, coriander leaves, and the additional walnuts.

6 to 8 servings

GREEN BEAN, ALMOND, AND MUSHROOM SALAD

This elegant salad combines three foods with distinctive textures: crisp, fresh green beans; porous, subtle mushrooms; and crunchy almonds. The contrast—of saturated and unsaturated fresh, crisp vegetables—is luscious.

  1 pound green beans, trimmed and cut into 2-inch lengths
  1 cup Mary's Basic Salad Dressing (page 260) or Vinaigrette (page 261)
  ½ pound fresh mushrooms
  ½ cup slivered almonds
  3 to 4 green onions, both white part and green, minced, or 2 tablespoons minced fresh chives (optional)
  1 to 2 tablespoons minced fresh parsley or marjoram
  ½ cup alfalfa sprouts (optional)

Steam the beans until bright green and crisp-tender and rinse under cold water to stop the cooking. Toss with the salad dressing and refrigerate for an hour or two.

Just before serving, toss the mushrooms, almonds, green onion, and parsley with the beans. Top with sprouts, if you wish, and serve.

6 to 8 servings

BROWN RICE SALAD

This is one of my most popular salads; the combination of rice, vegetables, and nuts is pure ambrosia. It keeps well, refrigerated, for a few days and can be presented in a bowl or, more elaborately, molded in the shape of a ring and filled with another salad.

(continued)

1 cup raw brown rice

2 cups water

½ teaspoon salt

Pinch of saffron (optional)

Juice of ½ lemon

3 tablespoons olive oil

1 green pepper, seeded and diced

1 red pepper (if available), seeded and diced

4 radishes, sliced

½ cucumber, peeled (if waxed or bitter) and diced

½ cup pignolia (pine nuts), sunflower seeds, or chopped walnuts

¼ cup Roasted Soybeans (page 87)

1 rib celery, minced

½ cup chopped fresh parsley

¼ cup other chopped fresh herbs (tarragon, marjoram, basil, thyme, fennel), if available

½ cup freshly grated Parmesan cheese

5 green onions, both white part and green, chopped

1 head leaf or romaine lettuce, leaves separated, then washed and drained

1 recipe Mary's Basic Salad Dressing (page 260) or Vinaigrette (page 261)

For the garnish:

½ cup sprouts (alfalfa, sunflower, mung, lentil)

Tomato wedges or halved cherry tomatoes

Hard-boiled egg slices

Sliced or whole pitted ripe olives

Chopped green onions

Chopped fresh herbs

Cook the rice with the water and salt as directed on page 25, adding the saffron, lemon juice, and olive oil when you reduce the heat before covering. Allow the rice to cool and combine with the remaining salad ingredients except the lettuce, dressing, and garnishes. Toss with the salad dressing; correct the seasoning.

In a bowl: Line a bowl with lettuce leaves. Place the rice salad over the leaves in a mound. Top with sprouts and garnish with tomato wedges or cherry tomatoes and sliced hard-boiled eggs, black olives, green onions, and fresh herbs.

Molded in a ring: Pack the rice salad into a well-oiled ring mold and chill for several hours. Line a platter with lettuce leaves. Dip the mold into warm water for a few minutes, then unmold onto the platter. For a protein-complementary meal, place another leguminous salad—such as Marinated

Lentil Salad (page 252), Garbanzo Bean Salad (page 254) or Mixed Bean Salad (page 252)—in the middle. Or fill the center with tomato wedges or cherry tomatoes, sprouts, herbs, and sliced hard-boiled eggs.

6 to 8 servings

TOMATOES AND FRESH HERBS

1 recipe Mary's Basic Salad Dressing (page 260) or Vinaigrette (page 261)
3 to 4 ripe, red tomatoes, peeled and sliced thin
3 green onions, both white part and green, sliced
¼ cup chopped fresh basil
2 tablespoons chopped fresh parsley
1 tablespoon chopped fresh tarragon or 1½ teaspoons dried
2 tablespoons freshly grated Parmesan cheese (optional)
1 cup alfalfa sprouts

Set aside ¼ cup of the salad dressing. Toss the tomatoes, green onions, and herbs in the remaining salad dressing. Place in a bowl or on separate plates and sprinkle with Parmesan if you wish.

Toss the alfalfa sprouts in the remaining dressing and sprinkle over the tomatoes. Serve immediately or chill and serve.

6 to 8 servings

WATER CRESS AND MUSHROOM SALAD

Juice of ½ lemon
½ teaspoon dry mustard or 1 teaspoon prepared Dijon-style mustard
1 small clove garlic, minced or put through a press
¼ teaspoon dried tarragon
Salt, preferably sea salt, and freshly ground pepper
½ cup olive oil
1 to 2 bunches fresh water cress
½ pound fresh mushrooms, sliced

Combine the lemon juice, mustard, garlic, tarragon, and salt and pepper; stir in the olive oil. Toss with the water cress and mushrooms just before serving

6 to 8 servings

SALADE MIMOSA

1 to 2 hard-boiled eggs, peeled
Salt, preferably sea salt, and freshly ground pepper to taste
1 tablespoon chopped fresh dill
1 tablespoon fresh marjoram or basil, chopped
1 tablespoon chopped fresh parsley, plus additional for garnish
Other fresh herbs of your choice
3 green onions, both white part and green, sliced
1 head Boston lettuce or mixed greens, washed and drained
1 tomato, cut in wedges
⅔ cup Mary's Basic Salad Dressing (page 260)

Press the eggs through a sieve and toss with salt and pepper, the herbs
and the green onions. Just before serving, toss together the lettuce c
greens, tomato, and salad dressing and sprinkle on the herb-egg mixture.
Garnish with more chopped fresh parsley and serve.

6 to 8 serving

BEET AND ENDIVE SALAD

The colors alone make this a divine salad. Beets are sweet and crunchy
they contrast with the slight bitterness of the endive.

1 pound beets, unpeeled, leaves removed and 2 inches of stem left on
½ pound endive, leaves separated, then washed and drained
3 green onions, both white part and green, chopped, or 3 tablespoons chopped
fresh chives
Chopped fresh parsley to taste
1 recipe Orange Juice Dressing (page 263), Vinaigrette (page 261), or Cucum
ber Cream Dressing (page 261)

Steam the beets until crisp-tender. Run them under cold water, then
peel and cut into matchsticks, slice thin, or grate.
Combine the beets with the endive, green onions, and parsley and toss
with your choice of dressing (I recommend the Orange Juice).

6 to 8 servings

FIG AND MINT SALAD

It's hard to find fresh figs in this country. However, you may know
somebody with a fig tree in his yard; they are abundant in the South.

can't think of anything that compares with fresh figs when they are ripe. They have a subtle, exquisite flavor.

1½ dozen fresh figs, stems clipped off and cut in half lengthwise
1 tablespoon chopped fresh chives (optional)
1 tablespoon chopped fresh mint
¾ cup Orange Juice Dressing (page 263), Mint Dressing (page 264), omitting the garlic, or good fresh cream
1 head Boston lettuce, leaves separated, then washed and drained
Handful of sunflower seeds (optional)

Prepare the figs and toss gently with the chives, mint, and your choice of dressings or the cream. Chill.

Line a salad bowl with the lettuce leaves and fill with the figs, or place pieces of lettuce on individual plates and the figs on top.

Sprinkle with sunflower seeds, if you wish, and serve.

6 to 8 servings

SPINACH AND CITRUS SALAD

The sweet juice of oranges or tangerines bursts into every bite of this luscious combination.

¾ pound fresh spinach
½ pound fresh mushrooms, sliced
2 oranges, peeled and white membranes removed, then sectioned, or 2 tangerines, peeled, sectioned, and seeded
½ cup Roasted Soybeans (page 87) (optional)
Handful of sprouts (alfalfa, mung bean, lentil)
Salad dressing of your choice (see below)

Wash and stem the spinach; pat the leaves dry. Toss with the mushrooms, orange or tangerine sections, and roasted soybeans. Just before serving, add the sprouts and toss with the dressing of your choice (I like Mary's Basic Salad Dressing [page 260], Vinaigrette [page 261], Tahini Dressing [page 264], or Orange Juice Dressing [page 263]).

Note: You can add other vegetables to this salad, if you wish.

6 to 8 servings

GADO-GADO OVER BROWN RICE, WITH SPROUTS

An interesting, exotic Indonesian salad, *gado-gado* is not for people with aversions to peanut butter or ginger. The textures here are wonderful:

crunchy peanuts, in a creamy, pungent sauce, topping a salad of rice and vegetables. It's very rich, so balance out the rest of your meal accordingly.

For the rice and vegetables:
   1 to 1½ cups cooked brown rice (½ cup raw; see page 25)
   ½ cucumber, peeled (if very waxy or bitter) and chopped
   ½ green pepper, seeded and chopped
   Salt, preferably sea salt, and freshly ground pepper to taste

For the gado-gado sauce:
   ½ onion, chopped fine
   3 cloves garlic, minced or put through a press
   ½ cup raw peanuts
   1½ tablespoons peanut or safflower oil
   ½ cup boiling water
   1 cup crunchy organic peanut butter
   1½ tablespoons mild honey
   ¼ teaspoon Tabasco
   Juice and grated rind of 1 lemon
   2 tablespoons freshly grated gingerroot or 2 to 3 teaspoons ground ginger
   1 bay leaf, crushed
   Salt to taste
   2 tablespoons grated coconut
   1½ cups milk

For the Garnish:
   ½ large head Boston lettuce, leaves separated, then washed and drained
   Handful of sprouts (alfalfa, mung, lentil)
   1 tomato, cut in wedges
   Radish roses

Combine the rice, cucumber, and green pepper and sprinkle with salt and pepper; set aside.

In a wok, large skillet, or 2-quart saucepan, sauté the onion, garlic, and peanuts in the oil until the peanuts are lightly browned. Stir in all the other sauce ingredients except the milk and cook over a medium flame, continuing to stir, until the peanut butter has melted and blended in with the other ingredients.

When the sauce is bubbling gently, carefully stir in the milk. Blend well and cook for about 5 more minutes over a low flame.

Arrange the lettuce leaves on a platter and place a mound of the rice mixture on each leaf, topping with a generous amount of the *gado-gado* sauce. Sprinkle with sprouts and arrange the tomato wedges and radish roses among the lettuce leaves for a colorful garnish.

6 to 8 servings

POTATO-EGG SALAD WITH CHILLED BROCCOLI

More yellow and "eggy" than the familiar potato salad, this also shines with the bright green broccoli and bright red tomatoes.

½ bunch broccoli, trimmed and cut in florets
6 hard-boiled eggs, peeled
3 large potatoes, unpeeled, steamed and diced
4 ribs celery, chopped
1 green pepper, seeded and chopped
4 green onions, both white part and green, sliced, or ½ onion, minced
¼ cup chopped fresh parsley
  Salt, preferably sea salt, and freshly ground pepper to taste
1 cup Mary's Basic Salad Dressing (page 260), made with an additional table-spoon Dijon-style prepared mustard, or to taste
1 cup Blender Mayonnaise (page 259) or Tofu Mayonnaise (page 260), more to taste
½ head leaf lettuce or romaine, leaves separated, then washed and drained
2 tomatoes, cut in wedges, or ½ pint cherry tomatoes
¼ cup whole almonds
  Fresh parsley sprigs for garnish

Steam the broccoli briefly, until it is a bright green color. Remove from the heat immediately and rinse in cold water; the broccoli should be crisp.

Chop or mash the hard-boiled eggs. Combine with the potatoes, celery, green pepper, green onions, and parsley. Add salt and pepper and toss with the salad dressing; toss again with mayonnaise. Add more mustard if you wish.

Line a large platter or salad bowl with the leaf lettuce or romaine leaves. Mound the potato salad in the center, then arrange the broccoli in a ring around the edge (the green color will look beautiful against the potato salad). Inside this ring, place a ring of tomato wedges or cherry tomatoes interspersed with almonds. Scatter the remaining almonds over the middle of the salad, with a sprig of parsley here and there.

Cover and chill before serving.

6 to 8 servings

MIXED BEAN SALAD

1 to 1½ cups each cooked garbanzo beans, kidney beans, and white navy beans
(½ cup each dried; see page 25)
1 to 1½ cups cooked black beans (½ cup dried; see page 25) (optional)
1½ cups green beans, cut into 1-inch pieces and steamed briefly
1 cup yellow wax beans, cut into 1-inch pieces and steamed briefly
1 Bermuda onion, sliced thin
1 clove garlic, minced or put through a press
1 teaspoon chopped fresh dill
½ cup sunflower seeds (optional)
1 green pepper, seeded and chopped
1 recipe Mary's Basic Salad Dressing (page 260) or Vinaigrette (page 261)
Freshly ground black pepper to taste
½ teaspoon ground cumin (optional)

Combine the beans, onion, garlic, dill, sunflower seeds, and green pepper in a salad bowl. Pour the salad dressing over the bean mixture and add freshly ground pepper to taste and the cumin, if you wish. Toss well, cover, and refrigerate for several hours, tossing every once in a while to bind the oil and vinegar and to make sure the salad marinates evenly.

Serve with a protein-complementary soup or salad—Egg-Lemon Soup (page 111), Cream of Wheat Berry Soup (page 109), Brown Rice Salad (page 245)—or with plain couscous, an *excellent* accompaniment, or with Mixed Grains Bread (page 38) and a soup.

6 to 8 servings

MARINATED LENTIL SALAD

This dish is always a hit. The usual comment I get from guests and cooking students is: "I never thought of doing this with lentils!" Then they go back for seconds.

1 onion, chopped fine
3 cloves garlic, minced or put through a press
¼ cup olive oil
1 pound dried lentils, washed
2 quarts water
Pinch of cayenne pepper
2 bay leaves
1 teaspoon salt, preferably sea salt
Freshly ground black pepper
2 cups Mary's Basic Salad Dressing (page 260), made with olive oil and extra Dijon-style prepared mustard

3 tablespoons wine vinegar
½ head romaine or leaf lettuce, leaves separated, then washed and drained
2 to 3½ cups cooked brown rice (1 to 1½ cups raw; see page 25) or steamed couscous (see page 25) (optional)

For the garnish:
   Fresh parsley
   Sunflower seeds
   Alfalfa or lentil sprouts
   Black olives
   Tomato wedges

In a 4-quart stock pot or Dutch oven, sauté the onion and 2 cloves of the garlic in 2 tablespoons of the olive oil. When the onions are tender, add the lentils, water, cayenne, and bay leaves and bring to a boil. Add the salt and freshly ground pepper, then reduce the heat and cover. Simmer for 45 minutes to 1 hour, until soft but not mushy. Drain and allow to cool.

Mix together 1½ cups of the salad dressing, the remaining garlic, the vinegar, and the remaining olive oil. Toss with the cooked lentils and refrigerate for several hours.

Place a bed of lettuce on a platter and top with the marinated lentils. Toss the cooked brown rice or couscous with the remaining salad dressing and place in little mounds around the lentils, or in a ring.

Garnish with fresh parsley, sunflower seeds, sprouts, olives, and tomato wedges.

6 to 8 servings

GRATED CARROT SALAD

The colors and flavors here go beautifully with curries.

3 tablespoons wine vinegar or cider vinegar
3 tablespoons mild honey
½ teaspoon salt, preferably sea salt
½ cup plain yogurt, homemade (see page 259) or commercial
½ cup Blender Mayonnaise (page 259)
3 cups finely grated carrot
½ cup currants
1 head leaf lettuce, leaves separated, then washed and drained
3 tablespoons ground Roasted Soybeans (page 87)

Combine the vinegar, honey, salt, yogurt, and mayonnaise. Stir well, then toss with the grated carrot and currants.

(continued)

Mound helpings of the salad on crisp leaves of lettuce on individual plates, or line a bowl with lettuce and fill with the salad.

Top with ground roasted soybeans and serve.

6 to 8 servings

GARBANZO BEAN SALAD

For the beans:
  2 cups dried garbanzo beans
  6 cups water
  1 teaspoon dried thyme
  1 clove garlic, minced or put through a press
  1 carrot, chopped
  1 onion, chopped
  2 sprigs fresh parsley
  ½ teaspoon dried rosemary
  1 bay leaf
  1 teaspoon salt, preferably sea salt

For the marinade:
  ½ cup dry white wine
  1 bunch green onions, both white part and green, chopped
  ¼ cup chopped fresh parsley or a combination of parsley and other fresh herbs
     (basil, marjoram, tarragon, thyme)
  1 recipe Vinaigrette (page 261)
  1 green pepper, seeded and sliced or minced
  ½ red pepper (if available), seeded and sliced or minced

For the garnishes:
  ½ head leaf lettuce, leaves separated, then washed and drained
  ¼ cup freshly grated Parmesan cheese
  1 cup grated Cheddar cheese (optional)
  1 cup alfalfa sprouts (optional)
  2 tomatoes, sliced or cut in wedges
  4 radishes, sliced
     Chopped fresh parsley

Wash the beans and soak them for several hours in the 6 cups water. Combine with the thyme, garlic, chopped carrot, chopped onion, the parsley sprigs, rosemary, bay leaf, and salt in a flameproof bean pot or large saucepan. Bring to a boil, then cover, reduce the heat, and simmer for 1 to 2 hours, until tender but not mushy.

Drain the beans and toss immediately with the wine, chopped green onions and parsley, and the vinaigrette. Add the green and red peppers and toss again. Chill for several hours, stirring every once in a while to redistribute the marinade.

Line a platter or bowl with leaf lettuce. Shortly before serving, toss the marinated beans with the Parmesan cheese and optional Cheddar cheese and sprouts. Place over the lettuce on the platter or in the bowl; decorate with tomatoes, radishes, and more chopped parsley.

Serve with a rice salad, such as Brown Rice Salad (page 245), or Crudité Salad (page 73) or a grain-y, cheese-y, or creamy soup—Cheese and Black Bread (page 106), Cabbage-Cheese (page 116), Egg-Lemon (page 111)—for a protein-complementary meal.

6 to 8 servings

SHREDDED FRUIT AND VEGETABLE SALAD

A brilliantly colorful salad, exploding with sweet and sour tastes.

2 carrots, grated
2 apples, cored and grated
2 ribs celery, grated
6 radishes, grated
½ head red cabbage, grated
1 cup raisins
½ cup chopped dried apricots
½ cup chopped dates
½ cup chopped almonds
½ cup lemon juice
1 cup plain yogurt, homemade (see page 259) or commercial
¼ cup mild honey
½ teaspoon salt, preferably sea salt
¾ cup safflower oil
½ head leaf lettuce, leaves separated, then washed and dried
   Toasted wheat germ
2 fresh peaches, peeled and sliced, for garnish

In a large bowl, combine the grated carrots, apples, celery, radishes, and cabbage with the dried fruits and the almonds.

Mix together the lemon juice, yogurt, honey, salt, and oil. Pour over the salad and toss.

Line a salad bowl with lettuce leaves and fill with the grated fruit and

256

vegetable mixture. Sprinkle with the toasted wheat germ and garnish with fresh peach slices, then chill before serving.

6 to 8 servings

COLE SLAW

½ head green cabbage, finely shredded
2 carrots, grated
1 recipe Sweet and Sour Dressing for Cole Slaws (page 264)

Toss the ingredients together. Chill and serve, or serve immediately.

6 to 8 servings

SAUCES AND DRESSINGS

Some of the recipes here are basics, dressings or sauces that are called for as ingredients in other recipes in this book—Blender Mayonnaise (page 259) and Homemade Yogurt (page 259), for example—and also stand alone; indeed, yogurt is one of the best, easiest breakfasts I can think of. Many, like Tofu Mayonnaise (page 260) and Green Dressing (page 263), serve not only as salad dressings but also make excellent dips for vegetables and spreads for sandwiches.

I don't use too many roux-thickened sauces. The one that I do relish is White Wine Sauce, so I'm including it below. It's irresistible.

Several of the salad dressings that follow can be made in advance, not those with fresh herbs, like Vinaigrette (page 261)—unless your salad or vegetables require marinating—but some of the creamy ones, like the mayonnaise-based dressings—Sunflower Seed Dressing (page 263), Tahini Dressing (page 264), Tofu Mayonnaise (page 260). Make enough for the week so you can put together a tasty salad every night without bother.

WHITE WINE SAUCE

This is an excellent sauce for egg and cheese dishes. It can be made a day in advance, and it freezes well.

1½ cups Garlic Broth (page 92) or Vegetable Stock (page 91)
1 cup dry white wine
5 to 6 dried dark mushrooms
3 tablespoons butter
3 tablespoons flour (whole-wheat pastry flour or unbleached white, or a combination)
Salt and freshly ground pepper to taste

Combine the broth or stock, wine, and dried mushrooms and simmer together in a saucepan for about 30 minutes. Strain the liquid and either

257

discard the mushrooms or set them aside for another purpose.

Heat the butter in a heavy saucepan. When it is bubbly, add the flour and cook for a few minutes over low heat, stirring. Slowly pour in the hot broth, stirring all the while with a whisk; keep on stirring until the sauce thickens. Continue to cook for 10 minutes over low heat after the sauce thickens, then season to taste with salt and pepper.

About 2½ cups

HOMEMADE APPLESAUCE

Wonderful by itself as a side dish or dessert, this makes a delicious topping for the Potato Pancakes on page 218.

  8 large apples, peeled and sliced
  2 cups water
1½ tablespoons lemon juice
  1 teaspoon ground cinnamon
  ½ teaspoon ground ginger
  ½ teaspoon ground cloves
  ½ teaspoon freshly grated nutmeg
  ¼ teaspoon ground allspice
  ¼ teaspoon ground mace
   Mild honey to taste

In a large saucepan, combine the apple slices, water, and lemon juice. Bring to a boil, then reduce the heat, cover, and simmer for about 30 minutes, or until the apples begin to fall apart.

Add the spices and honey to taste, then stir and continue cooking for 15 to 30 minutes, depending on how mushy you want your applesauce to be. Press with a potato masher, leaving some large chunks.

Serve hot or chilled.

3 to 4 cups, depending on size of apples and amount of honey

SWEET AND SOUR SAUCE

This sauce is fairly thin. Very easy to make, it takes only a matter of minutes to prepare.

It's a perfect dipping sauce for Egg Rolls (page 80) and for the Tempura'd Vegetables or Tofu on pages 81 and 84.

1 cup tomato puree
2 tablespoons soy sauce
¼ cup mild honey
¼ cup cider vinegar

1 tablespoon prepared mustard
2 tablespoons dry sherry

Combine all the ingredients in a small saucepan and heat through.

About 1¾ cups

HOMEMADE YOGURT (FROM ADELLE DAVIS)

When you make this, be sure you use either Dannon plain yogurt or a yogurt recommended by a natural foods store as a starter. The bacteria in most commercial brands isn't sufficient. If your yogurt does fail, it probably will be because you used the wrong kind of yogurt as a starter, or because your water bath was too hot or not warm enough.

1 quart plus 2 cups lukewarm water
3 to 4 tablespoons plain yogurt (see note above)
1½ to 2 cups spray-dried milk
1 large can (13 ounces) evaporated milk, skim or regular

Blend the 2 cups lukewarm water, yogurt, and spray-dried milk together until well combined, then pour into a large pitcher (one that holds at least 4 quarts) containing the 1 quart lukewarm water and the evaporated milk.

Pour into jars, cover, and place in a pan of lukewarm water. Place the pan in a warm place where the temperature will remain constant (over a pilot light, on a heater, in a cooler full of warm water). Cover the pan and leave for 3 to 4 hours, checking the water from time to time to make sure it retains its lukewarm temperature. Refrigerate when thick (in summer, 3 to 4 hours; in winter, 5 to 6).

About 2 quarts

BLENDER MAYONNAISE

1 egg
2 teaspoons red wine vinegar or cider vinegar
½ to ¾ teaspoon salt, preferably sea salt
½ teaspoon dry mustard or 1 teaspoon prepared English or Dijon-style mustard (see note below)
¼ teaspoon freshly ground pepper
1 cup salad oil
2 tablespoons lemon juice, or more to taste

Put everything except the oil and the lemon juice into a blender and blend at medium speed. With the blender on, add the oil in a very slow

260

stream, then add the lemon juice, using more than 2 tablespoons if desired. Store, refrigerated, in a well-sealed jar.

Note: If you like a touch of sweetness in your mayonnaise, use the English mustard here.

1 ¼ cups

TOFU MAYONNAISE

This is scrumptious as a dressing, mayonnaise, or dip. It's essentially a low-calorie mayonnaise, and will be a blessing for those who love mayonnaise but hate the calories. It lasts several days in the refrigerator and is so easy to make that you can have it on hand all the time.

Juice of ½ lemon
2 tablespoons wine or cider vinegar
1 clove garlic, minced or put through a press (optional)
1 teaspoon Dijon-style prepared mustard
¼ cup Blender Mayonnaise (page 259)
1 teaspoon *miso* paste or tamari
1 to 1½ cups cubed tofu
Salt and freshly ground pepper to taste
2 tablespoons olive oil
2 to 4 tablespoons plain yogurt, homemade (see page 259) or commercial

Combine all the ingredients, using 2 tablespoons yogurt, in a blender and blend until smooth. Use more yogurt to thin the dressing out, if desired.

About 1½ to 2 cups

MARY'S BASIC SALAD DRESSING

Juice of 1 lemon
2 tablespoons wine vinegar or cider vinegar
1 clove garlic, put through a press or mashed and minced
½ teaspoon dry mustard or 1 teaspoon Dijon-style prepared mustard
¼ teaspoon salt, preferably sea salt
Freshly ground pepper to taste
½ teaspoon dried marjoram
½ teaspoon dried tarragon
1 teaspoon chopped fresh herbs (basil, dill, thyme) (optional)
¾ cup safflower oil or a mixture of safflower and olive oil

Method no. 1: Combine the lemon juice and vinegar in a small bowl or a 2-cup Pyrex measuring cup. Stir in the garlic and mustard with a fork or whisk. Add the salt, pepper, and herbs and blend well, then whisk in the oil. Refrigerate if not using right away and stir well before tossing the salad.

Method no. 2: Do not stir the oil into the dressing. Toss your salad ingredients first with the lemon-vinegar-herb mixture, then with the oil.

About 1 cup

VINAIGRETTE

1 tablespoon freshly squeezed lemon juice
3 tablespoons wine vinegar or cider vinegar
1 clove garlic, minced or put through a press
½ teaspoon dry mustard or 1 teaspoon Dijon-style prepared mustard
¼ teaspoon dried tarragon or 1 teaspoon chopped fresh herbs (basil, tarragon, dill, parsley, chervil)
¼ teaspoon dried marjoram or dried basil
¼ teaspoon salt, preferably sea salt
  Freshly ground pepper to taste
¾ cup olive oil

Method no. 1: Combine the lemon juice and the vinegar, then stir in the garlic and mustard with a fork. Add the herbs, salt, and pepper; whisk in the olive oil. Stir well or shake vigorously in a covered jar before tossing your salad.

Method no. 2: Do not blend the oil into the dressing. Toss your salad ingredients first with the lemon-vinegar-herb mixture, then with the oil.

About 1 cup

CUCUMBER CREAM DRESSING

½ cucumber, peeled and grated
½ cup Mary's Basic Salad Dressing (page 260) or Vinaigrette (page 261)
¼ teaspoon salt, preferably sea salt
½ cup plain yogurt, homemade (see page 259) or commercial, or buttermilk

Toss the grated cucumber together with 1 tablespoon of the salad dressing and the salt; let sit for 15 minutes.

(continued)

Rinse the cucumber and squeeze dry, then mix with remaining dressing and stir in the yogurt.

About 1 ¼ to 1 ½ cups

POPPY SEED DRESSING

Good with Avocado and Citrus Salad (page 239).

Juice of 1 lemon
2 to 3 tablespoons wine vinegar or cider vinegar
2 tablespoons mild honey
1 teaspoon Dijon-style prepared mustard
¼ to ½ teaspoon salt, preferably sea salt
¼ teaspoon freshly ground pepper
⅔ cup safflower oil
3 tablespoons poppy seeds

In a blender or electric mixer, combine the lemon juice, vinegar, honey, mustard, salt, and pepper. While the blender is running, slowly pour in the oil. Stir in the poppy seeds.

About 1 ½ cups

CURRY DRESSING

½ cup Blender Mayonnaise (page 259)
1 cup plain yogurt, commercial or homemade (see page 259)
1½ to 2 teaspoons curry powder
½ teaspoon turmeric
½ teaspoon chili powder
¼ teaspoon ground ginger
¼ teaspoon paprika
  Salt, preferably sea salt, to taste

Stir all the ingredients together. Chill.

1 ½ cups

GREEN DRESSING

½ cup fresh spinach leaves, more as desired
1 small clove garlic, put through a press

2 tablespoons chopped green onions, both white part and green, or fresh chives, more if desired
1 tablespoon chopped fresh dill, more if desired
1 teaspoon fresh tarragon or ¼ teaspoon dried, more if desired
3 tablespoons chopped fresh parsley, more if desired
½ cup plain yogurt, homemade (see page 259) or commercial
2 tablespoons lemon juice, more as desired
½ cup Blender Mayonnaise (page 259)
　　Salt, preferably sea salt, and freshly ground pepper to taste

Blanch, drain, and chop the spinach leaves, then puree in a blender with the garlic, green onion, and other herbs, using the yogurt and lemon juice to liquefy. (Alternatively, you can chop the herbs very fine and put them through a sieve.)

Stir this mixture into the mayonnaise; add salt and freshly ground pepper as needed. Add more herbs and spinach if you desire a darker, greener dressing, and add more lemon juice if you want it more tart.

About 1 to 1¼ cups

SUNFLOWER SEED DRESSING

This is one of my favorite dressings. It goes beautifully with sprouts salads, slaws, and green salads, and can also serve as a dip.

⅓ cup sunflower seeds
1 clove garlic
　　Salt, preferably sea salt, and freshly ground pepper to taste
1 tablespoon chopped fresh herbs (parsley, tarragon, thyme, dill)
2 tablespoons lemon juice, more to taste
1 cup plain yogurt, homemade (see page 259) or commercial

In a blender or food processor, grind the sunflower seeds fine, almost to a butter. Add the garlic, salt and pepper, and herbs, then blend in the lemon juice and the yogurt and mix until you have a smooth sauce. Adjust the seasoning.

About 1½ cups

ORANGE JUICE DRESSING

Good with green salads, especially those with citrus, and fruit salads, and especially good with Avocado and Citrus Salad (page 239), Beet and Endive Salad (page 248), and Fig and Mint Salad (page 248).

(continued)

264

⅓ cup fresh orange juice
   Juice of ½ lemon
¼ to ½ teaspoon salt, preferably sea salt
½ teaspoon dry mustard or 1 teaspoon prepared Dijon-style mustard
⅔ cup vegetable or safflower oil

Mix together the orange juice, lemon juice, salt, and mustard; blend in the oil.

About 1 cup

MINT DRESSING

1 cup plain yogurt, homemade (see page 259) or commercial
3 tablespoons lemon juice
1 tablespoon chopped fresh mint
   Salt, preferably sea salt, to taste
1 small clove garlic, minced or put through a press (optional)

Combine all the ingredients in a blender, or chop the mint fine and stir it into the other ingredients.

About 1¼ cups

TAHINI DRESSING

Good on spinach salads.

¼ to ½ cup sesame tahini, to taste
1 recipe Mary's Basic Salad Dressing (page 260) or Vinaigrette (page 261)

Blend the tahini with the salad dressing in a blender or with a whisk.

About 1¼ to 1½ cups

SWEET AND SOUR DRESSING FOR COLE SLAWS

¼ cup mild honey
¼ cup wine or cider vinegar
½ teaspoon salt, preferably sea salt
½ cup plain yogurt, homemade (see page 259) or commercial

Stir together the honey, vinegar, and salt; blend in the yogurt.

1 cup

THE GREAT VEGETARIAN TURKEY AND OTHER HOLIDAY DELIGHTS

~~~~~

Thanksgiving Menu

Corn Chowder (page 267) *or* Pumpkin Soup (page 267)

The Great Vegetarian Turkey (page 268), with "Gravy" (page 270) *or* White Wine Sauce (page 257)

Fruited Sweet Potato Casserole (page 270) *or* Creamed Mashed Potatoes (page 271)

Waldorf Salad (page 272)

Creamed Peas and Pearl Onions (page 272)

Pumpkin or Sweet Potato Pie (page 273)

Mince Pie (page 273)

It will come as no surprise to you that Thanksgiving, a holiday that is centered around eating, is my favorite. If I'm not cooking for my own friends on that day (or on any feast day), I'm cooking for somebody else's.

Shopping for Thanksgiving dinner during the first year of my "supper club," I found the fruit stands in Austin well stocked with large, gourdlike cushaw squash. To me they had the size and shape of small turkeys, so I brought one home and stuffed it. I baked it, then decorated it with turkey feathers and vegetables. A carrot, steamed briefly and fastened to the neck of the squash with toothpicks, served as a beak. A piece of lettuce, also attached with toothpicks, served as a comb. This extraordinary creation turned out to be such a spectacular sight that I later made it and served it on a public television show in Austin.

The "turkey" squash itself is not part of the meal, but the stuffing baked inside it has all the appeal of the traditional turkey stuffing, redolent with sage. You don't have to go through all the trouble of stuffing a squash; the stuffing can be baked in loaf pans. But the "great vegetarian turkey" is not too difficult an undertaking, and it's very dramatic—and fun!

About the Menu

Most of the foods that we are used to seeing at Thanksgiving appear on this menu. I chose corn chowder because I associate Thanksgiving and harvest time. Another possibility for a soup is pumpkin soup (or, if you prefer, the Apple-Spice Soup on page 136). Pumpkin has to appear somewhere on the menu, after all, and this might be more appealing than the traditional pumpkin pie—even one as delicious as I consider mine!

Sweet potatoes are another Thanksgiving regular. The fruited sweet potato casserole is scrumptious and certainly more special and interesting than candied sweet potatoes. I recommend it highly. If you prefer sweet potatoes in your dessert, make the sweet potato pie.

If you are concerned with protein complementarity, the corn chowder is the best choice for this meal. The stuffing is high in protein, but the chowder would give it a good boost.

About the Schedule

Thanksgiving dinner—or Christmas dinner or any festive meal—is quite an undertaking for one person. A potluck supper is a good idea for this occasion, but if you are doing the whole show, here is the order in which to do things:

Make the pies the day before. You can also assemble the fruited sweet potato casserole the day before (cover tightly and refrigerate until baking time).

Start bright and early Thanksgiving morning. You can make the Waldorf salad before or after you stuff the squash. Make the stuffing, and while it cooks prepare your soup. By the time the soup is simmering, the stuffing should be cooked and you can go ahead and stuff the squash. Bake the "turkey" close to dinnertime or a little before, giving yourself time to adorn it with feathers and so on. The peas and onions should be cooked close to eating time, as should mashed potatoes. If you have not had time to make the sweet potato casserole in advance, put it together after you prepare the "turkey."

PUMPKIN SOUP

1 fresh pumpkin (2 pounds)
4 cups milk
¼ cup mild honey, or to taste
1 tablespoon molasses (optional)
2 tablespoons butter
½ teaspoon freshly grated nutmeg, or to taste
½ teaspoon ground cinnamon
½ teaspoon ground mace
½ to 1 teaspoon curry powder
¼ teaspoon ground ginger
1 teaspoon salt, preferably sea salt
2 tablespoons maple syrup (optional)
½ to 1 cup orange juice
    Finely grated rind of 1 orange (optional)
1 cup light cream, whipped (optional)
2 tablespoons sunflower seeds or ground pecans

Cut the pumpkin in half, then scrape out the pulp and seeds and cut into pieces. Steam for 15 to 20 minutes, or until soft. Run under cool water and peel away the skin; the skin will peel away easily. Puree, a few pieces at a time, in a blender or food processor. (Alternatively, cut in half, remove seeds and pulp, and place in a pan, cut side down. Bake for 1 hour at 325 degrees.)

In a large, heavy-bottomed stock pot or Dutch oven, stir together the pumpkin, milk, honey, molasses, and butter over low heat until well blended. Stir in the nutmeg, cinnamon, mace, curry powder, ginger, salt, and maple syrup, then simmer gently for 15 minutes; do *not* allow the mixture to boil.

Slowly add the orange juice and rind. Simmer, stirring often, for 10 minutes. Correct seasonings and stir in half the whipped cream.

Serve hot, or cool and chill well. Garnish with the remaining whipped cream and the sunflower seeds or ground pecans.

6 to 8 servings

CORN CHOWDER

Corn chowder is rich and creamy, a perennial favorite made with corn, milk, and potatoes. The green pepper lends a nice crunch, and the kernels of corn are bursting with juicy sweetness that flows into the creamy stock.

This is a protein-rich soup, good to serve with bean and vegetable dishes. Preparation goes fairly quickly. You can easily remove the cor from the cob by running a knife down between the kernels and the col you'll be amazed at how much corn you can get.

1 potato, unpeeled and diced
2 cups Vegetable Stock (page 91)
  Salt, preferably sea salt
2 tablespoons butter or vegetable oil
1 onion, chopped
2 tablespoons flour (whole-wheat pastry flour or unbleached white, or a comb nation)
2 cups fresh corn kernels (from 3 to 4 ears of corn)
1 green pepper, seeded and diced
1 quart milk, enriched with 3 tablespoons spray-dried milk
  Freshly ground pepper to taste
½ cup grated Cheddar or Swiss Gruyère cheese (optional)

In a small or medium-sized saucepan, simmer the potato in the stoc with a little salt until tender.

Heat the butter or oil in a stock pot or Dutch oven and sauté the onio until tender. Stir in the flour, blend well, and continue to sauté, stirring for 2 to 3 minutes more. Stir in the potato in its liquid and bring to a sim mer. Stir until you have a smooth sauce, then reduce heat and add th corn, green pepper, and the enriched milk. Bring to a gentle simmer—d not let it boil—then cover and cook for 20 minutes. Add salt and pepper t taste and simmer another 5 minutes. Add the grated cheese and stir until i melts.

Serve immediately.

6 to 8 serving

THE GREAT VEGETARIAN TURKEY

For the stuffing:
1 cup dried lentils
1½ onions, chopped
2 cloves garlic, minced or put through a press.
1 cup raw brown rice
1 cup raw millet
2 tablespoons safflower or vegetable oil
1 cup chopped almonds, raw cashews, or pecans
¼ cup sunflower seeds
½ cup yellow cornmeal, preferably stone-ground
2 ribs celery, chopped

2 cups broccoli florets, steamed briefly until bright green
2 teaspoons dried leaf sage
2 teaspoons ground celery seed
1 tablespoon tamari, or to taste
  Salt, preferably sea salt, and freshly ground pepper to taste
1 cup whole-wheat bread crumbs, more if necessary

For the "turkey" (optional):
1 large cushaw or Chinese squash (about 10 pounds)
1 small head Boston or leaf lettuce, leaves separated, then washed and drained
  Turkey feathers
1 small, whole carrot, steamed briefly

Cook the lentils, with ½ chopped onion and half the minced garlic, as directed on page 25. Drain and reserve 1 cup of the liquid.

Cook or steam the rice and millet as directed on page 25.

Sauté the remaining onion and garlic in the safflower or vegetable oil, along with the nuts and sunflower seeds, until the onion is tender.

Mix all the ingredients together in a large bowl, adding more bread crumbs or some of the reserved liquid from the lentils as necessary to make a thick, stiff mixture.

Preheat the oven to 350 degrees.

Stuffing the squash: If you are using the squash, set it in a roasting pan with a little water and steam it for about 30 minutes. Rinse in cold water, then, with a sharp knife, cut a semicircular piece out of the "rump" of the squash, making sure to remove the whole piece intact so that it's easy to replace. (It should be a big enough piece so you can stick your hand or a large spoon inside the squash to remove the seeds and stringy pulp.) Scoop out the seeds and pulp, and brush the insides with butter.

Now stuff the squash with as much stuffing as you can squeeze in (putting any leftover stuffing in one or more oiled 1-quart loaf pans). Fit the piece you removed back into its place, and set the squash upright in an oiled roaster. If the squash doesn't stand upright, cut a *thin* horizontal slice off the bottom, taking care not to cut through the rind, so the squash will have a flat surface to rest on.

Bake for 1 hour in the preheated oven, along with the pan or pans of extra stuffing. Remove from the oven and place on a platter lined with most of the lettuce leaves. Stick the turkey feathers in the "rump." Attach the steamed carrot to the "head" with toothpicks for the "beak," and make a "comb" out of the remaining lettuce leaves.

Surround the "turkey" with leftover stuffing. Once everyone has had a good look, remove the semicircular "rump" and serve the stuffing with "Gravy" (see below) or White Wine Sauce (page 257).

Alternative presentations: Place the stuffing in four 1-quart oiled loaf pans, two well-oiled Bundts, or a large oiled casserole and bake for 1 hour. Unmold from the Bundts onto a platter and surround with colorful steamed vegetables. Or hollow out a pumpkin, fill with the mixture and bake for 45 minutes at 350 degrees. Surround with lush, sensuous vegetables and serve.

About 25 servings (4 quarts stuffing)

"GRAVY"

3 tablespoons safflower oil or butter
2 tablespoons grated onion
3 tablespoons flour (whole-wheat pastry or unbleached white, or a combination)
2 cups Vegetable Stock (page 91) or Tamari-Bouillon Broth (page 91)
Pinch of dried rosemary
2 tablespoons soy sauce (reduce if using Tamari-Bouillon Broth; use to taste)
Salt, preferably sea salt, to taste
Freshly ground pepper to taste

In a medium-sized saucepan, melt the oil or butter and sauté the grated onion for a few minutes. Add the flour to make a roux and cook, stirring, for a few minutes, until just beginning to brown.

Slowly pour in the stock, stirring all the while. Stir until thickened, then add the rosemary and simmer gently for 10 minutes, stirring often. Stir in the soy sauce, salt, and pepper to taste.

2 cups

FRUITED SWEET POTATO CASSEROLE

3 medium sweet potatoes
3 tablespoons butter
½ cup mild honey
½ cup sunflower seeds or slivered almonds, or a mixture of both
2 teaspoons ground cinnamon
2 apples, cored and sliced
½ cup raisins or currants

3 bananas, sliced
1 teaspoon cornstarch or arrowroot
Juice of 1 orange, warmed

Steam the sweet potatoes in 1 inch of water until tender but not mushy, about 15 to 20 minutes. Drain and slice, peeling if the skin is bitter.

Preheat the oven to 350 degrees; oil a 2-quart baking dish.

Arrange the potato slices in a layer in the prepared baking dish. Dot with bits of the butter and brush with some of the honey.

Setting aside about 2 tablespoons of the sunflower seeds and/or almonds and 1 teaspoon cinnamon for the topping, combine the apples, raisins, and remaining sunflower seeds and/or almonds and cinnamon. Layer this mixture on top of the sweet potatoes; dot with butter and brush with honey. Layer the banana slices over the apple mixture.

Dissolve the cornstarch or arrowroot in the orange juice and stir in any leftover honey and butter. Reserving a little of this mixture for basting, pour the rest over the bananas. Sprinkle with the reserved cinnamon and sunflower seeds and/or almonds.

Bake in the preheated oven for 30 to 45 minutes, until the banana layer is just browned, basting a few times with the orange juice during the baking.

Serve hot.

6 to 8 servings

CREAMED MASHED POTATOES

6 medium potatoes, peeled and cut in half
2 tablespoons butter
⅓ cup milk
Salt, preferably sea salt, to taste
Paprika (optional)

Steam the potatoes until tender, about 30 minutes. Drain and mash with a potato masher, a fork, or a ricer. (You can also mash by putting them through the grater blade of a food processor—don't use the steel blade, or they'll become gummy.) Stir in the butter, milk, and salt. Place in a warm serving dish and sprinkle with paprika. Serve immediately; or, if you can't serve right away, keep warm by placing, covered, in a pan of hot water.

6 servings

WALDORF SALAD

3 apples, cored and diced
3 ribs celery, diced
1 cup Tokay grapes, cut in half and seeded, or seedless green grapes (optional)
1 cup broken walnuts or pecans
½ cup raisins
¾ cup Blender Mayonnaise (page 259)
¼ cup plain yogurt, homemade (see page 259) or commercial

Toss all ingredients together and chill.

6 to 8 servings

CREAMED PEAS AND PEARL ONIONS

1 pound pearl onions, peeled
1 to 2 cups fresh peas
5 tablespoons butter
5 tablespoons whole-wheat flour
2 cups hot milk
½ teaspoon salt, preferably sea salt, or to taste
   Freshly ground black pepper
3 tablespoons dry sherry
2 tablespoons chopped fresh parsley
½ cup sliced mushrooms, sautéed in butter
   Pinch of cayenne pepper

Steam the onions and peas, separately, on a rack over water (they must be cooked separately because the peas steam more quickly than the onions). Reserve 1 cup of the steaming liquid.

Melt the butter in a medium-sized, heavy-bottomed saucepan; stir in the flour. Stir the roux over medium heat for 2 to 3 minutes, making sure it doesn't brown. Slowly whisk in the hot milk and the 1 cup liquid from the peas and onions. Stir over medium heat until the mixture reaches the boiling point and you have a smooth, thick sauce. Season with salt, freshly ground pepper, and the sherry.

Add the peas, pearl onions, and sautéed mushrooms to the cream sauce. Stir together, and add a very small pinch of cayenne; correct the seasoning. Garnish with parsley and serve.

6 to 8 servings

PUMPKIN PIE

The unusual addition of molasses makes this a dark and delicious pie.

½ recipe **Whole-Wheat Pie Crust** (page 149)
 3 **eggs**
1½ cups cooked, puréed **pumpkin** (see page 267)
1½ cups milk, enriched with 3 tablespoons spray-dried milk
 2 tablespoons **butter**
⅓ cup plus 1 tablespoon mild **honey**
 2 tablespoons **molasses**
1½ teaspoons **vanilla** extract
1½ teaspoons ground **cinnamon**
 ½ teaspoon ground **ginger**
 ¼ teaspoon ground **mace**
 ¼ teaspoon ground **cloves**
 ¼ teaspoon freshly grated **nutmeg**
 ¼ teaspoon **salt**, preferably sea salt
   Whipped cream, plain yogurt, or vanilla ice cream

Preheat the oven to 350 degrees.

Roll out the crust to fit a 9- or 10-inch pan; brush the pie shell with one of the eggs, beaten, and prebake for 5 minutes. Remove from the oven and turn the heat up to 425 degrees.

Blend the remaining eggs with the rest of the ingredients (except, of course, the whipped cream or other garnishes) and pour into the pie shell. Bake at 425 degrees for 10 minutes, then reduce the heat to 325 degrees and bake for another 30 to 40 minutes.

Cool and serve with whipped cream, plain yogurt, or vanilla ice cream.

One 9- or 10-inch pie

SWEET POTATO PIE

Substitute cooked, mashed sweet potatoes for the pumpkin and follow the above recipe.

One 9- or 10-inch pie

MINCE PIE

I've had mince pies that have been too sweet for me. There's really no need for much additional sweetener here, as the dried fruits and the fruit juice contain so much natural sugar already.

(continued)

1 recipe Whole-Wheat Pie Crust (page 149) (see note below)
⅓ cup currants
½ cup raisins
1 cup dry sherry
2 tart apples, peeled and chopped
⅓ cup chopped, pitted prunes
⅓ cup chopped, dried apricots
¼ cup chopped, pitted dates
½ cup broken pecans or walnuts
    Juice and grated rind of ½ orange
    Juice and grated rind of ½ lemon
¼ cup apple cider
½ teaspoon ground cinnamon
½ teaspoon ground cloves
¼ teaspoon freshly grated nutmeg
1 tablespoon brandy
¼ cup mild honey
3 tablespoons whole-wheat flour or whole-wheat pastry flour
½ to ¾ cup plain yogurt, homemade (see page 259) or commercial, or heavy cream, whipped

Preheat the oven to 350 degrees.

Roll out half the pie-crust dough and fit it into a 9- or 10-inch pie pan, reserving the other half for a lattice topping. Follow the directions on page 150 and prebake the pie shell for 5 minutes, then remove from the oven and turn the heat up to 375 degrees.

Cover the currants and raisins with sherry and soak while preparing the other ingredients, or for 15 minutes. Pour off the sherry.

In a large saucepan, combine the apples, raisins, currants, prunes, apricots, dates, nuts, orange juice and rind, lemon juice and rind, and apple cider. Bring to a simmer, then cover and cook over low heat for 20 minutes. Add the spices and brandy and stir in the honey; simmer another 5 minutes. Stir in the flour and mix well.

Pour the filling into the pie shell and spread it evenly. Roll out the other half of the crust and make a lattice topping.

Bake at 375 degrees for 40 minutes, then serve, topped with plain yogurt or whipped cream.

Note: If you wish a sweeter crust, add ¼ cup date sugar along with the flour.

One 9- or 10-inch pie

DESSERTS

Desserts are treats by definition, and can be the most extraordinary part of a meal. Most in this chapter are uncomplicated. You will find fruits and liqueurs used often; fresh fruit alone, or fruit and cheese will often suffice after a meal, and you should feel free to omit the liqueurs called for in many of these recipes. You'll recognize some of these desserts as protein complementary, with an abundance of eggs and/or milk, perfect after a vegetable-oriented meal (don't forget that this course is often the easiest place to add protein). Others, such as the simple fruit desserts, are light and most welcome after a heavy meal.

A dessert will lose its magic if you serve it while people are still full from the dinner. Allow a little time to elapse after the last course, then serve it. I also find that very sweet food should not follow too quickly upon the heels of a main dish. So sit back and digest for awhile; make tea or coffee; then you and your guests will really appreciate the grande finale.

Though liqueurs are high in sugar, none of these desserts call for refined sugar as such. I've often read about unrefined sugar and heard it advertised, but I've rarely seen it. It's usually expensive, and difficult to track down. You may have also heard of date sugar and been tempted to use it. I sometimes do in baking (in fact, I suggest its use here for a sweeter whole-wheat pie crust), but it's unsatisfactory for most things because it doesn't dissolve.

I use honey, replacing sugar with it in all recipes. There are a few things one needs to know for honey cookery, rules that apply to all kinds of dishes. The first and most important is *use mild honey*. I think the reason so many "health food" desserts are so bad is that they're dominated by the taste of a strong honey. There are many, many kinds; their taste and scent comes from the flowers that are the source of the nectar from which the honey is made. Some are strong, some mild. I'm no authority on all the different kinds of honey, but I do know from my experience what some of the strongest ones are and which mild ones to watch for. Orange blossoms, lavenders, sage, and buckwheat make very strong honeys; clover, cotton, and acacia make mild ones. Color is a good indicator: the lighter, clearer, and more golden the hue, the milder the honey. Dark oranges and browns are strong. Mild honey has a slightly waxy taste, too, or maybe it's that the taste of the wax isn't dominated by the other strong scents and flavors. Shop around, taste and find a mild one; if you can't, use about one-quarter less than the recipe calls for.

Honey often crystallizes, especially in cold weather. Keep it in a glass jar, and to melt it down place the jar in a heavy-bottomed saucepan. Fill the pan with water and place over a low flame. Let the water around the jar simmer until the honey is melted down.

To convert any recipe using sugar to a honey recipe, use one-quarter less honey than the amount of sugar called for, and decrease the total liquid content by one-eighth.

Molasses is another important sweetener. Its flavor is so strong that it acts as a spice as well, and should only be used when called for. Like honey, molasses comes in different strengths, which are discernible by the color. Dark, thick molasses is very strong, and the lighter ones are milder, with a less spicy sweetness.

Choose your fruits according to the season. You will be hard pressed to find good melons in the fall and winter, or good pears in the spring and summer. Choose carefully. Unripe pineapple is a disaster, as are unripe melons. I've heard of various methods for testing certain fruits for ripeness; mine are simple and straightforward. I smell, feel, and look. Bananas should be yellow, not green, and even a few brown spots are good to indicate that they are really ready. Pineapples, melons, peaches, pears, apricots, nectarines, and persimmons should smell sweet and fragrant, as if you could almost taste them. Thump watermelons—they should have a hollow resonance. Look carefully at the color and choose the reddest strawberries, the pinkest peaches, the deepest purple plums. Feel the fruit carefully; it should be firm but not hard, as if it were about to burst with juice, and it should give you the feeling that if you squeezed it it would burst. If it's soft and bruises at the lightest amount of pressure, it's not good. Search for local fruit stands, which are more apt to have ripe fruit than are supermarkets. The more locally grown fruit you can get, the better.

BANANAS POACHED IN WHITE WINE

My most frequent dessert choice for catered dinners. It can be made early on the day you wish to serve it, and kept either in or out of the refrigerator (warm it up before serving. It's easy and quick; I have often gone to a catering job with the ingredients and made poached fruit while the soup and main dish were being served. This is a sweet, enticing compote. My guests have always loved it.

Juice of ½ lemon
3 to 4 ripe but firm bananas, cut in half lengthwise and then into 2-inch lengths
2 cups semidry white wine
1 tablespoon vanilla extract
1 stick cinnamon
½ cup mild honey
½ cup raisins or currants
½ cup dried apples
½ teaspoon freshly grated nutmeg, or to taste
¼ cup slivered almonds (optional)
½ cup heavy cream, whipped and flavored with vanilla extract

In a bowl, combine the lemon juice and enough water to cover the bananas. Cut the bananas and drop into the water (the acidity of the lemon juice will prevent the bananas from discoloring).

Combine the wine, vanilla, cinnamon stick, honey, raisins, and dried apples in a medium-sized saucepan and bring to a simmer. Simmer for 5 minutes, covered.

Meanwhile drain the bananas. Add them to the mixture in the saucepan, along with the nutmeg. (If the bananas are not completely covered add a little water.) Simmer, covered, for 10 minutes, then add the slivered almonds and remove from the heat. Remove the cinnamon stick and add more nutmeg, if you wish.

Serve warm, topped with the vanilla-flavored whipped cream.

6 to 8 servings

PEARS POACHED IN RED WINE WITH A TOUCH OF CASSIS

These can also be prepared hours in advance and reheated, or served at room temperature. The dish may be made a day in advance, but the pears will be firmer if cooked the same day you are serving them.

(continued)

3 firm, ripe pears, peeled, cored and sliced
Juice of ½ lemon
2 cups red wine
½ cup mild honey
½ cup raisins
¼ cup *crème de cassis*
1 stick cinnamon
¼ cup slivered almonds (optional)
½ cup heavy cream, whipped

Prepare the pears and drop them into a bowl containing the lemon juice and enough water to cover.

Combine the wine, honey, raisins, cassis, and cinnamon stick in a medium-sized saucepan. Cover and simmer for 5 minutes, removing the cinnamon stick when the 5 minutes are up.

Drain the pears and drop them into the simmering liquid. Add the slivered almonds and simmer, covered, for 10 to 20 minutes.

Serve warm, topped with whipped cream.

6 to 8 servings

ITALIAN FRUIT COMPOTE

This compote can be made several hours before you wish to serve it.

½ cup seedless raisins or currants
½ cup semidry or sweet white wine
1 apple
1 pear
Juice of ½ lemon
1 banana
½ cup dry white wine
1 teaspoon vanilla extract
⅛ teaspoon ground cinnamon
3 tablespoons mild honey, or to taste
1 small bunch red grapes, halved and seeds removed (if you want to take the time)
1 small bunch seedless green grapes, halved
4 figs, dried or fresh, chopped
¼ cup Marsala
½ cup heavy cream, whipped and flavored with vanilla extract (optional)

Soak the raisins or currants in the semidry or sweet white wine; dice he apple and the pear and toss with the lemon juice.

Slice the banana and simmer in the dry white wine with the vanilla, cinnamon, and honey for 5 minutes.

In a large chilled bowl, preferably glass, toss all the above ingredients (except the whipped cream)—the apples and pears, the bananas in their wine, the raisins in theirs—together with the grapes, figs, and Marsala; you might want to add a little more honey.

Chill until ready to serve, and top, if you wish, with a little vanilla-flavored whipped cream.

6 to 8 servings

DRIED FRUIT COMPOTE

Make sure you taste this before you add honey. I find that it's sweet enough without the addition of anything further.

This keeps for several days in the refrigerator. Like fruit soup, it makes a good leftover, because the syrup becomes sweeter as the fruit loses its sugar.

1 pound mixed dried fruits (figs, prunes, apricots, pears, peaches, raisins, apples)
4 cups water
  Juice of ½ lemon
2 tablespoons brandy
  Mild honey to taste
½ cup yogurt, homemade (see page 259) or commercial, or heavy cream, whipped
3 tablespoons slivered almonds

Combine the dried fruit and water in a 3- or 4-quart saucepan. Bring to a simmer and cook for 30 to 40 minutes, covered.

Add the lemon juice, brandy, and honey to taste and serve hot, warm, or chilled, topped with yogurt or whipped cream and slivered almonds.

6 to 8 servings

ORANGES GRAND MARNIER

This dish always comes as a delightful surprise to my guests. What looks like plain sliced oranges turns out to be a perfect combination of sweet citrus and heady liqueur with the marvelous zip of fresh mint.

Oranges Grand Marnier can be made at any time prior to your dinner. I once made five gallons for a wedding and served it in a punch bowl. The oranges looked beautiful, and the leftover fruit lasted for several days.

(continued)

4 oranges
2 to 3 tablespoons chopped fresh mint, plus additional for garnish, if desired
2 to 3 tablespoons slivered almonds
¼ to ½ cup Grand Marnier
Grated coconut (optional)

Simultaneously peel the oranges and cut away the membranes by cutting the peel off in a spiral, using a very sharp knife and cutting all the wa
through to the pulp. Slice the oranges crosswise.

Place in a decorative bowl and toss with mint and Grand Marnie
Cover and refrigerate for an hour or more. Before serving, toss again wi
the almonds and more fresh mint, if you wish. Serve sprinkled with grate
coconut, if desired.

Note: For dramatic impact, these can be flambéed. Heat a little Gran
Marnier and brandy in a saucepan. When it is warm, light it and careful
pour it over the fruit. Or, you can warm the brandy and Grand Marnie
pour it over the fruit, and then light it.

6 to 8 serving

MELON AU PORTO

1 or 2 cantaloupes, depending on the size, or 1 Crenshaw melon
1 to 2 tablespoons port per serving, to taste
Juice of 1 to 2 limes
Lime wedges for garnish

Cut the melons in half and remove the seeds. Cut into large slices (on
melon should yield six to eight slices, depending on the size of the melon
Now make several crosswise slashes, about 1 inch apart, down *to* the rin
but not through it, across each slice. Place the melon on a platter or on in
dividual plates and squeeze lime over each piece, then spoon 1 to 2 table
spoons port over each.

Serve garnished with lime wedges.

6 to 8 serving

WATERMELON-FRUIT EXTRAVAGANZA

This can be made up to four hours in advance and chilled, covered.

½ watermelon (see note below)
1 cantaloupe, halved and seeded
1 honeydew melon, halved and seeded

½ pound seedless green grapes
2 to 3 tablespoons fresh mint leaves, plus additional for garnish
½ pint berries in season
3 peaches, sliced
Slivered almonds for garnish

Remove the meat from all the melons with a melon-ball spoon or regular spoon (being careful not to damage the watermelon shell, since you will be using it for your fruit bowl), and toss with the grapes, berries, and mint in a very large bowl. Discard the cantaloupe and honeydew rinds.

Scallop the edge of the watermelon shell with a very sharp knife. Fill it with the melon ball–fruit mixture, top with peach slices, and garnish with mint leaves and almonds.

Place on a tray and surround with any extra fruit mixture.

Note: If you want a basket, start with a whole watermelon. Cut a handle across the top, then cut around the sides (see illustration). Remove the two top pieces on either side of the handle and cut away the flesh under the handle. Proceed as above, and scallop only the sides.

12 servings

PINEAPPLE BOATS

Fruit-Filled Pineapples

2 pineapples
1 pint strawberries, stemmed and sliced
½ pound seedless green grapes
½ pound fresh or dried figs, sliced
4 peaches, sliced
1 tablespoon fresh mint leaves, plus additional for garnish

Cut the pineapples in half lengthwise with a very sharp knife, leaving the leaves intact. Scoop out the fruit with a grapefruit knife, without cutting through the skin. Cut away the core, discard, and cut the fruit into chunks.

Toss all the fruits together, along with the 1 tablespoon mint leaves, and place back in the pineapple shells. Chill and serve on a platter, garnished with additional fresh mint leaves, scooping the fruit out of the shells and into chilled bowls for serving.

6 to 8 servings

PEACHES MARSALA

3 to 4 firm, ripe, sweet peaches
Marsala to cover
Fresh mint and sliced strawberries (optional) for garnish

Drop the peaches into boiling water to cover for 1 minute, then drain and run under cold water. Peel off the skins; they will come off easily. Slice the peaches and place in individual wine glasses or dessert dishes.

Cover the peaches with Marsala and serve, garnished with fresh mint and, if you wish, sliced fresh strawberries.

6 to 8 servings

RASPBERRIES IN RED WINE

2 pints raspberries
Red wine to cover

Wash and drain the berries and place in wine glasses. Cover them with red wine and serve.

6 to 8 servings

GRAPEFRUIT WITH PORT

⅓ to ½ cup port
3 to 4 grapefruit, preferably Texas Ruby Reds, cut in half, sectioned, and, if you wish, edges scalloped
Strawberries, mint, and orange slices for garnish

Spoon 1 tablespoon port over each grapefruit half. Garnish with strawberries, mint, and orange slices and serve.

6 to 8 servings

PINEAPPLE WITH KIRSCH

Use only the finest kirsch for this recipe. I recommend Rauthaus.

1 ripe pineapple, skinned, cored, and chunked
1 cup sliced strawberries
⅓ cup kirsch
Fresh mint for garnish

Toss the pineapple and strawberries with the kirsch and serve garnished with fresh mint.

6 to 8 servings

BAKED APPLES

6 to 8 large, tart apples
½ cup raisins
⅓ cup mild honey, approximately
    Ground cinnamon, freshly grated nutmeg, and ground allspice to taste
½ cup chopped almonds
    Apple juice or cider
1 stick cinnamon (optional)
½ cup heavy cream (optional)

Preheat the oven to 350 degrees.

Core the apples from the top, not cutting all the way through the bottom but cutting out a cone shape, so that you have a large hole in the top that narrows as you reach the bottom.

Fill each cavity with raisins and dribble in some honey, up to a tablespoon per apple. Sprinkle with cinnamon, nutmeg, allspice, and almonds.

Butter a baking dish and place the apples in it, with the open end of the cone up. Pour apple juice or cider into the pan so the pan is half full. If you wish, place a stick of cinnamon in the cider. Bake in the preheated oven for about 45 minutes, basting every 15 minutes with the apple juice.

If you want a richer dish, pour a little cream over the apples before serving.

6 to 8 servings

GRAIN-STUFFED BAKED APPLES

Mix together the raisins, honey, and spices with the almonds and 1 cup cooked brown rice or other cooked grains. Moisten with a little milk and fill the apples with the mixture. Bake as above.

BASIC DESSERT CRÊPES

Use these crêpes for the two desserts that follow. They can also be used for any number of other dessert-type fillings.

(continued)

⅓ cup water

⅔ cup milk

⅓ cup Grand Marnier or orange juice, or a combination

3 eggs

3 tablespoons sesame oil or melted butter (omit if using an inverted crêpe pan)

¼ teaspoon salt, preferably sea salt

1 cup whole-wheat pastry flour (or half whole-wheat pastry flour and half unbleached white)

Put all the ingredients except the flour in a blender and turn on. Add the flour and blend at high speed for 2 to 3 minutes. Refrigerate for at least 2 hours and at the most a day ahead. (If you do not have a blender, beat up the eggs, then beat in the liquids and the salt. Gradually beat in the flour with a wire whisk. Let the batter rest for 2 hours.)

Make the crêpes according to the directions on pages 173–74.

20 to 30 pancakes

SPICED FRUIT- AND NUT-FILLED CRÊPES

These crêpes, all assembled, freeze quite successfully. Wrap them tightly in buttered foil and keep them in the freezer for up to two months. They will thaw in an hour at room temperature, in 30 minutes in a 350-degree oven.

The filling can be made up to a day in advance, covered, and refrigerated. Or it can be frozen for up to a month. The sauce will keep for two days in the refrigerator.

1 recipe Basic Dessert Crêpes (see above)

For the filling:

3 tablespoons butter

½ to 1 teaspoon ground cinnamon

½ teaspoon freshly grated nutmeg

2 apples, peeled and diced

1 banana, diced

½ cup raisins

½ cup chopped almonds

3 tablespoons mild honey

1 teaspoon vanilla extract

1 tablespoon brandy

2 teaspoons dark rum

For the sauce:

3 tablespoons maple syrup
2 tablespoons *crème de cassis* liqueur
1 cup plain yogurt, homemade (see page 259) or commercial

Have the crêpes stacked and ready to be filled. Heat the butter and stir in the cinnamon and nutmeg. Add the apples and sauté, stirring, for 5 minutes. Add the banana, raisins, and nuts and sauté for 5 minutes more. Stir in the honey, vanilla, brandy, and the rum. Taste for spiciness and sweetness, then cook for a few minutes more, until the apples are cooked through.

Remove from the heat. Place 2 tablespoons filling on each crêpe and roll up. Place the crêpes in a buttered baking dish, cover with foil, and warm in a low oven.

Serve topped with a sauce made by stirring the syrup and cassis into the yogurt.

6 to 8 servings

ORANGE DESSERT CRÊPES

These are irresistible. The filling is like a cake icing, buttery and rich, with heady orange and almond flavors. Very easy and elegant, especially when you flambé them, turn the lights down low, and bring in your serving dish bright with the beautiful blue flames. They can be assembled a day in advance and refrigerated, tightly covered, but should be baked just before serving.

1 recipe Basic Dessert Crêpes (see page 283)
  Juice of 2 oranges
½ cup Grand Marnier
¼ pound (1 stick) unsalted butter, softened
¼ cup mild honey
¼ teaspoon almond extract
¼ cup almonds, ground in a blender
1 tablespoon grated orange peel
¼ cup brandy
  Slivered almonds and chopped fresh mint for garnish

Have the crêpes stacked and ready to be filled. Preheat the oven to 350 degrees.

Strain the orange juice and combine it with ¼ cup of the Grand Marnier. Cream the butter with the honey and beat in the orange juice–Grand Marnier mixture by spoonfuls; you can use an electric beater, a whisk, or a fork. Stir in the almond extract, the ground almonds, and the grated orange peel.

Spread a generous layer of the orange butter on each crêpe. Fold the crêpe in half, then fold in half again, so the shape is a quarter circle. Place in a buttered baking dish. (Alternatively, you can make a *gâteau* by buttering each crêpe and stacking them one on top of the other.) Heat through in the oven for 10 to 15 minutes.

Combine the brandy and remaining Grand Marnier in a saucepan and warm over a low flame. Either light the liqueur while in the pan and pour it flaming over the crêpes, or pour the warm liqueur over the crêpes and light. If you wish, continue spooning the blue-flaming liqueur over the crêpes until the flame goes out.

If you have made a *gâteau*, cut in very thin pie-shaped wedges to serve. Garnish with slivered almonds and chopped fresh mint.

6 to 8 servings

BAVARIAN CRÈME AU CAFÉ

This has been an immensely successful dessert at my house. The mint extract makes it especially delightful. It's so light that guests don't feel "weighed down" even after having seconds.

There are several steps involved here, and I recommend that you make it the day before you wish to serve it, though it will keep for several days and can be made as little as five hours before serving. It has a melt-in-your-mouth consistency that makes it a good complement to any kind of meal, light to heavy, though naturally you wouldn't want to serve it after an egg-oriented meal. It's a protein-rich dessert as well.

 5 eggs plus 3 egg yolks, at room temperature
 ¾ cup mild honey
 2 tablespoons (2 envelopes) unflavored gelatin
 ½ cup strong coffee
 1½ cups milk
 ½ teaspoon peppermint extract
 4 tablespoons Kahlúa
 1 teaspoon vanilla extract
 2 teaspoons brandy
 ¼ teaspoon cream of tartar
 ⅛ teaspoon salt, preferably sea salt
 1 cup heavy cream, chilled

This recipe involves several steps, so it will help to have the necessary equipment ready.

For the custard: A heavy-bottomed saucepan for heating the
         egg yolks and milk
         A whisk
         A wooden spoon
         A small pan for heating the 1½ cups milk
         A small bowl or pan for dissolving the gelatin
         in the coffee
         A strainer set over a 3-quart bowl
         A candy thermometer
For the egg whites: A clean, dry egg beater or baloon whisk
         A large bowl
         A spatula
For the whipped cream: A clean, dry egg beater or whisk, chilled
         A 1-quart bowl, chilled

A 2-quart decorative mold or soufflé dish or 8 ramekins

Making the custard: Separate the eggs, placing the whites in the large
bowl for the egg whites and the yolks, plus the three extra, in the saucepan
(keep the whites you didn't use in a covered jar in the refrigerator). Gradually whip the honey into the yolks and beat until the mixture is frothy.

Dissolve the gelatin in the coffee in a small bowl or pan, stirring well to
make sure all the crystals are dissolved. Set aside in a pan of water on the
stove.

In another saucepan, heat the milk over medium heat until you see the
surface begin to tremble; do not allow it to boil. Now dribble the milk
slowly into the egg yolks, beating all the while with a whisk.

Place this mixture over a low to medium flame (if you're not working
with a heavy-bottomed saucepan, the flame should be low) and heat
through, stirring with a wooden spoon all the while, until it begins to
thicken. (Under no circumstances let this mixture boil, as that will curdle
the egg yolks. If the eggs do begin to curdle, remove the pan from the heat
immediately and stir vigorously, then return to the heat.) As the temperature reaches 168 degrees, the mixture will begin to thicken and steam. Stir
until the mixture is creamy and coats your spoon evenly, then remove from
the heat and stir for 1 minute to cool.

Heat the coffee-gelatin mixture through over a pan of water to dissolve
again, then add it to the custard, carefully scraping every last bit out of the
bowl or pan with a rubber spatula. Strain the mixture into the 3-quart
bowl, then stir in the peppermint extract, 2 tablespoons of the Kahlúa, the
vanilla, and the brandy and set aside.

Beating the egg whites: Start to beat the egg whites. As they begin to foam, add the cream of tartar and the salt. Beat until the egg whites form stiff, shining peaks, then stir one-fourth into the custard and gently fold in the rest.

Beating the cream: Leaving ½ cup of the cream in the refrigerator to chill further, beat the remainder in the chilled 1-quart bowl, circulating the beater or whisk to incorporate as much air as possible. (If your bowl and beater are not chilled, place the bowl over ice water.) Beat the cream until doubled in volume and until it adheres softly to a spoon when lifted, but not until it is stiff.

Stir the Bavarian cream mixture so it begins to set evenly. If you don't do this, the gelatin will settle at the bottom. Allow it to cool for about 5 minutes, stirring every minute or so, then gently fold in the whipped cream.

Pour the Bavarian cream into the mold of your choice or into individual ramekins. (If you are using a soufflé dish, you may have to prepare a collar [see page 159], although you need only do this if you have more cream than the soufflé dish will hold. If you are using a decorative mold, rinse it with cold water, fill with the mixture, and refrigerate.) Cover well and chill for 4 to 5 hours, or overnight. Keep chilled until you are ready to serve.

Just before serving time, whip the remaining cream and flavor it with the remaining Kahlúa. Serve the Bavarian cream in the soufflé dish or ramekins, or unmolded on a serving plate. (To unmold, dip in very hot water for a few seconds and reverse onto a chilled serving plate; refrigerate again to set.) Top with the Kahlúa-flavored whipped cream.

6 to 8 servings

BAVARIAN CREAM TARTLETS

The Bavarian cream can also be served in individual tart crusts. Fill the baked crusts with the Bavarian cream and refrigerate. (I prefer the cream by itself, though, as it has such a light, special flavor.)

Dessert Soufflés

A puffed-up dessert soufflé, right out of the oven, is one of the most elegant and dramatic desserts I can think of. With all the eggs and milk, it's also one of the most healthful. This is definitely a place to incorporate protein into your meal. Soufflés can follow any meal that doesn't call for many eggs.

Dessert soufflés, like main-dish souffles, may be assembled up to two hours in advance and held, covered.

APRICOT SOUFFLÉ

1 pound dried apricots
  Milk or cream for blending
½ teaspoon vanilla extract
2 tablespoons Cognac or ⅓ cup apricot liqueur (optional)
¼ cup mild honey, or to taste
6 eggs plus 2 egg whites, at room temperature
  Salt, preferably sea salt
¼ teaspoon cream of tartar
1 cup heavy cream, whipped and flavored with vanilla extract or Cognac

Soak the apricots in water to cover overnight, or for at least several hours. Place in a saucepan and bring to a boil, then lower the heat and cook for 5 to 10 minutes.

Pour off the water and puree through a food mill or in a blender or food processor. (If you need some liquid for the blender, add a little milk or cream.) Stir in the vanilla and the Cognac or apricot liqueur and taste for sweetness; add the honey. Separate the eggs and beat in the yolks, one at a time; add ½ teaspoon salt. Heat through over very low heat for 3 to 4 minutes, then remove from the heat and cool slightly. (The soufflé mixture can be refrigerated at this point, tightly covered.)

Preheat the oven to 375 degrees; butter a straight-sided soufflé dish.

Beat the 8 egg whites, adding a little salt and the cream of tartar after they begin to foam, until they form stiff, shiny peaks. Stir one-quarter of the egg whites into the apricot mixture, then fold in the remainder. Spoon the mixture into the prepared soufflé dish and bake for 30 minutes, until brown and puffed.

Serve immediately, topped with the vanilla- or Cognac-flavored whipped cream.

6 to 8 servings

GINGERBREAD SOUFFLÉ

Imagine the sweet spiciness of gingerbread in a downy soufflé. A little of the sauce settles at the bottom, becoming cakey, and the top becomes crusty as the soufflé bakes. So, to capture all the gingerbread goodness, scoop all the way to the bottom of the dish as you serve.

This impressive dessert also makes a delicious, puddinglike leftover.

3 tablespoons butter
1 teaspoon freshly grated gingerroot or ½ teaspoon ground ginger
1 teaspoon ground cinnamon
3 tablespoons unbleached white flour, or a combination of unbleached white and whole-wheat pastry flour
¾ cup hot milk
1 tablespoon mild honey
Salt, preferably sea salt
1 tablespoon dry sherry
¼ to ⅓ cup finely cut preserved ginger or ginger marmalade
3 to 4 tablespoons molasses
5 eggs plus 1 egg white, at room temperature
¼ teaspoon cream of tartar
Whipped cream or vanilla ice cream

Melt the butter and sauté the ginger for 1 minute, then stir in the cinnamon and add the flour. Stir together to make a roux and cook, stirring with a wooden spoon, for 1 minute. Slowly pour in the hot milk; whisk over low heat until the mixture is thickened. Remove from the heat and stir in the honey, ¼ teaspoon salt, sherry, preserved ginger or ginger marmalade, and molasses. Separate the eggs and beat in the yolks, one at a time. (The soufflé mixture can be refrigerated at this point, tightly covered.)

Preheat the oven to 400 degrees; butter a 2-quart soufflé dish.

Beat the 6 egg whites until they form stiff, shiny peaks, adding the cream of tartar and a pinch of salt when they begin to foam. Stir one-quarter of the beaten egg whites into the sauce, then fold in the remaining egg whites. Pour into the prepared soufflé dish and bake for 25 to 30 minutes.

Serve immediately, topped with whipped cream or vanilla ice cream.

6 to 8 servings

SOUFFLÉ GRAND MARNIER

1 orange
1 sugar cube (optional)
3 tablespoons butter
3 tablespoons unbleached white flour

½ cup hot milk
¼ cup orange juice, heated
4 eggs, separated, plus 2 egg whites, at room temperature
3 tablespoons orange marmalade
6 tablespoons Grand Marnier
⅛ teaspoon salt, preferably sea salt
¼ teaspoon cream of tartar
1 cup heavy cream

Rub the orange with the sugar cube to remove the zest, or use an orange zester; set aside. Peel off the remaining part of the skin and slice the orange into thin rounds; set aside for garnish.

In a heavy saucepan, melt the butter and stir in the flour. Cook for 1 minute, then slowly pour in the milk, orange juice, and zest, stirring constantly with a whisk. Beat with the whisk until smooth.

In a small bowl, beat together the egg yolks, the marmalade, and 4 tablespoons of the Grand Marnier. Stir a little of the milk/orange juice mixture into the yolk mixture, then pour the yolk mixture into the saucepan. Beat over low heat for 1 minute, then remove from the heat and allow to cool. (The soufflé mixture can be refrigerated for a day or so at this point, tightly covered.)

Preheat the oven to 375 degrees; butter a 2-quart soufflé dish.

Beat the 6 egg whites until they begin to foam, then add the salt and cream of tartar. Continue to beat until the egg whites are stiff and form shiny peaks.

Stir a small amount of the egg whites into the soufflé mixture and fold in the rest; pour into the prepared soufflé dish. Bake for 30 to 40 minutes.

Toward the end of the baking time, whip the cream and flavor it with the remaining Grand Marnier. Serve the soufflé immediately, topped with the Grand Marnier-flavored whipped cream and decorated with the sliced oranges.

6 to 8 servings

LIGHT CHEESECAKE

This is not the intense, ultrarich cream-cheese cake that we know and love, but it does have that wonderful cheesecake melt-in-your-mouth quality. If you can't find mild honey you shouldn't attempt this, because the taste of a strong honey will overpower the other flavors.

(continued)

Butter for the pan
¼ cup wheat germ
1 teaspoon ground cinnamon
4 eggs
1 pound ricotta
½ cup plain yogurt, homemade (see page 259) or commercial
½ cup mild honey, or to taste
2 teaspoons vanilla extract, or to taste
3 tablespoons lemon juice, or to taste
½ teaspoon salt, preferably sea salt
2 tablespoons unbleached white or whole-wheat pastry flour

Preheat the oven to 350 degrees.

Butter an 8-inch spring-form pan or baking pan generously. Combine the wheat germ and cinnamon and pour into the pan, then turn the pan so that the mixture coats all of the sides and the bottom in a thin layer. Pour off excess or shake the pan to layer it evenly over the bottom. Refrigerate.

Beat the eggs in a blender or mixer and blend in the ricotta, yogurt, honey, vanilla, lemon juice, salt, and flour. Taste and add more honey, lemon juice, or vanilla if you desire. Pour into the prepared pan and bake in the preheated oven for 45 minutes to 1 hour. When you see the top just beginning to brown, turn off the oven; leave the door closed and let the cheesecake sit in the oven for another hour.

Remove from the oven and refrigerate overnight or for at least several hours before cutting.

6 to 8 servings

MILLET-RAISIN PUDDING

Millet is such a pleasing grain, very high in nutrients. This protein-rich dessert also makes a good breakfast; it's the kind of dish you might want to keep on hand, covered, in the refrigerator, for a nourishing snack. The flavors and textures here are wonderful, and the pudding has a heavenly aroma.

1 cup raw millet
3 cups water
¼ teaspoon salt
⅔ cup spray-dried milk
¼ cup mild honey
1 teaspoon vanilla extract
½ cup grated coconut
½ cup raisins

Preheat the oven to 350 degrees; butter a 2-quart casserole.

Combine the millet, water, and salt in a medium-sized saucepan and bring to a boil. Immediately remove from the heat and drain off some of the water into a blender. Blend in the spray-dried milk, then the honey and the vanilla. Pour back into the pot with the millet and stir in the coconut and the raisins.

Pour the millet mixture into the prepared casserole. Cover with foil or a lid and bake for 1 hour.

When you remove the casserole from the oven, the liquid will still be bubbling at the bottom of the baking dish. Allow the pudding to cool and absorb the remaining liquid before serving.

6 to 8 servings

INDIAN PUDDING

Indian pudding is an old American recipe. Cornmeal was referred to by the Pilgrims as "Indian"; hence the name. Recipes for it occur in cookbooks as far back as the seventeenth century, and often call for the addition of "a little Indian."

This is a spicy dessert, high in protein; it makes a good leftover.

1 quart milk, scalded
6 tablespoons yellow cornmeal, preferably stone-ground
⅓ to ½ cup molasses (depending on the strength of your molasses and your taste for it)
2 to 3 tablespoons mild honey
4 eggs, beaten
1 teaspoon salt, preferably sea salt
1 teaspoon ground ginger
½ teaspoon freshly grated nutmeg
3 tablespoons butter
½ cup raisins

Preheat the oven to 325 degrees; butter a 2-quart casserole, soufflé dish, or Dutch oven.

Bring the milk to the boiling point in a 2- or 3-quart heavy-bottomed saucepan. Pour in the cornmeal in a slow stream, stirring all the while with a whisk or wooden spoon. Bring to a gentle boil and cook over low heat, stirring, for about 15 minutes, until the mixture is thick and creamy (it should have the consistency of a runny cream-of-wheat). Add the molasses and honey and cook for another 5 minutes.

(continued)

Remove from the heat and stir in the beaten eggs, the salt, ginger, nutmeg, butter, and raisins; mix well.

Pour the pudding into the prepared casserole, soufflé dish, or Dutch oven and bake for 1 to 1½ hours, until a knife comes out clean and the top is just beginning to brown.

6 to 8 servings

Fruit Pies

APPLE, PEACH, OR PEAR PIE OR TARTS

1 recipe Whole-Wheat Pie Crust (page 149) (see note below)
5 cups peeled, sliced apples, peaches, or pears
½ cup mild honey
⅛ teaspoon salt, preferably sea salt
1 tablespoon cornstarch or arrowroot, dissolved in a little water
½ teaspoon ground cinnamon
½ teaspoon freshly ground nutmeg
¼ teaspoon ground allspice
1 teaspoon vanilla extract
1 tablespoon lemon juice
1 tablespoon brandy or Calvados (apple brandy)
1 beaten egg or 2 tablespoons milk, mixed with a little ground cinnamon

Preheat the oven to 350 degrees.

Roll out half the pie-crust dough to fit a 9- or 10-inch pie pan, saving the second half of the dough for a lattice or regular top crust (or roll out the whole amount and fit in several tart pans). Following the directions on page 150, prebake in the preheated oven for 5 minutes, then remove the pan from the oven and raise the oven heat to 450 degrees.

Combine the sliced fruit with all the other ingredients except the egg or milk. Place in the pie shell (or tart shell) and cover with a lattice or regular top crust, pricking the regular crust to allow steam to escape. Brush the lattice or top crust with the egg or milk mixture.

Bake at 450 degrees for 10 minutes, then turn down the heat and bake at 350 degrees for another 30 minutes. Serve warm or cooled.

Note: If you prefer a sweeter crust, add ¼ cup date sugar to the flour.

One 9- or 10-inch pie or several smaller tarts

BERRY OR CHERRY PIES

1 recipe Whole-Wheat Pie Crust (page 149) (see note page 294)
2 tablespoons cornstarch
¼ cup water or orange juice
4 cups berries or pitted cherries, washed, stemmed, and picked over
½ to ⅔ cup mild honey
2 tablespoons lemon juice
2 tablespoons *crème de cassis* or other fruity liqueur (use kirsch for cherry tarts)

Preheat the oven to 350 degrees.

Roll out half the pie pastry and fit it into a 9- or 10-inch pie pan, saving the other half for a lattice topping (or roll out the whole amount and fit in several tart pans). Follow the directions on page 150 and prebake the shell or shells for 5 minutes, then remove the pan and raise the oven heat to 450 degrees.

Dissolve the cornstarch in the water or juice. Combine with the berries or cherries and other ingredients and turn into the pie crust (or tart shells). Cover with a lattice topping and bake at 450 degrees for 10 minutes, then turn the heat down to 350 degrees and bake for another 30 minutes.

One 9- or 10-inch pie or several smaller tarts

PECAN PIE

When I was growing up in Connecticut, pecan pie was a rare treat. I now have the luxury of living in Texas, where pecan trees grow in my back yard and spill their pecans all through the fall. Pecan pies are no longer rare, but they are still very special.

½ recipe Whole-Wheat Pie Crust (page 149)
4 tablespoons (½ stick) butter or ¼ cup safflower oil
⅔ cup mild honey
¼ cup molasses
3 eggs
1 teaspoon vanilla extract
1 tablespoon rum
¼ teaspoon freshly grated nutmeg
½ teaspoon salt, preferably sea salt
1 to 1¼ cups broken pecans plus ¼ cup whole pecan meats

Preheat the oven to 350 degrees.

Roll out your crust to fit a 9- or 10-inch pie pan; follow the directions on page 150 and prebake the crust for 5 minutes, then remove the pan and raise the oven heat to 375 degrees.

Cream the butter or oil with the honey and the molasses; beat in the eggs. Add the vanilla, rum, nutmeg, and salt. Set aside the ¼ cup whole pecan meats and stir the broken ones into the pie mixture. Pour the mixture into the pie shell, and with the remaining nuts make a design on the surface of the pie.

Bake at 375 degrees for 35 to 40 minutes, until a knife comes out clean when inserted in the center.

One 9- or 10-inch pie

BAKLAVA

This rich, flaky Middle Eastern pastry is time consuming, but worth the effort. You won't find this quite as sweet as *baklava* you may have eaten before, because it does not call for a large amount of refined sugar. But the honey syrup poured on when the sizzling *baklava* comes out of the oven makes it quite rich.

This can be assembled up to a day before you bake it, and will stay fresh after baking for up to three days if wrapped in foil or plastic.

    4 cups (about 1 pound) very finely chopped nuts (almonds, walnuts, pecans)
    ⅓ cup date sugar
    1 teaspoon vanilla extract
      Grated peel of 1 lemon or orange
 1½ cups wheat germ
    ¼ cup sesame seeds
    ¾ teaspoon ground cloves
    1 tablespoon ground cinnamon
    ½ cup melted butter
    1 pound filo dough
 1¼ cups mild honey
    2 cups water
    3 tablespoons lemon juice

Preheat the oven to 350 degrees.

Combine the nuts with the date sugar, vanilla, grated lemon or orange peel, wheat germ, sesame seeds, ground cloves, and half the cinnamon. Place in a large measuring cup or divide into four equal portions.

Brush a 2- or 3-quart oblong baking dish with some of the melted butter and arrange a layer of filo dough in it, allowing the edges to extend over the sides of the pan. Place another layer of filo on top of this and butter it. Repeat with four more sheets of filo, buttering every other one. Butter the sixth sheet and sprinkle with some of the remaining cinnamon. Spread one-quarter of the nut mixture over this and enclose it by folding the overlapping edge of the *top* sheet of filo (that is, the one directly under the filling) over it all the way around.

Layer three more sheets of filo over the nut mixture, buttering each one. Sprinkle the third one with cinnamon and spread on another layer of the nut mixture. Fold the edges of the three sheets of filo over this mixture. Then bring the overlapping edge of the filo underneath the first layer of filling up over this second layer, so you are enveloping not only the filling but the filo beneath this second layer (see illustration). Continue in the same way with the remaining filo and nut mixture, so that you have four layers of the filling with three buttered sheets of filo between each one. Use the overhanging edges of filo from the bottom layer if you can, but if they won't reach after a while, just use the edges underneath the layer in question. When you place the final sheet of filo on top you will wrap it around the whole assemblage from the top.

Layer on the remaining filo, buttering every other layer. Just before you add the last sheet, bring all the remaining overhanging edges from the bottom, if there are any, up over the top of the *baklava*, then cover with the last sheet of filo. Brush with butter and sprinkle with cinnamon, and tuck the edges into the sides of the pan.

With a sharp knife, make diagonal cuts, about 2 inches apart and ½ inch deep, across the *baklava*. Turn the pan and make diagonal cuts the other way, so you get a pattern of diamond-shaped pieces about 2 inches long.

Place in the preheated oven and bake for 1 hour.

Meanwhile, make a syrup by combining the honey and water in a large heavy-bottomed saucepan; cook for 10 minutes. (It is important to use a large saucepan because the water and honey mixture will bubble up tremendously when it reaches the boiling point.) Stir in the lemon juice, remove from the heat, and allow to cool.

When the *baklava* is golden brown and crisp, remove it from the oven and, using a sharp knife, cut all the way through to make diamond-shaped pieces. Immediately pour the cooled syrup over the hot *baklava;* it will make a satisfying sizzling noise as it saturates the pastry.

Cool and serve.

Note: This yields 4 dozen pieces in a 3-quart baking dish and about 30 pieces in a 2-quart dish.

2½ to 4 dozen pieces

MOIST CARROT CAKE

This is especially showy if made in a Bundt pan and iced with fluffy whipped cream. I have even used this recipe for a traditional tiered wedding cake.

¾ cup safflower or vegetable oil
1 cup mild honey
4 eggs
¼ cup brandy
1 teaspoon vanilla extract
¼ cup soy flour
1¼ cups whole-wheat pastry flour
1 cup unbleached white flour
1½ teaspoons baking powder
1½ teaspoons ground cinnamon
1½ teaspoons freshly grated nutmeg
½ teaspoon ground cloves
½ teaspoon salt, preferably sea salt
½ pound carrots, grated
1 cup sunflower seeds, chopped pecans, or chopped walnuts
1 cup heavy cream, whipped and flavored with 1 teaspoon vanilla extract
Fresh flowers or fruit and nuts for garnish

Preheat the oven to 350 degrees.

Cream the oil with the honey until the mixture is fluffy. Beat in the eggs, brandy, and vanilla.

Sift together the flours, baking powder, spices, and salt. Stir into the liquid ingredients and beat until the mixture is smooth, then stir in the grated carrots and the seeds or nuts.

Butter a Bundt pan generously (or use two loaf pans). Pour in the batter and bake at 350 degrees for 1 hour, until a toothpick inserted in the center comes out clean.

Let cool in the Bundt until it pulls away from the sides of the pan, then, holding a cake rack tightly over the pan, reverse the pan and allow the cake to fall out onto the rack. Let cool, then carefully lift from the rack and place on a plate. Ice the cake with the vanilla-flavored whipped cream and decorate with flowers or fruit and nuts. Chill until ready to serve.

Note: If you are not serving it right away, stick toothpicks in the cake and cover with plastic wrap. The toothpicks will keep the plastic off the whipped cream (and keep the whipped cream off the plastic). Keep refrigerated.

12 to 16 servings

FRUIT AND SPICE CAKE

For the cake:
¾ cup mild honey
½ cup safflower oil
3 eggs
2 teaspoons vanilla extract
½ cup milk, buttermilk, or plain yogurt, homemade (see page 159) or commercial, more if necessary
1 cup whole-wheat pastry flour
1 cup unbleached white flour
½ cup soy flour
½ cup wheat germ
½ teaspoon salt, preferably sea salt
4 teaspoons double-acting baking powder
1 teaspoon ground cinnamon
½ teaspoon freshly grated nutmeg
½ teaspoon ground allspice
2 apples, cored, peeled, and sliced thin
1 banana, sliced
½ cup sunflower seeds, chopped pecans, or chopped walnuts

For the icing:
½ pint strawberries, washed and stemmed
12 ounces cream cheese
   Honey to taste
   Nuts and fresh flowers (optional) for garnish

Preheat the oven to 350 degrees; oil a 9 x 13-inch baking pan or a 10-inch Bundt pan.

Cream together the honey and oil until the mixture is fluffy. Beat in the eggs and stir in the vanilla and milk, buttermilk, or yogurt.

Sift together the flours, wheat germ, salt, baking powder, and spices. Add to the liquid mixture a cup at a time and beat well. (The mixture should be runny, like regular cake batter; if it is too stiff add a little milk or buttermilk.) Fold in the sliced apples and banana, then the seeds or nuts.

Pour into the prepared pan and bake for 45 minutes, or until a toothpick comes out clean when inserted in the center. Let the cake cool in the pan for 10 minutes, then invert on a cake rack to finish cooling. (Be careful; the cake is moist and heavy.)

For the icing, puree a little more than half the strawberries, setting the rest aside for garnish, in a blender or food processor. Add the cream cheese, and blend until you have a smooth mixture. Add honey to taste.

(continued)

When the cake is cool, spread the cream cheese mixture over it. Decorate with strawberries and nuts and, if you wish, with flowers.

12 to 15 servings

CAROB MARBLE CAKE

Although carob *isn't* chocolate, it does resemble it in flavor and color. This cake, with its rich icing, has fooled many guests at my house, as have the Carob Brownies on page 301.

For the cake:
¾ cup mild honey
½ cup safflower oil
4 tablespoons (½ stick) butter
3 eggs
2 teaspoons vanilla extract
1 cup buttermilk or milk
½ teaspoon salt, preferably sea salt
2 teaspoons double-acting baking powder
1¼ cups sifted whole-wheat pastry flour
½ cup sifted unbleached white flour
½ cup carob powder

For the icing:
4 tablespoons (½ stick) butter
⅓ cup spray-dried milk
½ cup carob powder
¼ cup mild honey
1 teaspoon vanilla extract
¼ cup milk
  Water (optional)
  Peppermint extract (optional)

Preheat the oven to 325 degrees; butter and flour two round 8- or 9-inch layer pans and, if you wish, cut waxed paper to fit the bottoms.

Cream the honey with the safflower oil and butter until fluffy. Beat in the eggs, vanilla, and the milk or buttermilk, then sift in the salt, baking powder, and whole-wheat pastry flour. Beat until the batter is smooth.

Divide the batter in half. Into one half beat the sifted unbleached white flour; into the other beat the carob powder. Drop alternate spoonfuls of the white and carob batter into the pans, so that you have a checkerboard pattern. Then, with a knife, swirl the carob into the white batter in paisley curls.

Bake for 45 minutes to an hour, or until a toothpick comes out clean when inserted in the center. Cool in the pans for 10 minutes, then remove from the pans and cool on a rack.

While the layers are cooling, prepare the icing.

Cream the butter with the spray-dried milk and the carob powder, then beat in the honey, vanilla, and milk. Beat until smooth. Thin out with water, a tablespoon at a time, if it seems too thick for you, and add, if you wish, *one* drop of peppermint extract.

Frost the cooled cake layers.

8 to 12 servings

CAROB BROWNIES

½ cup safflower oil
½ cup mild honey
3 tablespoons molasses
2 eggs, beaten
1 teaspoon vanilla extract
¾ cup whole-wheat pastry flour
1 teaspoon double-acting baking powder
½ teaspoon salt, preferably sea salt
½ cup carob powder
¾ cup chopped nuts or sunflower seeds
½ cup raisins

Preheat the oven to 350 degrees; oil a 9-inch-square baking pan.

Cream the oil, honey, and molasses and beat in the eggs and the vanilla. Sift together the flour, baking powder, and salt. Stir into the liquid mixture, then add the carob, nuts or seeds, and raisins and mix well.

Spread the batter in the prepared pan and bake for 30 minutes, or until a toothpick comes out clean when inserted in the center.

Allow to cool in the pan, then cut into squares. Wrap in plastic or foil if not serving right away.

9 to 12 brownies

STRAWBERRY AND CASSIS SHERBET

This sherbet is a frozen meringue flavored with strawberries and cassis. The reason I have added cassis is that nowadays it's hard to find ripe, full-bodied strawberries. The cassis gives the sherbet a delightful lift.

If you've never made a meringue before, you will be amazed by the chemical transformation that occurs. I couldn't believe it, the first time I made one, as I beat in the hot syrup and watched the fluffy egg whites become satiny and smooth. The change is nothing short of miraculous, and for me it was especially exciting to see that I could do this easily with a honey syrup.

Be sure to make your syrup in a large saucepan, more than double the volume of your honey and water. It will bubble up furiously; I have carelessly clogged up many a burner with the overflow. Also keep the heat moderate or your syrup will caramelize.

3 cups strawberries, fresh, washed and stemmed, or frozen
3 to 4 tablespoons lemon juice
½ cup *crème de cassis*
3 egg whites, at room temperature
  Scant ¼ teaspoon cream of tartar
  Pinch of salt, preferably sea salt
⅓ cup water
¾ cup mild honey
  Fresh mint, fresh sliced strawberries, and lime slices for garnish

Puree the strawberries in a blender and stir in the lemon juice and the cassis. Set aside.

Put the egg whites into a clean, dry 3-quart bowl or in the bowl of an electric mixer. Begin to beat the egg whites slowly. When they start to foam, add the cream of tartar and the salt and beat into stiff, shining peaks. Set aside (or if you have a free-standing mixer, turn it down to low speed), and prepare the syrup as follows:

Bring the water and honey to a boil in a large heavy-bottomed saucepan over medium heat. Tilt the pan to combine the honey and water evenly and to obtain a clear liquid. Boil rapidly to the "soft ball" stage on a candy thermometer (238 degrees).

Now, beating at moderate speed, dribble the hot syrup into the egg whites. Continue beating at high speed for 5 minutes or so: you will see the egg-white mixture go through a miraculous metamorphosis and become a satiny meringue. Continue beating until the egg whites are cool and form stiff, satiny peaks when a bit is lifted with a spoon. Gradually beat the strawberry-cassis puree into the meringue.

Turn into a shallow pan or ice trays and freeze for an hour or so, until mushy and almost set (let soften if frozen solid). Scrape into a mixing bowl and beat vigorously (or at high speed with an electric mixer) to break up the ice crystals. Turn back into the pan or trays and repeat the process again in an hour. (This second blending may be omitted, but your sherbet may still have ice crystals as a result.) Now turn into a serving bowl, a mold, or individual cups and cover. Freeze at least 2 hours for individual portions, 4 hours for bowls or molds.

Allow the sherbet to soften slightly in the refrigerator before serving; individual servings will take 10 minutes to soften, and a large bowl will take 20 minutes. If you wish to unmold the sherbet, dip it into warm water and reverse onto a chilled platter. Cover and return to the freezer for 30 minutes to set the "dribbles," then refrigerate for 20 to 30 minutes before serving.

Serve garnished with mint, fresh sliced strawberries, and slices of lime.

8 to 10 servings

Assorted Cookies

Once they have cooled, store these cookies in airtight containers.

WHEAT GERM AND OATMEAL COOKIES

¾ cup mild honey
½ cup safflower or vegetable oil
1 egg
2 teaspoons vanilla extract
½ teaspoon ground cinnamon
¼ teaspoon freshly grated nutmeg
½ cup grated coconut
1 cup wheat germ
2 cups rolled oats
1 cup raisins
½ cup whole-wheat pastry flour
½ teaspoon salt, preferably sea salt

Preheat the oven to 350 degrees.

Cream together the honey and oil, then beat in the egg and vanilla. Stir in the cinnamon, nutmeg, coconut, wheat germ, rolled oats, and raisins; sift in the flour and the salt.

Drop by scant tablespoonfuls onto oiled baking sheets, about 1 inch apart, and bake for 12 minutes. Cool on racks.

4½ dozen cookies

ALMOND GEMS

¾ cup safflower oil or butter
⅓ cup mild honey
1 teaspoon almond extract
½ teaspoon vanilla extract
Grated rind of 1 lemon
1 cup almonds, toasted and ground
2 cups whole-wheat pastry flour
¼ teaspoon salt, preferably sea salt

Preheat the oven to 400 degrees.

Cream together the oil or butter and the honey. Add the almond extract, vanilla extract, and lemon rind, then stir in the toasted, ground almonds. Sift in the whole-wheat pastry flour and the salt, and blend well.

Drop by teaspoonfuls onto oiled baking sheets, 2 inches apart, and bake for 10 to 12 minutes, until golden brown. Watch closely; these burn easily. Cool on the cookie sheets (they'll fall apart if you handle them while hot).

3 dozen cookies

GINGERSNAPS

This batter is very thick and sticky, like refrigerator dough. It's important to press these out very thin, or they won't "snap."

¼ cup safflower oil
¼ cup mild honey
½ cup molasses
1 egg
2½ cups whole-wheat pastry flour
¼ teaspoon salt, preferably sea salt
1 teaspoon ground cinnamon
1 tablespoon ground ginger

Preheat the oven to 350 degrees.

Cream together the oil, honey, and molasses, then beat in the egg. Sift together the whole-wheat pastry flour, salt, cinnamon, and ground ginger. Add to the liquid ingredients and mix well.

Drop by scant tablespoonfuls onto oiled cookie sheets, about 2 inches apart. Take a glass or jar and dip the bottom into cool water, then press out the cookies very thin. Keep wetting the glass to avoid sticking.

Bake for 10 to 12 minutes; cool on racks.

4 to 5 dozen cookies

ANISE AND BRAZIL NUT COOKIES

½ cup date sugar
½ cup mild honey
¼ pound (1 stick) butter
2 eggs
1 teaspoon ground aniseed
1 tablespoon grated orange rind
½ teaspoon salt, preferably sea salt
1 cup flour, half whole-wheat pastry flour and half unbleached white
½ cup wheat germ
1 cup finely chopped Brazil nuts
½ cup currants (optional)

Preheat the oven to 350 degrees.

Cream together the date sugar, honey, and butter. Beat in the eggs, aniseed, orange rind, and salt. Sift in the flours and wheat germ and stir in the Brazil nuts and optional currants.

Drop this runny batter by teaspoonfuls onto oiled baking sheets, about 1 inch apart, and bake for 10 to 12 minutes. Cool on racks.

6 dozen cookies

PEANUT BUTTER AND BANANA COOKIES

These are the best and most original peanut butter cookies I've ever tasted. The batter is very runny, but don't worry about this, because that's what makes these cookies as light as they are; they literally melt in your mouth. However, if you want a stiffer, heavier cookie, add ¼ cup whole-wheat flour or unbleached white flour to the recipe, and delete 1 teaspoon baking powder.

These cookies are very soft and cakelike.

¼ cup safflower oil
⅔ cup mild honey
2 eggs
½ teaspoon vanilla extract
½ to ⅔ cup peanut butter, to taste
1 cup mashed, very ripe banana (about 1 large banana)
¾ cup whole-wheat pastry flour
2 teaspoons double-acting baking powder
½ teaspoon salt, preferably sea salt

Preheat the oven to 350 degrees.

Cream together the oil and the honey. Beat in the eggs, vanilla, and peanut butter, then stir in the mashed banana. Sift together the flour, baking powder, and salt and stir into the liquid mixture. Blend well.

Drop onto oiled baking sheets by scant tablespoonfuls 1 inch apart and bake for 12 to 15 minutes. Cool on racks.

4 dozen cookies

INDEX